NATURAL LANDSCAPING

P9-CCA-854

NATURAL LANDSCAPING

Gardening with Nature to Create a Backyard Paradise

Sally Roth

Rodale Press, Inc.
Emmaus, Pennsylvania

A FRIEDMAN GROUP BOOK

© 1997 by Michael Friedman Publishing Group

Published in 1997 by Rodale Inc.

All rights reserved. No part of this publication may be reproduced or transmitted in any form or by any means, electronic or mechanical, including photocopy, recording, or any other information storage and retrieval system, without the written permission of the publisher.

The information in this book has been carefully researched, and all efforts have been made to ensure accuracy. Rodale Inc. assumes no responsibility for any injuries suffered or for damages or losses incurred during the use of or as a result of following this information. It is important to study all directions carefully before taking any action based on the information and advice presented in this book. When using any commercial product, *always* read and follow label directions. Where trade names are used, no discrimination is intended and no endorsement by Rodale Inc. is implied.

Printed in the United States of America. Rodale Inc. makes every effort to use acid-free ♾, recycled ♻ paper.

Library of Congress Cataloging-in-Publication Data

Roth, Sally.
  Natural landscaping : gardening with nature to create a backyard paradise / Sally Roth.
      p.   cm.
  "A Friedman Group book"—T.p. verso.
  Includes bibliographical references (p.   ) and index.
  ISBN 0–87596–704–3 (hardcover : alk. paper)
  1. Natural landscaping   I. Title.
SB439.R675   1997
712'.6—dc20
                                                           96-5912

ISBN 0–8759–885–6 (paperback)

Distributed in the book trade by St. Martin's Press

Color separations by Colourscan
Printed by Quebecor World

  4 6 8 10 9 7 5   hardcover
2 4 6 8 10 9 7 5 3 1 paperback

NATURAL LANDSCAPING
Gardening with Nature to Create a Backyard Paradise
was prepared and produced by
Michael Friedman Publishing Group, Inc.
15 West 26th Street
New York, NY 10010

**Michael Friedman Publishing Group
Editorial and Design Staff**

Editor: Susan Lauzau
Art Director: Lynne Yeamans
Designer: Kevin Ullrich
Photography Editors: Emilya Naymark, Deidra Gorgos

Rodale Organic Living Books

Executive Creative Director: Christin Gangi
Art Director: Patricia Field
Content Assembly Manager: Robert V. Anderson Jr.
Copy Manager: Nancy N. Bailey

Cover Designer: Nancy Biltcliff
Front Cover Photographer: Susan Seubert
Back Cover Photographer: Paul Rezendes (left),
  Bill Marchel (right)

We're always happy to hear from you. For questions or comments concerning the editorial content of this book, please write to:

  Rodale Book Readers' Service
  33 East Minor Street
  Emmaus, PA 18098

Look for other Rodale books wherever books are sold. Or call us at (800) 848-4735.

For more information about Rodale Organic Living magazines and books, visit us at **www.organicgardening.com**

For Gretel and David

Acknowledgments

My first thank-you must go to my mother, Mary Bohus Roth, who taught me how to see the many small wonders of the world. Eating green onions, complete with the taste of dirt, is a great first memory to carry with me.

Another debt of love and gratitude is due to my husband, Rick Mark, a true companion who loves the natural world as much as I do. From my wedding bouquet of fresh-picked wildflowers to frogs swimming in the bathtub and harbor seals on the rocks, you've known what matters most.

Thanks also to my daughter, Gretel Hartman, who can catch a crayfish in her bare hands faster than lightning, and to my son, David Roth-Mark, who notices the smallest ant. It's been wonderful to watch you learn the thrill of discovery.

I'm especially grateful for the special friendship of Pauline Hoehn Gerard and Deborah Baker Burdick, who saw me through the highs and lows of birthing this book. Thanks, Pauline, for belly laughs and birthday morning walks on your home place, and for a safe place to put the possums. Thanks, Deb, for lotuses in the moonlight and bad girls on the porch. Sister girlfriends, you mean more to me than I can ever say.

Thanks also to Arlene Porter and Bob Brooks, for books and friendship; to Mark Trela, for sharing a love of plants; to T. J. Bloechl, for coffee and a listening ear; to Jim Stinson, for always being ready to go look at fireflies; to Ann Gillihan, Jean Hadley, and Rosie Broz, for conversations to think about; and to Randy Pease, for words and music. Thanks to Ellen Phillips and Susan Lauzau, for sensitive and skillful editing. And last but in no way least, thanks to Jim Epler, the Angel Man, who helped point my steps toward the naturalist path.

CONTENTS

INTRODUCTION
8

Chapter 1
LANDSCAPING
WITH NATURE
*Inspiration and Ideas for the Landscape
You Really Want*
10

Chapter 2
A FIELD OF FLOWERS
*Creating Meadow
and Prairie Gardens*
28

Chapter 3
GARDENS UNDER TREES
*Creating Woodland and
Shade Gardens*
68

Chapter 4
POOLS, STREAMS, AND
WATERFALLS
Creating Water and Bog Gardens
104

Chapter 5
BIRDSONG IN THE GARDEN
*Attracting Songbirds
and Hummingbirds*
144

Chapter 6
BEAUTY ON THE WING
Attracting Butterflies and Moths
182

Chapter 7
SPECIAL FEATURES FOR
EVERY GARDEN
Paths, Walls, and Finishing Touches
210

Chapter 8
NATURAL GARDENING BASICS
*From Building Great Soil to
Winterizing for Wildlife*
234

RESOURCES FOR NATURAL LANDSCAPING
250

USDA PLANT HARDINESS ZONE MAP
252

INDEX
253

INTRODUCTION

I've always been a gardener, and I've always been a naturalist. But it took me many long years to realize that I could be both at the same time.

For more than a decade, I tried to make my gardens look like the centerfold of some glossy magazine—perfectly designed, perfectly planted, perfectly groomed. In a word, perfect.

I liked the look of those gardens well enough, and I sure enjoyed the praise that visitors threw my way, but the prettiness of my flowers didn't seem to be quite enough. It always felt as if something was missing.

My morning routine should have given me a clue. By seven in the morning, before I'd had my coffee and while the grass was still spangled with dew, I'd be outside. First I'd do a quick stroll around the garden to see what was coming into bloom or bud. I'd pull a few weeds here and there and look for seedlings sprouting in the mulch, but I didn't waste much time in the garden because my real morning destination was the woods and fields behind our house.

By the time I got there, mist would be rising off the field, moving in ragged wisps as if it were alive. Spiderwebs, their secret presence betrayed by beads of moisture, stretched across the tips of plants like jeweled ornaments. So fragile, so beautiful, so temporary—I'd stop in awe, touching the silk with a fingertip. Then, of course, I'd have to crouch down and find the spider, usually waiting under a leaf near one of its web's guylines.

Sometimes a rabbit would streak out in front of my feet, and the field was always filled with birds, burbling wrens, scolding red-winged blackbirds, orioles in the scattered trees, goldfinches and buntings, and my favorite, the humble, brown song sparrow with its sweet little voice.

I knew all the cycles of the wild places—when the first strawberry would ripen, when to wear long pants for blackberry picking, when to look for baby bunnies creeping out to nibble grass at dawn, when to listen for the cheep of nestlings or the creak of a katydid, when to walk down in the dark to catch a glimpse of owls.

There was always something going on in the woods and fields, and I loved it. The morning flew by, and it was always a surprise to feel the sun's heat on the back of my neck, the signal that it was getting on toward ten o'-clock, and time to go home.

Little by little, I borrowed ideas from my favorite wild places and implemented them in my garden. Spring wildflowers were the first to make the move, then oxeye daisies and a few other field flowers. But most of my favorite wild things were too pushy for my garden. They didn't know they were supposed to stay in one place, and they'd hop around with abandon, stretching their fast-moving roots or seeding themselves wherever they wanted.

Such lack of control! At first I thought it couldn't be tolerated, and I ripped out the wildlings that wouldn't behave. Then came the summer when the common milkweed I'd planted along the picket fence threatened to swamp the irises and hardy geraniums. Ready to do battle, I waded in among the thicket of milkweed stems, only to find that the leaves were hung with magic green lanterns, the small, ethereal chrysalises of the monarch butterfly. A few flashy striped caterpillars were still munching on the big oval leaves.

Of course I couldn't pull out the milkweed. Instead I moved the sissy plants to another area, and I let the milkweed overtake that patch of the garden. I moved in some equally feisty goldenrod, ironweed, asters, and beebalm—all of them from our wild field—and before long I had a new favorite part of the garden.

I can't say that was my epiphany, but it was a start. Over the next few years, my garden evolved from a traditional semiformal showpiece to a place of wilder, natural beauty. Because I used Mother Nature's plantings as a guide, my garden quickly became an inviting habitat for birds, butterflies, toads, incredible insects, and a host of other fascinating creatures.

I still had plenty of beauty and flowers, but now my garden was also filled with life. In the mornings, I'd spend hours in my garden, just as satisfied as when I was

The joys of a natural landscape include the rich assortment of colors, the variety of songs, and the daily dramas of nature in your own backyard. In creating a garden for your own enjoyment, you'll also be establishing a haven for creatures of the meadows, waterways, and woodlands.

out in the wild. By being able to observe at close range, without making a special trip, I learned wonderful things—how birds weave grasses, how rabbits pull fur from their chests to line their nests, how hummingbirds collect spider silk, how bugs fight to the death, how plants create their own territories.... The list is endless, because the natural world is full of constant surprises.

By bringing nature into my garden, I brought everything that's most important to me right home to my front yard. This small plot of earth hardly counts in the grand scheme of things. It's a drop in that old bucket. Yet when I see the multitude of life that this little garden nurtures and protects, I can't help wondering "what if." What if there were a million drops in the bucket? What if every subdivision made the switch to natural landscap-

ing? What if every city street held a secret garden full of wild things? It took just one year for indigo buntings to discover this place. It took three years for meadowlarks to return to the hill behind this house, where once they nested by the dozens.

Before animal rehabbers were common, I used to argue with a scientific friend about the value of a single bird. "What does fixing one bird's broken wing matter?" he'd ask. "We should just wring its neck. Won't make any difference in the big picture."

"Every bird counts," I'd protest.

I still believe it. Every bird, every butterfly, every lizard. We're all tied together, even if the threads are invisible. Creating and living in a natural landscape makes me feel a part of it all.

Chapter 1

LANDSCAPING WITH NATURE
Inspiration and Ideas for the Landscape You Really Want

A natural landscape blends the best of both worlds: the grand vision of nature and the guiding hand of the gardener.

Green-and-gold makes a great edging plant, and it blooms 'til frost.

Anatural landscape nurtures the gardener. It brims with life, creates its own moods, and sows its own surprises. From the first hummingbird at the columbine to the last golden leaves of Carolina allspice, from the song sparrow nest in the prairie rose to the chipmunk stuffing its cheeks with elderberries, every day brings a new feast of simple pleasures.

Most of us don't have the good luck of inheriting a yard that's filled with big old shade trees, a patch of woods, wonderful wildflowers, and a trickling brook. The traditional yard is dotted with a few young shade trees, a handful of shrubs, and gardens of flowers or vegetables. That's a good starting point. Once you take stock of what you have, you'll be surprised by how easy it is to build on your yard's existing foundation.

Even if your yard is nothing but lawn, you can still make a wonderful, inviting home for wildlife in less time than you think. Starting with a blank canvas can be even more fun, since you get the pleasure of creating something that's truly yours.

A New Perspective

Whenever I want to create or expand a garden, I start by counting my riches—the shrubs, trees, and plants I already have. While I'm taking inventory of my plants, I'm also thinking of their potential as food and shelter for wildlife.

Take some time to stroll around your yard and consider it from the wildlife's point of view. Does a robin nest in your young red maple? Is a cardinal feeding its young in the rosebush? Are chipmunks living along the stone wall? Look for places where birds build nests or seek shelter at night. Inventory the nooks and crannies that might be used by rabbits, chipmunks and ground squirrels, or other small animals. Check out the plants on your property for their shelter and protective cover potential. Does a spruce stand proud in front of your house? Is there a group of rhododendrons or a privet hedge? Does a vine cover a wall or a fence? Do you have a thorny patch of blackberries or other bramble fruits or perhaps a large shrub rose?

Think about food sources around your place. Remember to look beyond the obvious fruits and nuts. Even if all you have is a solitary shade tree, it can feed and shelter hundreds more critters than you've ever imagined. A single

MAKE A CHECKLIST

You'll be surprised by how many parts of your yard already fit into a natural landscape. Check off the features you already have:

- ❑ **brushpile**
- ❑ **compost pile**
- ❑ **fence**
- ❑ **flower garden**
- ❑ **hedges**
- ❑ **herb garden**
- ❑ **mature trees**
- ❑ **meadow area**
- ❑ **pond or other water feature**
- ❑ **shrubs**
- ❑ **sitting spot**
- ❑ **stone or timber wall**
- ❑ **vegetable garden**
- ❑ **"weedy" corner**
- ❑ **young trees**

Now circle the features on the list that you don't currently have, but would like to add. Use the checklist as a starting point for planning your natural landscape.

tree is a wildlife refuge all by itself. You may never have noticed the flowers a tree produces in spring, but they hum with honeybees or draw swarms of tiny insects, which in turn are sought by wood warblers and other bug-eating birds. The leaves are fodder for caterpillars, which turn into butterflies and moths.

Meanwhile, in the great food chain of life, those caterpillars, plus countless insects on leaves and bark, become food for birds, as well as for some other, odder creatures, such as arboreal lizards and tree frogs. I remember the first time I saw a young five-lined skink (a little striped lizard with a bright blue tail) resting on the bark of our oak. It looked frozen and immobile, but it was actually hunting. When a beetle trundled along, the skink flicked out its tongue and popped the beetle down

LOOKING THROUGH WILD EYES

It's an eye-opener to put yourself in the mind-set of a small animal. You need a whole new perspective once you realize that you're nothing more than a tasty morsel to a myriad of hunters. Suddenly the problem is not how to find food, but how to get to it without being eaten yourself. Scout around your property to see what sheltered pathways are already offered. Watch the birds come to your feeder, and see how they move from one sheltering shrub or tree to the next. You'll soon see that safe movement and shelter are vital parts of the picture.

Perhaps the most beautiful of all bluebirds, the western bluebird is splashed with rich chestnut on its upper back. Birdhouses will attract nesting pairs. In fall, large flocks congregate in western foothills and mountains.

Building a Small Mammal Shelter

The antics of rabbits, chipmunks, and other small mammals are a delight to watch. By supplying an abundance of natural foods and a safe place where they can hide from predators, you can easily encourage these interesting creatures to take up year-round residence in your garden.

Create an inviting home for small mammals like chipmunks and ground squirrels with a loose pile of stones. Add sections of PVC pipe in the pile as you build, making sure that the ends of the pipe are left open. Those holes and tunnels are mighty inviting to small mammals.

Life at the bottom of the food chain isn't easy. Hungry hawks, owls, housecats, and other predators are always on the prowl for small mammals. Give these endearing creatures a fighting chance by constructing safe havens here and there in your garden. A loose pile of rocks will give them plenty of crevices for fast getaways.

Chipmunks are quick to discover a natural garden, especially if it includes fruits, nuts, and seeds. With a bit of patience, you can entice these easily tamed creatures to eat from your hand or lap. Shelled nuts are always a favorite.

Like other lizards, this spotted whiptail appreciates sunny rocks, fences, and other sites where it can soak up the sun. Lightning fast, lizards primarily eat insects. Some crush the eggs of ground-nesting birds and lap up the yolk.

The graceful habit and pretty foliage of Japanese maples, plus their small size and general indestructibility, make them versatile trees. Notice how the mounded forms of the plants in this garden mimic the shape of boulders or mountains.

the hatch. Trees also produce a bounty of seeds, nuts, or fruit—a banquet for wildlife.

Learning from Nature

Mother Nature is gardener supreme, but she's willing to share her tips and techniques. All we have to do is look and learn.

To begin your lessons, take a field trip—literally. And a woods trip, and a meadow trip, and a pond trip. Visit your favorite wild places, and try to pinpoint just what it is that makes them so appealing to both you and the wildlife that live or visit there. Tuck a small notebook and pen into your pocket so you can jot down impressions and ideas.

While it's easy to enjoy a favorite wild place, it's not so simple to put your finger on just what the appeal is. Here are some ideas for making those appealing elements clear.

- Sit quietly for a while and let the atmosphere of the spot sink in. Then start listing the elements that drew you to the place, beginning with generalities—the cool relief of green shade or the dappled play of light and shadow across a meadow.
- Take a minute to get in touch with all of your senses. There may be aspects your conscious mind has never noted—the smell of honeysuckle in the air, the background birdsong, the springiness of the young grass under your feet, or the visual appeal of hills and valleys. Perhaps it's the sound of water that's irresistible.
- Now get as specific as you can. Note the kinds of trees that make up the woods and what grows beneath them. Sketch the casual arrangement of boulders or a fallen log across the path.
- After you've been sitting quietly for a while, animals, birds, and other creatures will begin to show up. See if you can figure out what draws them to that spot.

The raspy voice of the squirrel tree frog of the Southeast sounds just like a scolding squirrel. These tiny frogs can change color in a flash, going from their usual green to brown or black. Southerners know them as "rain frogs," and say they sound off when the weather is about to change.

The colorful indigo bunting, commonly seen on telephone wires along country roads, nests in brushy fields or hedgerows throughout eastern North America. These useful birds eat thousands of pests, including cankerworms, caterpillars, beetles, and grasshoppers. Indigo buntings are one of the few birds that sing throughout the day, even in the dog days of summer.

MORE THAN MEETS THE EYE

The attractions of a wild place appeal to more of our senses than sight alone. It took me years to realize that one of the things I liked about walking in the woods was the earthy aroma of decomposing leaves. To me, the moist smell of humus is the essence of the woods—and it was missing in my own natural landscape. I had been raking the leaves in spring, carefully uncovering the heads of emerging wildflowers, and piling last year's leaves on the compost pile. When I stopped raking and allowed the leaves to accumulate and decompose wherever they settled, just as they do in nature, my woodsy garden began to smell like a woods. (And my wildflowers did better than ever.)

Animal Magnetism

If you delight in a wild place because of the creatures it lures, examine what it is that makes the place an attraction for those animals. Your answers will keep coming back to the same big three: food, shelter, and water. But now it's time to see how those needs can be answered in a multitude of ways. A winter woods is filled with birds because there is food there. Watch what attracts the jays, the chickadees, and the woodpeckers.

Sometimes the answer is clear: a drink of water or a tempting berry. But other observations will surprise you. You may see a bird stripping bark from a grapevine, a butterfly testing leaves to find just the right one for her nursery, or a striped ground squirrel visiting a cache of nibbles in an old bird nest.

Finding a Human Scale

If you didn't know any better, you'd think that a lump of golden agate I keep on my desk was nothing more than a pretty stone. You wouldn't know that every so often I rub that honey-colored rock and see surf crashing against sea cliffs, hear the thin cry of gulls wheeling over the sea, and dream of harbor seals lounging at the foot of black cliffs of lava rock. When I look into those clear amber depths, I sometimes see a whale spouting way out in the mist. That agate on my desk may be nothing special to you, but to me it's the Oregon coast.

LESSON OF THE FOOD CHAIN
❧❧

Observing nature doesn't always lead to the ending you might expect. Once I watched a beautiful, dark-eyed deer mouse pick its way to a giant mushroom. With whiskers twitching and bright eyes alert every step of the way, he finally stood up beside the mushroom, balancing one paw daintily on the cap. I thought he was planning on fungi hors d'oeuvres. Wrong! Quick as a flash, the mouse grabbed a big, shiny black beetle that had bored into the thick-fleshed cap. The sharp, little white teeth flashed, and with a crunch I could hear 6 feet away, the beetle was history. In a matter of seconds, the whiskery little nose searched out six beetles and devoured them all. Then the mouse sat back and meticulously cleaned his face.

Watching the food chain in action makes you see that the natural world is truly interconnected. From the threads of mushroom mycelium and the microscopic inhabitants of the soil community to the scurrying six-legged insects and the high-minded humans that walk our paths, everything really does work together.

My gardens are just as evocative. Glossy strawberry leaves, so shiny they look waxed, are more than a groundcover. Those strawberry plants, another reminder of my old home in Oregon, are a bit of a favorite wild place where I'd go to watch the sunset and the beavers and the elk that sauntered into the meadow.

That's the beauty of the human mind. Give us a few of the details, and we'll fill in the big picture from that vast store of memories and images. You can't transplant the woods or move a lake to your home grounds, but you can downscale your favorite things to fit your space.

If your favorite escape includes a rocky outcrop, you can strategically place a few boulders to echo the effect. The mass of stone and the solid texture will give your natural landscape some of the feel of the wild place. In the same way, you can put in a small pool or a pump-fed section of stream. A little grove of five hemlocks and spruces will suffice in place of a mountain forest.

It's incredibly gratifying to mimic nature. Remember what fun it was to build dams across a stream when you were a kid. Adding a single-tier waterfall—or any other natural feature—to your garden will give you immense pleasure.

Rocks add visual height to a garden, putting plants closer to eye level and making the garden more appealing. Perennials and moss that spread to cover the rocks and knit the plants together make the garden look well-anchored to the earth, as if it's been there forever.

Real-Life Landscaping

I'll admit it—I'm a plant addict. Put me in a nursery, and self-control flies out the window. I load up the cart with pots of perennials, lug last-ditch orphans from the almost-dead bargain bin, and heave shrubs into the trunk of my car.

I've heard all the advice from seasoned pros. When you want to start a new garden, they caution, plan everything out on paper first. Do the grading, the electric, the water piping, the concrete, wood, and stonework, and then—and only then—put in the plants.

They're right, of course. It's much easier to install a water garden or an arbor if you don't have to move a dozen plants out of the way first. I'll never forget the year I dug up and moved 40—count 'em, 40—wheelbarrow loads of plants to make way for an earth berm I knew was going to go there before I planted the garden. But the berm was three years away, and I wanted to have a garden now!

So have I managed to change my ways? Well, maybe a little. Here's what I've learned over the years.

Trust Your Instincts

You know whether something is attractive or not. Now all you have to do is figure out why. Landscapers use basic principles of unity, variety, balance, and proportion. But if you're intimidated by landscaping jargon, let nature be your landscape teacher instead. Wild places are a living laboratory of garden design. With a little practice, you can refine your innate sense of what looks natural and appropriate.

Take a field trip to your favorite wild places and think about what catches your eye. Do you focus on the field of tawny grass or on the green-black cedars that dot its edge? Can you see how both elements work together

LANDSCAPE FEATURES FROM NATURE

You'll design a better garden with nature as your guide. As you visit wild places, note the appeal of the following:

- grasses in a wildflower meadow
- the statue-like quality of solitary dead trees
- rocks partially buried in soil
- varying terrain, such as hills and valleys, woods and water, or mixed patches of meadow and trees
- vertical vines that add color, texture, and fragrance to trunks, rocks, and cliffs
- unexpected surprises, such as plants growing in crevices

to boost each other's impact? In the same way, you can see how a single focal point, like a lone tree in the middle of a field, draws your eye. Notice the graceful way a natural woods is layered, with tall trees blending into shorter ones, then stepping down to understory shrubs, and finally reaching to ferns, wildflowers, and other low-growing plants on the floor.

If you're lucky enough to have a natural rocky outcropping, or if you've trucked in some hefty specimens, nestle a variety of plants in and around them to visually tie them to the landscape and avoid big-rock-in-the-front-yard syndrome.

Transition from Grass to Woods

New plantings of young trees and perennials never look as lush as you'd like at first, but be patient. Once the plants have a few years of growth under their belts, your landscape will acquire a natural look, as open areas blend with groups of trees and shrubs.

STEP 1: *Plant trees and shrubs in groups, allowing elbow room between them according to their mature size. Rocks and groundcovers around the new plantings will make them show up better in the landscape.*

STEP 2: *As groundcovers spread and plants fill in at the feet of your trees and shrubs, the planting will become more inviting to birds, which are less inclined to visit isolated specimen trees than they are a sheltering group.*

STEP 3: *After eight to ten years in your garden, the trees and shrubs that once looked so puny will have grown into a wonderful new corner of beauty in your yard. Even better, you'll have created valuable edge habitat during the growing years. This zone of transition—where plants and shrubs gradually give way to mature trees and woods—is filled with life, attracting birds, insects, and other wildlife.*

In a natural landscape, plants are guided, not controlled. Here, creepers and sprawlers along the rocks and paths are allowed free rein. Shrubs and small trees mixed in among the perennials add to the natural look.

If you're a careful observer, you can learn a lot from nature. A friend who put in a pond once asked me to help him figure out why it still looked so artificial. He'd planted clumps of lilies and water plants in it, but something was still off. We took a look at his pond, then we drove out into the country to see natural ponds. He immediately recognized that it was the edge that was the problem. Look at the edges of wild ponds, and you'll see that plants grow both at the edge and into the water, blurring the line between the two elements. My friend's pond ended abruptly with an edge of stone that was handsome but screamed "man-made!" When he tucked shrubs and sprawlers among the rocks, drifting them outward in natural-looking groups, his problem was solved.

Your hand and eye will work together to create a landscape that feels as though it were designed by Mother Nature. I find it a big help to occasionally take snapshots as the garden is progressing. It's a lot easier to see "what's wrong with this picture" than it is to spot areas for improvement while you're distracted by the scent of a flower or a hummingbird zipping by.

This immature male Anna's hummingbird lacks the brilliant color of the adult male, which flashes hot pink on head and throat. Dozens of hummingbird species are native to the Americas; none occur in the Old World.

Structure First, Plants Later

Creating a pleasing garden without a basic structure is like trying to walk without a skeleton. If you plant first and design later, you'll always have that nagging feeling that something is missing. It is—the backbone.

The backbone, or framework, of your garden is made up of substantial objects that keep their importance all through the seasons. Paths, woody plants, and objects with substantial impact are the bones of the garden. Man-made objects carry a lot of weight—they draw our eye in the garden. Use them sparingly so you don't get a doodad effect. Here are some possibilities to structure your garden around:

- a wide path, with curves that create a sense of mystery and anticipation
- a wooden bench or a pair of chairs angled toward each other
- a fanciful birdhouse on a post

- a pedestal-type birdbath
- a bird feeding station
- a rustic trellis or arbor
- a hefty log
- a grouping of rocks
- a rock or timber wall

UNCOVERING YOUR GARDEN'S BONES

I find it easier to visualize the structure of my garden or my garden-to-be if I imagine it in winter. Suddenly it's clear where the bones of the garden are—the stand of miscanthus grass mellowed to warm tan, the young hemlocks, the weathered bench, the wrought-iron shepherd's hook hung with finch feeders. The contours of the land itself and the route of a path, too, are easier to imagine without the distraction of plants.

Foliage can be as colorful as plants, but don't overdo it. This single red-leaved Japanese maple adds enough color to anchor a large space. Notice how the tree adds an air of mystery to the bridge, making it even more inviting to visitors exploring the garden.

Making the Plan

Planning a garden design is a little like rubbing your stomach and patting your head at the same time. Placement of one element depends upon where the others are, so you'll need to think about several things simultaneously.

Start with the biggies: Decide where you want to put a fence, a wall, a pool, an arbor, or a sitting space. Then lay out a pleasant, winding walkway through your garden space. Include spots along the way for sitting or stopping, and widen the path where you want people to linger. (For more about designing paths, see page 219.)

Figuring out the priorities is something only you can do. If you're yearning for a waterfall, make it number one on the list of projects, even though you can accomplish a dozen smaller projects in the same length of time.

Once you have your master plan, you can work on your garden a little at a time. If your budget or your free time won't stretch far enough to include everything at once, work on your plan one stage at a time. Here's how to break it down:

1. Plant the trees and shrubs first, since they take years to mature.
2. Put in the paths.
3. Prioritize when you install the "hardscape" elements—walls, fences, arbors, pool, and paths. Here's where you can economize and install one element at a time as your budget allows.
4. Add the plants for the crowning touch. If you work on your garden in stages, you can also plant one section at a time as you get to it.

Do It in a Weekend

You'll get more pleasure—and less pain!—out of a project if you handle it at a reasonable pace. I break big projects into chunks that I can manage one weekend at a time. If I can't do it in a single weekend, I break it down still further so that it doesn't become simply overwhelming.

If you want to put in a pond, for instance, you don't need to cram the whole project into one session. Instead, plan to dig the hole one weekend and lay the liner and rim the pond the next.

2-D or 3-D?

If you can visualize your garden on graph paper, great. I can't. Converting my three-dimensional eyesight into a two-dimensional garden plan is something that doesn't come easily to me. I'm more of the hands-on, stand-back-and-take-a-look type. It's the same way I move furniture around in my living room. ("Hmmm; wouldn't that sofa look better over here?")

When I'm planning a new garden or adding a new element to an existing one, I use lightweight plastic lawn chairs or cardboard boxes, moving them around until I'm satisfied with the layout. It takes a little practice to squint at a couple of upside-down plastic chairs and see a rustic arbor draped with grapevines, but I find it easier than trying to plan on paper. If I'm designing the route of a path, I use a garden hose or a dribbled line of mulch and plenty of imagination to get an idea of how it will look.

▲ *Let your plants mingle with one another instead of keeping them in separate spaces. Flowers and foliage that weave together are not only attractive, they also help eliminate weeds by shading them out.*

▶ *In this water garden, spiky, upright foliage provides appealing contrast to the water. River stones provide a transition from land to water and create an inviting beach for birds and other garden visitors.*

The Bit-by-Bit Approach

When I decided to turn my front yard into a wildlife haven, I started with a budget of $100—not much in landscaping dollars. I knew it wouldn't stretch to let me do the whole front yard, so I started small, focusing on a grouping of berried shrubs. I planted three deciduous winterberry hollies in a single group, curving them around a flat-topped rock that held a clay saucer—an impromptu bird and chipmunk watering hole that served for years until I got around to putting in the stone recirculating basin on my master plan.

That was almost a garden all by itself, but I added wildflowers and spring bulbs around their feet for spring interest, then mulched with lawn mower–chopped oak leaves. I was pleased with the first step, and so were the birds. Bluebirds and thrushes arrived within weeks, feasting on the berries and splashing in the bath. When the berries were gone, the protective branches of the shrubs gave the birds at my nearby feeders a new place to perch.

BLOOMING WITH IDEAS

There's no need to consult a professional designer to learn about good combinations—unlimited possibilities are right in front of your nose. Think about the spring wildflowers, a summer meadow, or the last hurrah before frost. How can you improve on wild blue phlox and Dutchman's breeches with a few trilliums thrown in for good measure? What could be more beautiful than madder-purple fall asters and a sweep of goldenrod, decorated with filmy plumes of virgin's bower vine? If you want a beautiful combination, borrow from nature.

I've learned to jot down companion possibilities when I see them. No matter how often I think, "Oh, I'll remember that," I never do unless I write it down. I'm not organized enough to keep a nice neat notebook, but even a scrap of paper in the pocket of my jeans serves the purpose.

To make a big splash without a big budget, start with three or four inexpensive azaleas. Pink, red, white, and even purple look good together, or choose orange, yellow, and red as your color theme. But don't mix the two color groups unless you like clashing colors.

BACKYARD AS A WILDLIFE HABITAT

Think like a bird or a rabbit and you'll have a ready idea of what's needed to make a landscape appealing to wildlife—protective cover, food, and water. Supply these basics, and your backyard will soon be a fascinating place alive with birds, bugs, and animals.

You can adapt this plan according to how much space you have available in your own yard. Just adjust the size of the various elements.

Develop the plan one part at a time, if you like. You'll most likely want to start with the birdfeeding area, which will give you an immediate payoff.

Make permanent features like arbors and rock walls the first step of each section, to give it structure you can build around. Plant shrubs and trees as soon in your long-range plan as you can, because they will take the longest to fill in.

FEATURES

1. Street
2. Driveway
3. Hummingbird garden
4. Patio with potted fuchsias and geraniums
5. Shade garden
6. Bird feeding area with assorted feeders and a few shrubs
7. Corridor of mixed shrubs and trees, mostly deciduous with a few evergreens
8. Birdseed garden
9. Meadow or prairie garden
10. Sitting place
11. Rock wall (piled or unmortared)
12. Pond and bog garden
13. Naturalistic woodland
14. Brush pile
15. Shallow drinking/bathing station for birds that is made from rock and recirculating pump, including small waterfall for sound of water to attract birds
16. Butterfly garden
17. Grape arbor
18. Berry bushes: thimbleberries, blueberries, viburnums, and elderberries
19. House
20. Huckleberry, lowbush blueberry, and bearberry
21. Evergreen woodland of conifers, rhododendrons, azaleas, and hollies

The following spring, when my wallet was a little fatter, I added on to my original planting. I created a second planting near the first, but based it on blueberries and viburnums. By extending the planting of wild blue phlox (*Phlox divaricata*) and other wildflowers from one group of shrubs to the next, the two pieces merged into a single garden.

Gardening bit by bit lets me extend my garden whenever the time is right. Each new piece is a satisfying garden in itself, and the whole thing expands gradually. Best of all, it looks good right from the start. I keep it from looking schizophrenic by repeating colors and plants throughout. Spicebushes, for example, are a repeating theme that helps tie things together.

A CHANGING LANDSCAPE

A natural garden is a work in progress, not a finished masterpiece. Its life is interesting, and its face is beautiful, but even when you step back and say "Ahhh," the picture doesn't hold for long. Even the slowest-growing desert landscapes are always changing. Seeds drop and sprout, roots reach out and shoulder neighboring plants aside, voles uproot the groundcovers, birds strip the bark for nest-building—the cycle never ends. Relax and enjoy the process instead of fighting to capture a particular moment. With a natural landscape, instead of a static scene, you can look forward to a lifetime of surprises.

Choosing Plants

I choose the plants for my natural gardens differently than I would for a conventional garden bed or border. You'll find specific plant recommendations with each kind of natural garden in the following chapters, but here are my general criteria:

- Usefulness: Will it serve as food or shelter?
- Adaptability: Will it thrive without coddling?
- Beauty: Does it add beauty of form or color to the landscape?

It's interesting how my definition of beauty has changed as I've become more and more interested in natural landscaping. Although I can still admire a manicured perennial border, I sometimes have to stop myself from thinking of such a garden as the airhead of the gardening world—pretty but vapid. My wild gardens will never measure up in a centerfold contest, but they have a much deeper beauty to me. I feel closer to nature and more a part of the real world when I walk among them than I ever would in the most magnificent English castle garden. The life my wild plants bring to my garden is worth a million pretty perennial faces.

I don't mean to suggest that natural landscapes aren't good-looking. Many of the same plants that used to fill my traditional borders have found new homes in my wild gardens: Yarrows and sunflowers grace the meadow, columbines and coral bells cluster in the woodsy shade, and asters and phlox enliven the butterfly garden.

Vines like this clematis are treasured by Carolina wrens, sparrows, and housefinches, which will often nest in the shelter of their intertwined branches. Wrens also seek dense vines for protection from the elements on cold winter nights.

If a long period of bloom is what you want, plant a mix of wildflowers. When one kind slows down (notice the seedheads on the golden coreopsis at top right), others, like the blanketflower and yarrow here, will take its place.

But the atmosphere of a natural landscape is different from that of a traditional border. The plants are freer. They mingle with their neighbors and pop up from self-sown seed in the most unexpected places. In spring, I like to watch seedlings of shrubs and trees, brought in by birds or animals or waking from dormancy in the soil, unfold their first leaves as they crop up uninvited among the plantings. There's something so irresistible about a tiny oak or maple or a Virginia creeper seedling that I feel an apologetic pang if I have to yank one out of the ground.

In nature and in natural gardens, plant communities are always changing over time. Plants seed themselves or die out, vines ramble onward, stoloniferous plants expand their territories. This natural succession is a fas-cinating process to watch. One of the things I find most satisfying about turning to a natural landscape is that it is truly a living, evolving garden, not a static collection of plants arranged to suit the gardener.

In the pages to come, you'll find lots of ideas on how to create the types of natural garden you enjoy most: meadow and prairie gardens, woodland and shade gardens, water gardens, bird gardens, and butterfly gardens. You'll learn how to add all the finishing touches—walls, paths, and other fun and useful features like benches and arbors. And you'll find everything you need to know to plant and care for your natural landscape. Soon, your natural landscape will bring as much beauty and pleasure into your life—and the lives of wildlife around you—as mine has brought me.

Chapter 2

A FIELD OF FLOWERS
Creating Meadow and Prairie Gardens

A sweep of grasses spiked with blazing star and the clustered flowers of rattlesnake master gives this prairie garden the feel of America's legendary grasslands.

Rattlesnake master is related to the garden perennial called sea holly.

I start every morning with a stroll around the yard, and the first place I head is always my meadow garden. I like to visit it before the sun is high, when silken cups of spiderwebs still glisten with morning dew. It's the "wildest" garden on our place, and that may be part of the attraction. Because it requires so little intervention from me, the gardener, it's brimming with wildlife.

My current meadow garden is mostly a meadow, but it's also partly a prairie, thanks to native plants that sprang up from seeds and roots. It's a more casual effort than my previous meadow gardens, which I started from bare, prepared soil. This one began when we let a slope of fescue go wild. Not long after we stopped mowing the slope into lawn, prairie grasses appeared. These plants, including bluestems and switchgrass, showed their tenacity by growing back from roots that might have been anchored there for a hundred years, when my backyard was once a peninsula of prairie.

I transplanted clumps of blue mistflower and ironweed into the meadow that first year, but I needn't have bothered. In the first spring after we stopped mowing, these perennial wildflowers, along with a host of others, reclaimed their space, shooting up from roots that had somehow managed to survive years of mowing. Common wildflowers, like yarrow and asters, and uncommon surprises, like flowering spurge and rattlebox, sprouted among the grasses, and at the foot of the slope, where water lies after a heavy rain, soft rush and sedges took tentative hold.

Now in its third summer, my meadow garden looks almost as good as the best wild meadows—and to me, that's the surest sign of success. Maximilian sunflower and other perennial sunflowers are running through the tawny grasses, free to roam among royal purple ironweed and the big mauve puffs of tall Joe-Pye weed. Lower-growing mistflower at their feet looks like a haze of blue smoke from a distance. Swamp milkweed in the damp soil at the foot of the hill adds a touch of pink to the scenery.

Wild creatures moved into my meadow just as fast as the flowers. From early spring right through the dead of winter, more than 40 species of birds visit the meadow, searching out seeds and insects. I like to watch the downy woodpeckers hammer on the tall stalks of common mullein, cracking the seedpods to find overwintering larvae.

A pair of song sparrows wove a dainty cup of grasses in the pasture rose as soon as the prickly bush grew knee-high. Two pairs of field sparrows dueled over the meadow, then settled the territorial dispute by agreeing on an imaginary boundary right down the middle. In summer, bluebirds raise babies in the nest boxes in the meadow—except for the box close to the woods, which has been claimed by a pair of Carolina chickadees.

In summer, family and friends delight in watching the butterflies that dance over the flowers. It's as if there were two layers of flowers—one grounded, one airborne. I keep a running checklist in my head, and each year brings new species. It makes me think that somehow the word is being passed. The meadow isn't thick with "weeds," but I let pigweed and pokeweed grow, and even some nettles, so that butterflies will find suitable host plants to lay their eggs on. Milkweed is welcome for its exquisitely fragrant flowers and its stout leaves—caterpillar food. I keep a lookout for the tattletale signs of chewed leaves and droppings that reveal a caterpillar's presence. They're everywhere, is what I find: Almost every plant hosts one kind or another.

Red-tailed hawks and barred owls hunt the meadow, and sometimes we spot a coyote or red fox intent on mouse-catching. But my favorite wild thing is the terrestrial crayfish (or crawdad, as they're called around here) that moved in among the sedges. I've never seen this terrestrial resident, but the evidence is unmistakable: a 10-

inch-tall chimney of dribbled mud, looking very much like a child's sand castle. That tower hides the entrance to a burrow from which the crayfish emerges at night to nibble on plants.

Meadow or Prairie?

Which type of natural garden do you want, a meadow or a prairie? They are different, and the difference mainly lies in the balance of wildflowers and grasses. Picture the two, and you'll see what I mean.

Think meadow, and you think of a knee-high spread of flowers against a green background: pure white oxeye daisies and blue-eyed grass, vivid orange hawkweed punctuated by paper birches, buttercups in a solid swatch of yellow, clover and milkweed and butterflies. In a meadow, wildflowers often grow in big stretches, covering the ground in a wash of color. The grasses are

Get out your binoculars for a close-up look at how butterflies sip nectar. The magnification also makes the colors and scales of wings come alive. Intricately patterned butterflies, like this painted beauty, are amazing when seen through binoculars.

TRIPLE OCCUPANCY

Bluebirds are the bird of choice in a meadow garden. The open space and abundant food are just what they like. But birds aren't the only tenants that will make use of nest boxes. These simple wooden homes are prime real estate for all kinds of creatures. Here are a few you might find.

Butterflies. The roof overhang or the floor of the box is a good place for butterflies to shelter in a summer shower. I've seen monarchs hanging like dry leaves from the bottom of one of our boxes in early morning.

Flying squirrels. These big-eyed creatures of the night are much smaller than typical squirrels, and they can fit easily into a bird box. They prefer a den in a tree, but they take shelter occasionally in high-mounted boxes or use them as food caches. If you find nibbled acorns or nuts with a single, elliptical hole chewed in the shell, suspect a flying squirrel. They're much more common than most people think.

Lizards. After the bluebirds fledge from the boxes in my meadow garden, little striped lizards with bright blue tails take over. These are youngsters of the big, brown, five-lined skink, an arboreal lizard that usually hangs out in the treetops. The young skinks bask on the birdhouse roofs in the hot summer sun and slide inside faster than the eye can follow if they think you're watching them.

Mice. Every winter, dainty, white-footed deer mice commandeer one or more of the nest boxes in my garden. When I slide the top open, I'm greeted by a pair of bright black eyes and a whiskery nose that seems more affronted than afraid.

Black-eyed Susans and their cultivated cousins known as gloriosa daisies are old reliables in any meadow garden. The plants self-sow to create ever-larger colonies. Long-blooming flowers attract butterflies and many other insects.

Prairie wildflowers are tough enough to thrive without much coddling from the gardener. Here, purple coneflowers and penstemons add punch to the color mix.

background players, a lush green backdrop for the bright flowers. Often you hardly notice them.

Think prairie, and grasses are what come to mind first. Prairie grasses are big and showy, with as much presence as the wildflowers they share space with. The wind rippling through the prairie grasses caused early naturalists to call the prairie a sea of grass. A prairie has a more subdued beauty than a meadow. Flowers are interspersed among the grasses, their colors hazed and softened by the grass.

The Mood of a Meadow

A typical meadow is in a state of flux. No matter how wild and "natural" a meadow looks, it's almost always artificial, created by mowing or grazing. Except for western mountain meadows and a few rare natural eastern grasslands, meadows are almost all created by the hand of man. They usually start as an abandoned field or a pasture, a piece of land that was cleared of forest and turned to crops or forage. Because this land is an unnatural ecosystem, unlike the grasslands of the West or the prairies, plant succession tends to be speeded up. Species change quickly as more dominant plants move in.

Look at the next meadow you admire, and you'll see that it's dominated by goldenrod, milkweed, and other wildflowers that spread from the roots to form colonies. These clonal colonies can last for years, especially if the meadow is mowed every year or two.

Eventually perennial grasses claim more and more space and, if you stop mowing, trees and shrubs move in. Succession moves fast in the warm Southeast, where pines often show up in a meadow in as little as three years. The progression is slower in the North, where it may take decades before grasses give way to encroaching forest.

By supplying a little guidance and a yearly mowing, you can slow the succession and manage your meadow garden so that it stays a meadow. Many gardeners choose to mow their meadow or prairie every year, but biennial or even triennial mowing may be all you need. Meadows and prairies are forgiving gardens: I didn't mow our Midwest garden at all in its first three years, and it looks great. But to maintain vigor in the grasses and to control seedling trees, we'll mow in late winter with the blade set about 6 inches high. Regular mowing is the only thing that will keep your meadow a meadow.

Goldenrod and New England aster, one of Mother Nature's inspired combinations, decorate late summer fields and do just as well in a meadow garden.

The Nature of the Prairie

The natural prairie, which once stretched unbroken from Indiana to the Rockies, changes as it moves from west to east. In the West, where rain is scarce in the shadow of the mountains, the grasslands are known as shortgrass prairie. Low-growing grasses, mostly buffalo grass and grama grass, green up in spring and go dormant by summer when all of the moisture is used up. They leave behind a parched, yellow landscape dotted by sagebrush.

Moving east, with rainfall becoming more generous, the grassland changes to mixed prairie. Wildflowers become more plentiful, and little bluestem (a grass that is neither little nor blue) takes over. Stands of sumac dot the mixed prairie. They're gorgeous in the fall, when the shining leaves turn brilliant red and orange against the tawny grasses.

The tallgrass prairie, which takes over in the Midwest, is what most of us think of as a prairie. Grasses

MEADOW OR PRAIRIE: WHICH IS RIGHT FOR YOU?

Deciding whether to grow a meadow or prairie garden is a matter of personal taste. Most meadow and prairie plants will adapt and thrive under a wide range of conditions, including extremes of pH or precipitation. So, consider these questions to decide which type of garden is right for you.

Do you want mostly colorful flowers? If so, go for the meadow look. Fill your garden with annuals that will bloom their heads off until frost, then dig them under and replant for next year. Or plant a meadow with perennials that flower generously, like oxeye daisies, coreopsis, and black-eyed Susans.

Do you like the look of grasses? If you do, plant a prairie. The prairie look depends on wonderful grasses, and it is these plants rather than flowers that hold center stage much of the time. In summer, though, a prairie leaps into bloom with wildflowers that complement the height and habit of the grasses.

How tall a garden do you want? If you want a shorter planting, you'll most likely want a meadow. Prairie favorites like big bluestem, compass plant, and many others can easily reach head-height or taller. If you like the prairie look but prefer a shorter garden, look for plants that stay at the height you want. Prairie dropseed, grama grass, foxtail barley, butterfly weed, and blanket flower are just a few of the possibilities.

How much replanting and weeding do you want to do? To keep the floriferous look, a meadow garden needs more attention than a prairie planting. Meadows will naturally go toward grasses unless you guide them. Because of the abundance of grasses, prairie gardens look good even with minimal maintenance.

What are the natural grasslands in your area? Some gardeners choose meadow or prairie depending on what was once the natural ecology of their area. But that doesn't mean you shouldn't grow a meadow garden in Nebraska or a prairie garden in Connecticut. If that's what you like, why not?

A native of Europe, chicory has made itself at home in North America. Roots dug after flowering can be used as a coffee additive or substitute.

Look for common milkweed along North American roadsides as far west as Kansas. Pods open to release parachuted seeds that drift to start new plants.

dominate, and they're big ones—waist-high or better. Compass plant towers over the grasses as they bend to the wind, its leaves showing the way north. Lustrous Indian grass and big bluestem, with its angular seedheads like a three-toed turkey foot, dominate the tallgrass prairie. Flowers bloom from spring through fall in the prairie. In summer, the tallgrass prairie explodes with color, much of it purple and yellow. Bright sunflowers and goldenrods bloom with asters, blazing star, and purple coneflowers in a glorious summer finale.

A False Start

My first meadow garden was a flop. Like millions of other gullible folks, I was seduced by the mouth-watering picture on a canister of wildflower mix. Imagining a lavish spread of poppies and bluebonnets and a hundred other treasures, I shook out the seeds and a disappointing amount of filler material onto a patch of poorly prepared soil, then sat back and waited.

What I got was just what I deserved. Weeds shouldered aside the seedlings, and the existing turfgrasses, which I hadn't bothered to remove, came roaring back, burying the puny wildflowers.

I should have known better, but Mother Nature makes it look so easy. From one end of the country to the other, she shows off wherever there's a bit of sunny open space. When we see a hillside on fire with brilliant red Indian paintbrush, a sweep of goldenrod and purple asters, or a splash of sunflowers and shoulder-high bluestem grass, we don't stop to think that the natural display took years to develop. Being human, we go for instant gratification. And that's the mistake.

Unless you're willing to take what you may get—and depending on the seeds already in the soil, that could be delightful—starting a meadow or prairie garden is just like starting any other garden. You have to dig out or kill off the lawn grass. You have to choose appropriate plants and buy high-quality seed. You have to control weeds so that your wild youngsters have a chance. And you have to guide the garden.

Summer is the peak season for a meadow garden. For a glimpse of the tooth-and-claw world of nature, pull up a chair and watch the drama of predatory insects and spiders, which lurk in the flowers to take their share.

A Partnership with Nature

Mark Trela
New Harmony, Indiana

"Meadow gardening makes you a more careful observer," says Mark Trela, owner of Fragrant Farms in New Harmony, Indiana. "You become a student of nature," he says. "You can see the interplay of different insects, birds, rabbits, moles, voles—everything working together."

One thing Mark likes about being a partner with nature instead of an adversary: "Your role is to be much less invasive than you'd be in a traditional, more structured garden. It's more of a partnership."

Today's gardens look too much alike, says Mark. "You see the same types of plants, even the same cultivars, in garden after garden." But a meadow garden is different. It's always a work in progress and always includes an incredible diversity of plants, some invited, others happy accidents.

Mark's meadow gardens, which include several areas, none bigger than a quarter acre, begin with a combination of seeds and plants. He prefers not to go into an area with major equipment and rip it up. Instead, he digs by hand and often plants his wildflowers through existing grass. He mulches thickly around his new plants to smother the grass. After the first year, he says, "I just stand back and watch as things reseed and spread."

Grasses are crucial to a successful meadow garden, says Mark. They're the backbone of the garden, keeping it interesting in fall and winter. He's also fond of stalwart perennials like ironweed, monarda, and small, white, late-blooming heath aster. Self-sowing balsam and larkspur and stands of hollyhocks give his gardens an old-fashioned "grandma's garden" air. A beautiful, soft apricot–colored hollyhock bloomed one summer after years of mixed colors growing together. Mark liked it so much he saved the seed and grows it every year to perpetuate the strain.

Making a meadow garden requires a shift in perspective, says Mark. "In a typical, 'normal' landscape, we're not thinking in wholes anymore—it's something for the front and something for the back or the side. A meadow garden is a whole unit. As soon as you add coneflowers, black-eyed Susans, and milkweeds

to the grasses, you'll have butterflies and insects. And after them will come the birds. "Just by virtue of being there, a meadow garden becomes an ecosystem. It's an ecology of the whole, not just a few plants stuck in a traditional garden to attract butterflies who will only stick around long enough to eat."

Mark likes to use a lot of native plants in his meadow gardens. He not only finds the plants beautiful but also points out that they offer sustenance to many insects and birds. "Swamp milkweed is one of my favorites," he notes. "It has that beautiful, pale pink-purple color and the butterflies just love it. Cardinal flower is wonderful, too. Black-eyed Susans bloom all summer, and asters are really glorious in the fall. I love to watch the birds in the meadow. They're mostly small songbirds—a lot of sparrows, indigo buntings—coming for the bugs on the plants or the seeds later in the season. They make it alive."

Mark has a hard time naming a single favorite season for his meadow garden, because he finds beauty in it all year long. "In springtime, things are greening up, and there's that surge of growth. Flowers hit their peak in late June through midJuly, and the peak of flowers means the peak of insects. Then fall brings the rich, mellow colors of the grasses, and in winter,

Spires of foxgloves punctuate this shady garden. The biennial plants will self-sow, so there's always a new supply for next year.

there are the interesting shapes of seedpods and the rustle of dry grasses."

Unlike more formal gardens, meadow gardens are for everyone. Kids love meadow gardens, says Mark, especially young children, who will have fun playing among the grasses and flowers. "It's a great education," he says.

The changing nature of a meadow garden holds great appeal for Mark. "The fun part is watching it develop," he says. "It's a lot more interesting than just watching your grass grow."

"A meadow garden is a liberating experience," he says. "If you're a gardener who's been a slave to your landscape, you'll find the freedom of a meadow is a wonderful change. Things will get along fine without constant intervention. Plant just once and watch results over time instead of replanting every year. Let things go to seed. Let things develop over time."

A field trip through the garden yields such curiosities as the oddly shaped blossom of prairie clover.

Paths invite visitors through the garden. Mark makes the paths wide enough to accommodate a wheelbarrow or a pair of friends walking side by side. Wider paths invite lingering, while narrow paths tend to hurry you through the garden.

Ready for Commitment

Making a meadow or a prairie is a long-term commitment. If you plant a commercial seed mix, you may find the first year is the flashiest. That's because seed mixes include fast-growing annuals in liberal amounts. Even in nature, any bare ground is quickly covered by a flush of opportunistic annuals. Their mission is to set seed while they have a chance, so they grow and bloom fast. The annuals in your seed mix will make your meadow garden a burst of glory the first year.

But after that first splash of annuals, the garden undergoes a change in personality as perennials and grasses take over. In nature, flowers often dot grasslands rather than spread lavishly across them. It's a beautiful effect, but more subtle. If you want a longer or showier splash of color, then you need to plan for it. Include more perennials, or clear some space each year so that annuals can self-sow or so that you can sow them. In an established garden, sow annuals in fall so that they have a head start on outdistancing the competition in spring.

Figure on at least two years of guidance to get a meadow or prairie going on its own. Weeding chores are heavy the first year or two until the desirable plants fill in thickly. The payoff is that once you get the groundwork in place, this natural garden will sustain itself for years, changing over the seasons as the plant communities naturally evolve with little or no guidance from you. It's fun to watch as the balance shifts year after year. A natural garden is never static.

Learn to love your meadow or prairie garden in its natural state, so that you aren't always fiddling with it. If you're constantly weeding or clipping or rearranging, your "meadow" will become just another garden. Animals won't move in, birds won't nest, and you'll miss out on the whole cycle of life that makes meadow and prairie gardening so rewarding.

The Right Mix

A meadow or prairie planting is no place for prima donnas that need to be coddled. You want plants that can stand on their own. Search out vigorous plants that

(continued on page 43)

An occasional mowing will allow enough light to reach the ground so that annuals can sprout from self-sown seeds. Perennials also benefit from mowing.

SIX STEPS TO MEADOW STARTUP

Weeds are the worst enemy of young meadow plants. But these simple steps will get you growing—and get weeds going!

1. Strip or smother existing sod.
2. Till or turn the soil until it is smooth.
3. Water the area thoroughly with a fine to medium spray.
4. Wait for weed seeds to sprout. Slice off with the blade of a hoe, taking care not to disturb the soil. Repeat as often as you have patience for.
5. Sow meadow garden seed.
6. Weed until meadow seedlings are well on their way.

The Right Mix

A backdrop of trees provides contrast to the bright colors of a meadow garden, multiplying the impact. This edge-of-the-trees area is also a natural place for meadow plants to thrive, a transition from field to woods.

FAST SPLASH MEADOW MIX

If you're planting into bare soil, try this mix of easy-to-grow annuals for a big splash the first season. Mix the seeds together before sowing for a more natural look. Interplant your meadow throughout the season with perennials and grasses for more enduring color in the following years.

Baby blue eyes (*Nemophila menziesii*). Delicate low-growing charmer with sky blue flowers above ferny foliage.

Bachelor's-buttons (*Centaurea cyanus*). Branched, bushy plants with narrow leaves and generous, long-lasting blooms in true cornflower blue, pink, rose, white, and intense deep red-purple.

Black-bearded wheat (*Triticum turgidum*, Durum Group). A cultivated variety of wheat with cream-colored heads that bristle with long 4-to 6-inch awns, shiny dark black when mature.

California poppy (*Eschscholzia californica*). Stunning vivid orange (sometimes yellow) flowers like silken cups above beautiful, lacy gray-green foliage. Pink and purple cultivars are available, but nothing beats the common species for oomph.

Calliopsis (*Coreopsis tinctoria*). A graceful, knee-high plant with abundant gold, russet, mahogany, or two-toned daisies and ferny foliage.

Corn cockle (*Agrostemma githago*). Simple, silky flowers in vivid magenta-purple atop a branching, midheight plant with grayish foliage.

Field poppy (*Papaver rhoeas*). A beautiful common weed of European farm fields; the familiar red "Flanders poppy" with crinkled blossoms of zingy red on wiry stems.

Scarlet flax (*Linum grandiflorum*). Satiny deep red flowers in loose clusters atop a 2-foot plant. 'Rubrum' is a lovely variety.

'Sensation'-type cosmos (*Cosmos bipinnatus*). Tall or midheight, airy plants with fine, ferny foliage and wonderful blossoms in shades of pink, rose, and white.

Shirley poppy (*Papaver rhoeas*, Shirley strain). Heart-breakingly delicate flowers in watercolor shades of pink, white, rose, and red, some with petals rimmed in deeper color.

Tickseed sunflower (*Bidens aristosa*). Huge but airy branching plants reaching 4 to 6 feet tall and wide, absolutely inundated with masses of buttery yellow daisies.

Yellow cosmos (*Cosmos sulphureus*). Bright yellows, oranges, and reds that glow like fire; a branching but upright plant that usually stays midheight but in wild forms can reach 7 feet tall!

California poppy (*Eschscholzia californica*)

Calliopsis (*Coreopsis tinctoria*)

You can make your meadow or prairie garden as showy as you want by using a free hand with flowering plants. Every year I add new perennials to the gardens, just as I do in my more traditional beds and borders. I also move plants around within the garden in early spring, to fine-tune the color scheme or design. Need more deep purple on that side to play against the Maximilian sunflowers? No problem. Simply move in five young ironweeds from the nursery bed. One warning: Prairie plants can develop tremendous root systems. Either move them young (two years old or less) or let them stay where they are.

In a new garden, there's plenty of open space to direct-seed California poppies and other fast-blooming annuals. But after the first year or two, you may find it hard to ease new annuals into the garden unless you clear some space first. Even when open ground is at a premium, self-sown annuals often manage to find a roothold among the perennials. I'm often astonished at the vigor—or the lack of it—of some annuals. Pink

catchfly (*Silene armeria*), almost a weed in the mixed border, is one annual that I figured would hold its own. But it gave up in a single season. Snow-on-the-mountain (*Euphorbia marginata*), on the other hand, keeps going strong year after year, dropping its hard, round seeds and somehow finding room to grow. Surprises like that are part of the fun of natural landscaping.

Great Grasses

We gardeners are easily sidetracked by flowers, but if you look beyond the blooms in any natural meadow or prairie, you'll see that grasses are really the backbone of these wild areas. Wild grasses are as varied as wildflowers, and like wildflowers, they may be widespread or local in their distribution.

Walk through an old field in Pennsylvania or Connecticut, and you'll find timothy and orchard grass. Look along railroad tracks from Indiana to Nebraska,

This beautiful spread is typical of "meadow-in-a-can" seed mixes. It will be spectacular the first year, but will quickly fade out under competition. Think of it as a bed of annuals and replant every year or two.

As you get to know your meadow, you'll discover all kinds of interesting subtleties, like the delicate yellow flowers of Indian grass, shown here.

Big bluestem once covered many thousands of acres of the American tallgrass prairie, but today all that's left are small remnants along roadsides and railways. It's a reliable food source for wild birds and mammals.

and you might run across little bluestem, a misnamed grass that grows waist-high and turns a lovely, soft orange-red in fall, or big bluestem, a gangly grass that can stretch to 7 feet.

If you hike the basin and range country between the Rockies and the Sierra Nevada and Cascades, you'll find clumps of bluebunch wheatgrass and the lovely, soft-as-velvet downy brome, or cheatgrass, an invasive, imported annual grass that forms a silvery green carpet in early spring. Step over to California, and you'll see beautiful purple needlegrass, with long, silky hairs that hide sharp-tipped seeds.

Think of grasses like these and dozens of others as the background fabric of your meadow or prairie garden. Their colors blend together like a fine piece of Irish tweed: subdued shades of green, gold, purple, brown, and coppery pink melded into a tapestry, with wildflow-

ers standing out like bright threads embroidered against the fabric.

You can start grasses from seed or buy plants. Start with a sampling of the grasses that are native to your area. Specialty nurseries offer dozens of possibilities. Although it's slower to start from seed (many grasses take three years to reach a good size), I find it totally satisfying to look at a 6-foot-tall stand of big bluestem and remember the day it first sprouted in a plastic pot on my windowsill.

Grasses add appealing texture and soft color all year. I like to look over my prairie garden on an early spring morning, when the soft new grasses are spangled with dew. In summer, I watch the breeze move across like ripples on water. When the grasses turn tawny gold and russet in fall, I sometimes sit right in the middle of the garden, listening to the grasses singing in the wind.

Wildlife in Your Meadow or Prairie Garden

Meadows and prairies are not only beautiful but they're also alive. Bees and butterflies probe the flowers, spiders spin among the stems of grasses, birds seek shelter and sustenance, and a menagerie of small, furred creatures skitter among the stalks, hidden from predators' eyes.

Meadow and prairie gardens attract similar types of wildlife. Because the garden is undisturbed for long stretches at a time, it's inviting to birds and animals, even usually wary creatures. What your meadow or prairie may attract depends on where you live.

Birds, Birds, Birds

Birds will be your most visible visitors. In spring, your garden is likely to be claimed by nesting pairs of field sparrows, song sparrows, and other songbirds. In early summer, when nestlings hatch, parent birds will comb the plants, seeking caterpillars and other tasty morsels. Later in the season, goldfinches, buntings, and sparrows in a dozen shades of brown will visit for hours at a time, cracking seeds on the ground and hanging like parrots on the tips of grasses. Sunflowers are so popular in the meadow garden that birds will squabble over them. In winter, flocks of cardinals, juncos, and other songbirds seek shelter among the standing plants.

One of the most beautiful and most common residents of meadow and prairie gardens is the indigo bunting, a tiny bird the size of a chickadee with feathers of vivid sapphire blue. Indigo bunting feathers are iridescent: When they're not shining in the sunlight, they appear dull black. But when the bird swoops down against the grasses, you'll see a flash of electric blue. Indigos appreciate an undisturbed stand of plant stalks, where they can hide their tiny nest low to the ground. One year, they built a nest in a patch of fragrant mountain mint in my meadow garden; the next year, they nested among sunflowers.

It's not too hard to find bird nests if you pay attention to the parents. When they act agitated, chipping loudly at you, that means you're getting near the nest. Withdraw a bit and watch to see where the parent goes. Grassland birds nest on or near the ground, so be careful where you step. When you spot the nest, go no closer. It's an old wives' tale that human scent will make a bird

A white-throated sparrow in the garden is a sign that winter's on its way if you live in the East or South, but a harbinger of spring for Canada and the North.

Birds are the gardener's best friend. A single bird consumes hundreds of insects every day, and tens of thousands of insects in a season.

You'd think bright yellow goldfinches would be easy to spot, but the little birds are surprisingly easy to overlook among sunflowers and other colorful blossoms.

QUICK TIPS TO ATTRACT BIRDS

Birds are a wonderful bonus when you have a meadow garden. Imagine redwinged blackbirds clinging to the tops of tall perennials or the song of a meadowlark drifting across your yard. Here are some ways to ensure that birds will flock to your meadow.

- Plant flowers that set bird-attracting seeds. Annual and perennial sunflowers, all kinds of cosmos, and coneflowers are superb bird attracters.

- Allow a few weeds to grow. The seeds or fruits of lamb's quarters, pigweed, pokeweed, and ragweed are relished by birds.

- Let some sections of your garden remain undisturbed by humans or dogs. Birds are adept at hiding nests close to human activity, as long as the immediate area is untrafficked.

- Plant some perennials that spread into colonies. The leaves and stems create good cover for birds.

- Cut your meadow in late winter rather than in fall. Birds will seek food and shelter in standing plants throughout the winter.

- Set up nesting boxes. Bluebirds love meadow gardens.

- Let milkweeds stand until they fall naturally. The strong, silky fibers of their stems are a favorite source of nesting material.

- Keep cats indoors. House cats are a major predator of songbirds.

abandon its nest. But it's a fact that your scent trail may draw a curious predator to the eggs or nestlings. So enjoy the show, but keep your distance.

Sometimes your meadow or prairie may lure unusual birds. One March day, I was walking through my meadow garden when a woodcock rocketed up from under my feet. Normally a bird of the forest, he was on migration and had been drawn to a muddy part of the garden where the earthworms that make up his diet were plentiful. The ground was full of ¼-inch holes where his long, flexible bill had been probing.

Dozens of other birds nest in or visit meadow and prairie gardens. The bigger your garden, the better your chances of attracting a variety of species. Depending on where you live, you might see bluebirds, magpies, red-winged blackbirds, loggerhead shrikes, or even the oddly named dicksissel, who says his own name over and over.

I'll never forget the day I first heard a meadowlark singing in my meadow garden. I'd stepped outside to enjoy an early morning cup of tea when I heard a clear musical whistle from a post in the garden. There he was, a gorgeous meadowlark, his shining golden belly puffed out with territorial pride as he sang. Now, at last, I had a meadow.

Small Dramas

Out of sight, there's a whole civilization living in the nether regions of your meadow or prairie garden. In tunnels, burrows, and runways through the grasses and plants, furry creatures scoot along unseen by the eyes of humans and, they hope, predators.

But it's not only the furred and feathered who will be gathering food and raising a family in your meadow or prairie garden. On a smaller scale, there are thousands of life-and-death dramas being played out every minute.

Insects will be the first creatures to move into your garden. The six-legged world is immense and fascinating. Best of all, it's going on right under your nose. No need to sit still or be discreet. The bugs couldn't care less about your presence.

What I like best about prairie plants and summer meadow flowers is that they're tall, so I don't even have to stoop to see what's going on. Butterflies flirt or fight with each other, beetles glint metallic green in the sun, bees pat pollen into pouches on their legs. Wasps hunt for caterpillars to take home to their paper nursery chambers.

Spiders are great to spy on, especially for kids. They'll give you a close-up look at the beauty and terror of nature, from gossamer cups rimmed with morning dew to the death struggle of a moth in the web. Look for beautiful yellow crab spiders waiting in the center of a flower for an unsuspecting butterfly. If you see a wide leaf rolled under at the edge, peek inside, and you may find a nursery of tiny spiderlings.

I learned how spiders make their webs by watching them at work in my meadow garden. With one hind foot hooked to the previous strand, they lay down a new course of silk, going round and round faster than you would expect. It takes the bigger orb weavers less than an hour to make a 2-foot web.

East of the Rockies, lightning bugs on summer nights are taken for granted, but to those who grew up west of the mountains, they're magic. I didn't fully appreciate the splendor of fireflies—another name for these flying nightlights—until some cousins visited from Oregon. We were sitting out on a second-floor porch, looking down over a field, when suddenly the youngest child broke into our conversation. "What are all those little lights?" he demanded. He'd never seen lightning bugs before, and he was instantly charmed.

Orb weavers spin a classic web between plants or other supports. Stroll in your garden early in the morning when the dew outlines and reveals each web.

The fast, darting flight of dragonflies, and their ability to hover and dive, gives them a predator's edge over the mosquitoes and other insects they devour on the wing.

A prairie or meadow garden is full of insect voices in summer, with crickets, katydids, coneheads (yes, really), and grasshoppers tuning up. If you see an insect with long back legs with the toothed comb edge that indicate a singer, capture it in a jar and keep it overnight to listen.

Butterflies—Floating Flowers

The flat-topped flower clusters of yarrow, ironweed, and other meadow and prairie plants have a multitude of tiny flowers, and that's perfect for butterflies. These nectar-seekers are opportunists. As soon as your garden blooms, butterflies will be there.

Midsummer to late summer is peak butterfly time. That's when I find everything from tiny orange-bordered blues to velvety black swallowtails with wings almost 4 inches across. In late summer, when monarchs start to move through on migration, flurries of orange-and-black wings dance over the meadow.

Butterflies will be looking for places to lay their eggs as well as nectar to sip. They're specific in their needs: Monarchs lay on milkweed, pearl crescents like asters, American painted ladies seek out pearly everlasting for a nursery. That's because these are the plants their caterpillars eat. When they hatch, dinner's waiting.

Purple flowers hold as much attraction for butterflies as red and orange flowers do for hummingbirds. This monarch is probing the blossoms of rough blazing star, a native prairie species.

BUTTERFLY CHECKLIST

Some butterflies are found across the country, but others are very local. Monarchs, for example, are found all across the country; Baltimore checkerspots are found only where turtlehead grows. If you keep a checklist, you'll soon have a good idea of what lives near you. Depending on where you live and what's in your garden, you may see these butterflies.

❑ **Black swallowtail**
❑ **Buckeye**
❑ **Cabbage white**
❑ **Common blue**
❑ **Common sulphur**
❑ **European skipper**
❑ **Gray hairstreak**
❑ **Great spangled fritillary**
❑ **Green hairstreak**
❑ **Indian skipper**
❑ **Meadow fritillary**
❑ **Monarch**
❑ **Orange sulphur**
❑ **Painted lady**
❑ **Pearly crescentspot**
❑ **Red admiral**
❑ **Red-spotted purple**
❑ **Tiger swallowtail**
❑ **Viceroy**
❑ **Zebra swallowtail**

With wings closed, the painted lady reveals only a hint of her coloring.

The appeal of a meadow lies in its wildness. These beautiful plumes of goldenrod spread aggressively by roots to merge with other plants in a wildflower mix that will need no intervention from you to keep it looking good.

You can consult butterfly books to learn just what host plants will attract what butterfly, or you can play it by ear as I do. I've learned that just about any plant in my garden may be prime caterpillar territory for one butterfly species or another. I watch for telltale droppings or chewed leaves to find caterpillars. If I see an unfamiliar sort, I like to raise a couple in a jar, along with leaves of their host plant, and see what they turn out to be. It's a great feeling to carry a perfect, newly hatched butterfly outside, its delicate feet clinging to your fingertip, and set it free.

One year, I was tickled to see that my heliopsis had seeded itself with abandon. I couldn't wait to see the golden daisies come into bloom. Then a plague of small, spiny black caterpillars hit. In no time, most of my heliopsis was standing nude, its leaves stripped to the center vein. I cursed the caterpillars, then I captured a few to see what they would turn into. In two weeks, they hatched into coppery orange crescentspots, and I released them to join their siblings, who were fluttering

over the flowers. And the heliopsis? Leaves regrew and the plants bloomed just a bit later than usual, none the worse for wear.

Design Tips for Your Meadow or Prairie

Meadows and prairies are the most forgiving of gardens. Almost any combination of plants looks good, as long as you remember to plant plenty of grasses. There are no rules, except for what you find personally pleasing.

You'll want a big, wide stretch for your meadow or prairie. If your budget is limited, it's better to keep the size of your garden smaller than it is to spread your plants out too much. A 40-foot-square prairie garden filled with bloom is more satisfying than a sparse 100-foot patch that you have to live with for three years before it looks like anything. You can always enlarge the garden as cash permits.

(continued on page 54)

MEADOW GARDEN DESIGN

Create a meadow for long-term beauty by letting grasses and tenacious spreading perennials form the backbone. This meadow garden will thrive with only an occasional mowing to keep down the trees and shrubs that will be carried in by birds and the wind. The flowers include a mix of natives and foreigners, which have a tenacity that's welcome in this setting. Most of the flowers in this garden are perennials, which will need no maintenance from you to keep their good looks. The annual poppies, cornflowers, and corn cockles will sow themselves to rebloom year after year, but you'll need to keep an eye out for invading weeds and grasses. If you want, you can treat the annuals section of this garden (area 6 on the plan) as a flowerbed; collect the seed from your flowers at the end of the season, and in spring clear the soil and sow your saved seed. That way you're sure to get a burst of bloom every year. Plant in wide sweeps to get the maximum impact. Or you can alter the design but keep the planting list, and intermingle the plants for a more informal, less showy look.

PLANT LIST

1. Purple-top grass (*Tridens flavus*)
2. Dame's rocket (*Hesperis matronalis* 'Alba')
3. Heath asters (*Aster ericoides*)
4. Oxeye daisies (*Chrysanthemum leucanthemum*)
5. Bluets (*Houstonia caerulea*)
6. Field poppies, cornflowers, and corn cockles (*Papaver rhoeas, Centaurea cyanus*, and *Agrostemma githago*)
7. Goldenrods (*Solidago odora* and other *Solidago* spp.)
8. Black-eyed Susans (*Rudbeckia triloba, Rudbeckia fulgida*, and other *Rudbeckia* spp.)

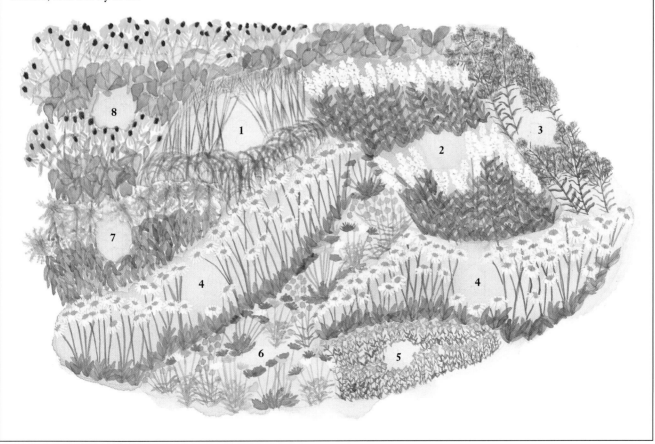

One Clover and a Bee

Mary Lee Sargent
Champaign, Illinois

"I've always been a gardener," says Mary Lee Sargent, who's earned her nickname of "Prairie Mary." "I grew up in the Dallas, Texas, suburbs, where everybody planted marigolds and petunias, and I loved that when I was a child. But as I got older, I got interested in wildflowers from going out into nature. Then I discovered prairies."

Mary Lee's love of prairie gardens and restoration led her to join Grand Prairie Friends, a Midwest conservation group. "A lot of rights-of-way and highways were getting bulldozed," she recalls. So, with the Prairie Friends, "we'd go ahead of the bulldozers and rescue plants before they got in there."

Mary Lee's prairie garden is an educational effort as well as a private delight. Her garden is located on the grounds of the New Harmony Inn, in historic New Harmony, Indiana, which Mary Lee had visited for years as a retreat. Although it's on land that's open to the public, Mary Lee retains a strong sense of personal identity with the prairie garden. "I feel like it's mine, all mine!" she laughs. "It definitely is my garden. I planned it, planted it, and maintain it, with just a little help from others."

The prairie garden sprouted in 1989 on bare ground that had once been woodland and river bottoms. The plot combines more than 55 species of plants drawn from dry, wet, and woodland prairie species, and covers a third of an acre.

"In the sunny part, I have lots of grasses and silphiums. I love the form of big bluestem—it looks like something that would be in a Chinese brush painting. And I'm just wild about compass plant (*Silphium laciniatum*). I love the color—a lemony yellow—and the sandpapery leaves. I like the hardiness of it, the adaptability, and its massiveness. And I love that the plant has a story behind it. Compass plant leaves are oriented north-south, so pioneers used it to get a bearing on direction.

"But I like the silphiums generally," says Mary Lee. "Their leaves have such wonderful rough texture, and the plants have great definition of form."

She grows silphiums in her home garden in Champaign, Illinois, as well as in the New Harmony prairie garden. "I have two plants in my home garden that stop people in their tracks," she says. "One is a great clump of delphiniums that puts on a show of blue every few years, and the other is the cup plant (*Silphium perfoliatum*). That's the plant that people stop and stare at. It has just a bower of golden bloom atop the plant."

The New Harmony garden needed a lot of care at the beginning, says Mary Lee. "It seemed like I was weeding constantly." But as the plants matured and began seeding themselves, she has found that the garden takes care of itself much of the time. She plans a week-long weeding session in May and burns the old growth once a year, usually in late winter. Friends help her tend the burn so that it stays under control. The remains of standing grasses and wildflowers burn quickly, leaving the prairie ready for new growth. She adds scores of new plants every spring and weeds out fleabane and other exotic invaders.

Her prairie is a garden for all seasons, but it's in early summer that it brings her a special kind of pleasure. "In late June, it's all so green, so lush. It's not even at full height, just chest-high, but to see the power of the life force in those plants.... It's a hopeful feeling."

The prairie has grown lush with maturity, and Mary Lee feels the garden more than fulfills her original intent of acquainting visitors to New Harmony with their prairie heritage.

"It's an educational place as well as an aesthetic and spiritual place," she says. Only one thousandth of one percent of the native prairie that existed in 1800 is still around today, she says—less than 2 square miles of prairie. "'Prairie' means 'meadow'," she points out, "and I used to find that a diminutive, when I think of what used to be. It seems sad that the word now fits." Although she loves to see her prairie garden in the full glory of its late summer beauty when it's a sea of golden bloom and grasses at full height, her view is

BEST GRASSES FOR PRAIRIE GARDENS

Grasses	Description	Conditions	Comments
Little bluestem (*Schizachyrium scoparium*)	2–5′ tall clumps of fine green leaves; turns vivid, warm rusty orange color in fall and holds that color till spring.	Sun to part light shade. Average, well-drained soil. Drought tolerant. Zones 3 to 10.	Tiny, fuzzy tufts of seeds along the stems catch the light. An eyecatcher in fall and winter, especially if planted in large colonies. Self-sows.
Big bluestem (*Andropogon gerardii*)	Large clumps of fine blue-green leaves from which arise slender stems topped with three-toed "turkey-foot" seedheads. Reaches to 7′.	Sun. Average well-drained soil. Zones 4 to 9.	One of the main grasses of the tallgrass prairie, and a beauty. Beautiful warm russet to bronze fall color.
Indian grass (*Sorghastrum nutans*)	Clumps of fine to medium foliage topped by slender panicles of golden tan flowers. Mellows to yellow and then rusty orange in the fall. Reaches to 5′.	Sun. Average well-drained soil. Zones 4 to 9.	Nice accent plant in a prairie, where it isn't as aggressive as the bluestems or cord grass. Self-sows.
Switch grass (*Panicum virgatum*)	Upright clumps of foliage topped by airy clouds of incredibly delicate flowers and seedheads. Mellows to beige in winter. Reaches 3–7′.	Sun. Average to moist soil. Tolerates poor conditions. Zones 5 to 9.	A lovely grass for the prairie garden. Seeds itself readily once established; weed out as necessary.
Cord grass (*Spartina pectinata*)	Fast-spreading grass with razor-sharp leaves, but beautiful at a distance, with a flowing mane of foliage. Yellow fall color. Reaches 4–7′.	Sun. Average to wet soils. Zones 4 to 9.	An aggressive spreader, and difficult to work around, so plant it in a spot that doesn't get much traffic.
Wheatgrass (*Agropyron* spp.)	Clumps of soft foliage with wheatlike flowers. Reaches to 3′.	Sun. Average to poor soils. Zones 5 to 9, depending on the species.	Can be very aggressive, not necessarily a bad trait in a natural prairie garden. Birds like the seeds. *A. magellanicum*, Magellan blue wheat grass, is an ornamental variety with blue-green foliage.
Stipa (*Stipa* spp.)	Graceful, beautiful grasses with wispy, silky, extremely long-haired seedheads. Most species grow to about 3′.	Sun. Average to dry well-drained soil. Zones 6 to 10, depending on species.	Exquisite seedheads catch the light like silken threads, but can poke animals and passersby.

Chapter 3

GARDENS UNDER TREES
Creating Woodland and Shade Gardens

Woodland gardens are filled with a blaze of color in spring, then mellow to a hundred shades of green for summer coolness.

Azaleas announce spring with a shout of color that wakes the woodland.

I've always liked surprises, and my woodland garden is full of them. Long before my perennial borders wake from winter slumber, I begin haunting the paths of my woodsy front yard. No wildflowers are chancing the weather yet, but the birds know spring is coming. This February morning, a pair of Carolina chickadees are courting, offering each other love songs in high, thin voices.

There's so much to watch in a woodland garden that the first wildflowers usually manage to take me by surprise. I know spring is here for sure when I come across a nosegay of dainty purple hepatica or a cluster of bloodroot flowers, their wide white stars held flat in the warmth of the sun. Once the wildflowers get going, there's something new every week. Watching them emerge from winter slumber into bud and bloom rejuvenates my spirit. As the flowers awake, the insects do, too. A humming noise leads me to a bevy of fat, slow bees bumbling about the pussy willows. They're right at nose level, but they're interested in pollen, not in me. At this height, it's easy to watch as they clean their dusty heads and pat the golden pollen into saddlebags on their legs.

My woodland garden is so full of life that I sometimes forget what it looked like just a few short years ago. When we moved into our little log house, the front yard was a lovely sweep of green lawn beneath old oaks and elms. (And yes, they're American elms—this area seems to be one of the last bastions against Dutch elm disease.)

Most passersby would have said our front yard was pretty, and it was, in a parklike way. But to me, that green perfection was boring. Except for a scattering of robins and an oriole nest swinging from the tulip tree, I couldn't find much life to look at in my own front yard. The sunny side yard had plenty of room for playing ball with the dogs and catch with the kids. Who needed a front yard that was just for show?

The Making of a Woodland Garden

Little by little, I replaced the greensward with a woodland garden. I started with a single bed, smothering the grass with an ankle-deep layer of chopped leaves and putting in a few special plants from my local garden center. I tried to limit my choices to berried shrubs for the birds (though I splurged on a star magnolia, which the dogs promptly chewed off to a nubbin).

When October came around, I took advantage of the bounty of fallen leaves and chopped them into bits with a few passes of the lawn mower. Then I piled them into new beds along a tentative web of paths. When I liked the look of things, I moved in young trees and shrubs—redbuds, sugar maples, wild hydrangeas, viburnums, and my favorite, spicebush—from the natural woods behind our house.

In just a few short years, my woodland garden is looking like a real woods. Young oaks, maples, and hickories have sprouted in the blanket of humus, and wildflowers are multiplying happily. Last year I had a spread of self-sown, sky blue phacelia that rivaled my favorite wild spot down the road. The "exotic" plants I added—Japanese painted ferns, a few azaleas, and some favorite Oregon wildflowers—don't seem out of place here because I chose them to fit the feeling of the natural landscape.

The Nature of a Woods

In eastern Pennsylvania, where I grew up, the woodland was mostly deciduous trees (hardwoods), with occasional stands of hemlock, white pine, or spruce (softwoods) to add variety and contrast. In fall, the hillsides blazed with red and orange maples and the clear yellow of birches and tulip trees, accented by the deep green of the

For some 50 years, Isabel Hill tended the land at Lanark, the 340-acre plantation where she lived. She discovered a small stream running through her woods and lined its banks with oakleaf and French blue hydrangeas. BELOW: Posed among a carpet of daffodils, Isabel Hill was passionate about the natural world, often working seven or eight hours a day in her garden.

A Garden Idyll

The late Isabel Hill spent her lifetime creating a magnificent garden on her family's plantation in Millbrook, Alabama. In June, her legacy will be transferred to the Alabama Wildlife Federation.

by Grace Collins Hodges   Photographed by Richard Felber

PORTRAIT BY MELISSA SPRINGER

Because of its fairy-tale quality, the story of the late Isabel Hill's garden might begin, "Once upon a time ..." In 1948, as a young bride, Isabel, known for her great beauty and her ability to charm the bark off trees, moved with her new husband, Wiley Hill, to Lanark, a now 340-acre plantation north of Montgomery in Millbrook, Alabama. Over the next 50 years, this pair, both city born and

bred, developed a deep love of the pastoral life, and Isabel uncovered a passion for gardening that lasted her lifetime.

Isabel and Wiley Hill began gradually, working together in the yard near their house, and it was just that, a yard, not yet a garden. They planted a Japanese magnolia outside their picture window and later moved it several times as they expanded the

Our tile,

Your vision.

CA Sun Valley · Costa Mesa · West Hollywood · Hayward · San Francisco NV Las Vegas TX Houston · Dallas GA Atlanta NC Charlotte NY New York · coming soon

HOUSTON
7055 Old Katy Road
Houston, TX 77024

ATLANTA
791 Miami Circle N.E.
Atlanta, GA 30324

DALLAS
11550 Newberry
Suite 300
Dallas, TX 75229

NORTH CAROLINA
11435 Granite Street
Suite M
Charlotte, NC 28273

product shown
Cote d'Or™

WALKER
ZANGER

*Your Life's**Tile** Resource.*™

Ceramic Tile · Stone Tile & Slabs · Mosaics · Terra Cotta · Glass Tile

Call **877.611.0199** to order a catalogue.   www.walkerzanger.com

conifers. Because the trees and shrubs of the understory aren't dense and can be easily pushed aside if need be, you can enter an eastern woodland just about anywhere, whether or not there's a deer trail to guide your feet. In spring and summer, the air is rich and earthy with humus; in fall, there's a delicious crunch of dry leaves underfoot. Sunlight slants through the branches and beneath the canopy, creating patterns on the woodland floor.

Not until we moved to the Pacific Northwest did I find out that all woods are not created equal. The forests in Oregon are almost entirely coniferous, I was stunned to find, not to mention two or three times taller than eastern hardwood forests. Gigantic firs and spruces loom like somber giants, their branches interwoven to create a constant twilight on the forest floor. It's a good thing hiking trails are so common in the Northwest, because these woods are nearly impenetrable. The underbrush of

wiry huckleberry, leathery-leaved salal, and waist-high ferns makes travel difficult except on paths. Instead of humus, the woods are aromatic with cedar and fir. Your footsteps are soundless on the thick, spongy carpet of needles.

Just about the time I got used to the deep, quiet cathedrals of the Northwest woods, we moved to southwestern Indiana—back to the hardwoods. We were so busy settling in and exploring our new surroundings (prairie flowers and grasses were a great distraction!) that it wasn't until my first Christmas in Indiana that I noticed that these woods, too, were different from my old Pennsylvania stomping grounds.

I like to cut my own greens for holiday decorations. But as I pulled on my boots that winter morning, I couldn't quite recollect where any evergreens were. Surely there must be a white pine in the woods behind our house, I thought, but after a morning of hiking, I

Footpaths are a must in the old-growth forests of the Pacific Northwest, where giant conifers can top 300 feet and the understory is thick with a tangle of vine maple, ferns, and young trees. A carpet of fallen needles muffles every footfall and soaks up the soft rain like a sponge.

Hardwood trees like these paper birches make a deciduous forest glow with glorious color in autumn. Common in northern forests from Alaska to Maine, they were "canoe birch" to Native Americans, who sewed the strong white bark over frames of cedar for their watercraft.

SHADE GARDEN OR WOODLAND GARDEN?

The line between shade and woodland gardens is easily blurred, but there are distinctions that make your garden a shade garden as opposed to a woodland garden or vice versa. These general ideas will help you decide which direction is right for you.

Shade Garden

- Can be created in a small or large space. Even a 2-foot-wide strip can be made into an appealing shade garden.
- Is generally more controlled in look and feel, although the degree of control is up to you.
- Usually consists of low-growing, low-maintenance plants, including lots of groundcovers and evergreens, so it looks good and green year-round.
- Is in shade almost all the time, in every season.
- Can be created anywhere you have part or full shade: where a tree or a building casts a shadow, between your house and your neighbor's, or on the north side of your home.
- Includes more "exotic" plants that wouldn't naturally grow in your area.
- Attracts birds and small mammals seeking food and shelter.

Woodland Garden

- Needs plenty of elbowroom to look natural. Fifty square feet is about the minimum, although you might create a strip of woodland garden (10 × 30 feet or more) along a walk or drive.
- Is more naturalistic in look and feel. At its finest, it looks like a piece of natural woods transplanted to your yard.
- Has a seasonal look that mirrors the natural woodland of your area.
- May change in sun or shade exposure, depending on the season.
- Needs trees for an underpinning. If your yard is graced by shade trees, or even a single good-size tree, you have the perfect foundation for a woodland garden. If you don't already have trees, you can add them.
- Includes many native species, but can also be rounded out with ornamentals that maintain the effect.
- Attracts nesting birds and mammals.

The hand of the gardener is evident in a shade garden, which has a more controlled "garden" look. Spring bulbs, camellias, and other flowering shrubs add color in spring, while the strong, sinuous shape of the tree is eye-catching at any season. Notice how it echoes the curving border.

The mossy path, abundant wildflowers, and young trees sprinkling this garden make it look as if Mother Nature were in charge here. In a woodland garden, where the soil is undisturbed most of the time, many wildflowers will gradually fill out into large colonies that mirror natural woodlands.

found that everything was indeed deciduous. This was new to me, so I got in the car to reconnoiter on the gravel backroads that run through the farm fields. Whenever I saw a conifer on the horizon—and you can see for miles in this flat land—I'd head toward it. Each time, the pine or spruce turned out to be in someone's front yard. Oddly enough, our corner of Indiana is bereft of conifers, except for the deciduous bald cypresses that dot the river bottoms.

Shaking my head in wonderment, I ended up clipping boughs from a prickly eastern red cedar along the hedgerow, missing those soft Oregon firs and Pennsylvania pines more and more with every "Ouch!"

Woodland or Shade Garden?

I call my front yard a woodland garden because I intended it to look like a natural woods. A little disorganization is fine with me: After having set the garden's foundation in place, I'm letting the garden go pretty much where it wants to.

As bright as a brand-new quilt, this pink and red medley is toned down by the cool greens of hosta and rhododendron, foliage effects that last long after the flowers fade. The azaleas will add their own neat, glossy leaves to set off the white-variegated hostas later in the season.

SAME PLANT, DIFFERENT LOOK

The focal point in my shade garden is a large 'Arnold Promise' witch hazel. The shrub stands proudly above creeping junipers and a mound of red-tinged dwarf cryptomeria, an evergreen with soft, springy foliage. I've grouped 'Arnold' with 'Morning Light' miscanthus (an ornamental grass) and evergreen bayberry. Most of the plants are separated, or at least restrained, so that they don't stray into each other's space, and the garden is neatly mulched with fine bark. At its feet is a groundcover of scalloped coltsfoot leaves cobwebbed with silver on their undersides.

'Arnold Promise' witch hazel also shows up in my nearby woodland garden, but it has a different personality there because of its companions as well as the garden style. In the woodland garden, 'Arnold' is just another shrub among many. I haven't set it up to hold the spotlight as I did in the shade garden because I wanted it to blend in with the woodsy look. In autumn, its golden leaves are part of the general extravaganza. Only in late winter, when its branches are strewn with crinkled ribbons of yellow flowers, does it really draw attention to itself.

Like other natural gardens, creating your own woodland is a learning experience. In the first year, you'll lay out beds and paths and settle plants into place. You may fool yourself into thinking that's your garden. But someone else's ideas are always at work in a naturalistic woodland—the best gardener of all, Mother Nature.

At the head of my driveway is a more controlled planting, and that one I call a shade garden. Each plant is carefully chosen and placed in a design I planned for texture and all-season color. No one would ever call it formal, but it has a more groomed look than my woodland garden, where plants mix and match among a free-form blanket of leaves. My shade garden is an ornamental planting, but it has a lot to offer wildlife, too: Myrtle warblers feast on the waxy bayberries, bees and other insects visit the coltsfoot when it blooms in early spring, and native sparrows tug off pieces of dried ornamental grass for their nests.

In years past, a shady yard used to be something to complain about. Most gardeners have wised up, although even today, I still hear people talking about how they can't grow anything in the shade. More than once, I must admit, I've found myself grabbing them by the arm while I evangelize about the pleasures of a shady garden.

Whether your style leans toward a densely textured planting of quiet evergreens or a blatant copy of Mother Nature's grand scheme, you can create a beautiful natural landscape in the shade. In both shade and woodland gardens, you'll enjoy the play of color and texture, the song of wind through the branches, and the trilling calls of courting birds.

The Shady Side of Gardening

If you're dreaming of a woodland or shade garden, you probably already have some shade. Maybe the garage casts a daylong shadow along a strip that you've tried to brighten with impatiens. Maybe your front yard boasts a beautiful old maple, with roots so thick and thirsty that nothing grows beneath it. Or perhaps the street side of your place is bordered by a tall hedge or fence that shelters you from traffic but casts quite a shadow.

Not all shade is created equal. Under a grove of firs, the shade is deep and constant. In my former woodland garden in Oregon, beneath firs and spruces, the wildflowers are true shade-lovers, adapted to the all-season dimness beneath the evergreens. They included tall white fairybells, wide parasols of incredibly fragrant vanilla leaf, lacy tangles of rosy pink fumitory, and a carpet of wood sorrel.

Light is dimmed under an oak or Norway maple, too, but it's a seasonal effect. When the tree bares its branches come autumn, whatever is beneath it will be in the sun.

In springtime, when the warming rays of the sun reach through bare branches of oaks and poplars, my

You can combine sun- and shade-lovers by matching their needs to the planting site. Keep in mind that the top "story" of plants will be in sun: Here, a flowering cherry gets its day in the sun while the rhododendron beneath it appreciates the shade cast by the tree.

GAUGING SHADE

Full shade, light shade, partial shade—the distinctions can get confusing. Here's how to tell them apart:

- Full shade is deep, all-day shade—the kind found beneath a Norway maple or a big oak or in a conifer forest. This is also the shade you'll find in the skyscraper canyons of a big city.

- Light shade is dappled, like the shadows found beneath fine-leaved trees like locust trees or birches. Some rays of sunlight filter through the fine leaves, creating shifting patterns of light and shadow all day long.

- Partial shade can mean light shade, or it can mean sun for part of the day and shade for the rest of the day.

- High shade means that trees have a high canopy of branches and a bare or almost bare trunk. This can be the case naturally, especially when a woodland is cleared for housing and the developer lets some trees remain for shade. Trees that grow in a woodland have fewer lower branches than those that grow in the open. High shade may also be a created condition, if you've limbed up your trees by sawing off the lower branches. The lack of low branches means that sunlight can slant through, reaching understory plants, except during the middle of the day, when the canopy will block the overhead sun.

favorite wildflowers wake into bloom. These are the so-called spring ephemerals, like snow white bloodroot and creamy Dutchman's breeches, pink-tinged spring beauties and toothwort, and wild blue phlox and dwarf delphinium. These plants need sun to bloom and form flowers for next year, which is why they grow naturally in deciduous woodlands. By the time the trees' and shrubs' leaves grow in, throwing the garden into shade, the spring ephemerals have gone dormant until the next year.

One of the most unsettling sights I've ever seen was a spring woods in full bloom—in August. Hordes of gypsy moths had completely defoliated the trees, and when the sunlight reached the forest floor, it woke the spring ephemerals. Rose-breasted grosbeaks and wood warblers were moving through the trees in their drab fall plumage, while beneath them bloodroot was blooming and mayapple was pushing up. It was downright weird.

The quality of shade, as well as its season, also varies. Beneath alders or birches, shade is dappled, with sunlight glancing through the leaves to speckle the ground in changing patterns. In the shadow of a garage or a neighboring building, however, shade is solid and unchanging.

If you're the type of person who loves details, you can keep a calendar that charts when your planned garden spot is in sun or shadow. And you can think about how the shade changes through the seasons, as the sun charts a higher or lower course through the sky.

A spot that gets morning sun in high summer, when the sun is northward and nearly overhead, may be in shade all day in autumn, when the sun slinks along close to the horizon. And vice versa, of course.

When you're planning a shade garden, there's no need to spend a year measuring the way the light shifts. Summer sun is the important factor. That's when the earth is tilted toward old Sol and the rays are most intense. Site your shade garden so that it will be out of the reach of the hot summer sun when it's at its peak, from 10 A.M. to 2 P.M.

Even a small spot can be a treasure when you add the sound of water to a woodland garden. Ferns find their niche among the rocks of this small waterfall. You can make your own in just one weekend.

Blooming in shades of rose, pink, cream, and even green, these hellebores, or Lenten roses, add unusual color to the early spring garden. Their sturdy foliage may be evergreen.

A shady nook lights up with warm golden foliage and a sprinkling of sunny flowers. The lacy foliage of yellow corydalis is a great companion for large-leaved hostas.

But unless you're new to the neighborhood, chances are you already know where and when the shade falls in your yard. That's where you hang the hammock in summer, where you can't grow vegetables or grass, or where the last bit of snow lingers.

Shade-loving plants are adapted to lower levels of light. Their foliage will burn in the sun, and their growth will suffer if the sun is too direct or lasts too long. But except for a few absolute "shademasters," most shade-loving plants will adapt to partial shade as long as they're protected from the most brutal rays of the sun.

Shady soils can be moist or dry, just like those in other parts of the garden. Tree roots can soak up an enormous amount of moisture, especially if it's been a while since the last rain—even an inch of rainfall can leave the soil under a tree barely moist after the roots wick it away. And where rainfall is scarce, the soil may be bone-dry. You can handle dry shade in several ways: Choose plants that will thrive in dry, shady conditions; use mulches to help slow evaporation; and dig in organic matter to help your soil retain more water. Columbines, hostas, impatiens, and astilbe all prefer moist soil, but many shade-lovers will thrive in dry conditions. Try stout, spiny bear's breeches (*Acanthus mollis*), tall, blue American bellflower (*Campanula americana*), fringed

bleeding heart (*Dicentra eximia*), the invasive but beautiful plume poppy (*Macleaya cordata*), and two hellebores, Corsican and fetid (*Helleborus lividus* var. *corsicus* and *H. foetidus*).

Start with Structure

Once you have your shady site picked out, it's time to do a little planning. As with any garden, you'll want to start by laying out the basic structure.

Paths in any garden are a major part of the garden framework, and they're what I always start with. Then I plan for height and "hardscape" elements like walls and structures, the other things that give a garden some backbone. (For more about adding paths, walls, and structures to your garden, see Chapter 7, beginning on page 210.) The last thing I do is plant evergreens to help the garden hold its shape in winter.

In my Indiana woodland garden, once I had an idea where the paths would go, I started planning the understory. I didn't want the three old shade trees to stick out like sore thumbs. I needed to step them down with a second layer of shorter trees, to provide a transition between the shade trees and lower-growing plants.

WOODLAND GARDEN DESIGN

Create a shady haven with a combination of shrubs, trees, and perennials that offer structure and beauty year-round.

Many of the plants in this garden offer colorful flowers as well as richly textured foliage. This garden offers all-season beauty, from earliest spring, when the star magnolias burst into bloom, to the glories of fall, when your shady spot will be glowing gold and orange.

In winter, the graceful forms of the deciduous shrubs and the weight of evergreens will give it structure until the seasons roll around again and the warming sun coaxes the ephemeral spring wildflowers into bloom.

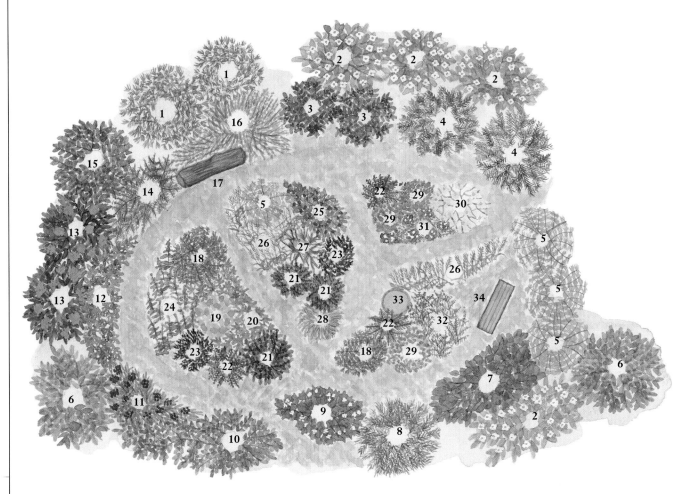

PLANT LIST

1. Deodar cedar (*Cedrus deodara*)

2. Flowering dogwood (*Cornus florida*)

3. American holly (*Ilex opaca*)

4. Hemlocks (*Tsuga canadensis*)

5. Spicebushes (*Lindera benzoin*)

6. Existing deciduous shade tree

7. Hazel (*Corylus avellana*)

8. Eastern white pine (*Pinus strobus*)

9. Thimbleberry (*Rubus parviflorus*)

10. Serviceberry (*Amelanchier laevis*)

11. Lowbush blueberry (*Vaccinium angustifolium*)

12. Waterleaf (*Hydrophyllum macrophylla* or *H. canadense*)

13. Rhododendrons (*Rhododendron* spp.)

14. Beaded woodferns (*Dryopteris bissetiana*)

15. Yellow birch (*Betula lutea*)

16. Heathers and heaths (*Calluna* and *Erica* spp.)

17. Log bench

18. Orange-flowered witch hazel (*Hamamelis* × *intermedia* 'Diane', 'Orange Beauty', or 'Copper Beauty')

19. American persimmons (*Diospyros virginiana*)

20. Virginia creeper (*Parthenocissus quinquefolia*)

21. Winterberry (*Ilex verticillata*)

22. Christmas ferns (*Polystichum acrostichoides*)

23. Black pussywillow (*Salix gracilistyla* var. *melanostachys*)

24. American bellflowers (*Campanula americana*)

25. Hearts-a-bustin' (*Euonymus americanus*)

26. Bottlebrush grass and fall Japanese anemone (*Hystrix patula* and *Anemone japonica*)

27. Dead tree

28. Golden hakone grass (*Hakonechloa macra* 'Aureola')

29. Whipoorwill azaleas (*Rhododendron periclymenoides*)

30. Star magnolias (*Magnolia stellata*)

31. Dutchman's breeches and bloodroot (*Dicentra cucullaria* and *Sanguinaria canadensis*)

32. Japanese painted ferns (*Athyrium goeringianum* 'Pictum')

33. Pottery bird bath (basin only) set on a rock

34. Bench

Note: All shrubs and planting areas can be underplanted with spring ephemeral wildflowers, such as wood anemone, rue anemone, mertensia, erythroniums, mayapple, Jack-in-the-pulpit, bloodroot, and others.

Adding an Understory

The layer of shorter trees and shrubs that surround mature trees in a natural woods is called the understory, and it's a vital part of a woodland—and a woodland garden. Many understory trees are actually understudies—youngsters of the dominant forest species that come into their own when an old patriarch keels over, creating an opening for more sun. These trees typically grow tall and spare, concentrating their energy on pushing upward toward the sun, not on growing side branches.

The more attractive understory plants for a woodland garden are shade-tolerant, midheight species that will grow and branch normally, even in the shadows. There are plenty of good choices, from eastern deciduous woodland natives like American persimmon and eastern redbud, to western species such as vine maple and Pacific yew, to foreign, shade-tolerant species, including China's golden-rain tree, the signature tree of the former Utopian community here at New Harmony and one of my favorites for landscaping.

The easiest way to choose understory trees for a woodland garden is to spend an afternoon looking at different stretches of nearby woods. The first thing you'll notice is that much of the understory is made up of youngsters—10-, 20-, or 30-year-old trees waiting to take the place of their elders. But you'll find lots of midheight possibilities, too.

THE FIRST LEAF

I used to marvel when my mother told me the names of things as soon as they sprouted, even before they had their first set of true leaves. But then I learned that when you spend a lot of time in your garden, you start to recognize the plants at younger and younger stages of growth. Now, with 30 years of gardening under my belt, I can tell a sprouting cosmos from a bachelor's-button as fast as my mother could.

But it wasn't until I started my woodland garden that I got to know the first leaves of woody plants. An impossibly tiny but perfect glossy red heart turned out to be the seed leaf of Virginia creeper. A single, big, wavy-edged flag of a seed leaf was silver beech. I was entranced. Now I look forward eagerly to next spring so that I can learn more trees from the first sprout.

SPOTLIGHT ON SPICEBUSH

One of the best plants for a shade garden or woodland is an all-American called spicebush (*Lindera benzoin*). It has a lovely, graceful shape, with sinuous, almost horizontal branching that creates a layered, wide-flaring form. The plant keeps its spare lines by self-pruning: Some branchlets near the ends of branches die back and drop off during the winter, keeping the silhouette clean instead of cluttered and twiggy. Wild plants vary from large, multitrunked shrubs to small, single-stemmed trees. No selections or named cultivars are available, but the untampered-with species is beautiful in any form.

All parts of the plant—flowers, stems, leaves, branches, and berries—have a delicious spicy scent. I like to crush a bit of leaf and rub it under my nose when I'm strolling in the garden.

Grouped or isolated in the garden, spicebush is good-looking year-round, but it has two seasons of absolute glory. In spring, its dark branches are studded with sulfur yellow clusters of bloom that outline the stems in glowing color. In fall, the simple oval leaves turn clear dandelion yellow, a dazzling effect in a woodland or garden.

When the leaves drop, shiny red berries stud the stems. Gray-cheeked thrushes, veeries, and other thrushes are especially fond of the berries, and once they find them, they'll strip a plant in a matter of days. But keep a few berries for yourself. They're beautiful in a vase, if you can bear to clip a branch, and they smell great when bruised between your fingers.

In winter, the graceful silhouette of dark umber spicebush branches stands out. In summer, its leaves are sought by spicebush swallowtail butterflies, which lay their eggs on the foliage. The large caterpillars sport a pair of fearsome false eyespots to fool the birds.

Like many native American shrubs, spicebush isn't usually stocked by garden centers. Although a Japanese species is beginning to come into vogue, American spicebush is still an unknown in most of the gardening world. You'll have to order it from a specialty nursery like those listed in "Resources for Natural Landscaping" on page 250.

In our Indiana woods, I jotted down my favorites: persimmon, sassafras, redbud, dogwood, Kentucky coffee tree, and blue beech. If you don't know the names of your local trees, take a field guide with you, or collect leaves to identify later.

Beneath the layer of midheight trees come shrubs of all sizes, including those that cross the line to small tree status, such as fringetree and spicebush. I always run out of space long before I run out of possibilities—there are so many good choices, it's hard to stay focused. Choose those that personally appeal to you, but try for a mix of fall foliage, flowering, and evergreen plants, while keeping an eye out for those with good winter form. If a plant incorporates more than one good trait, hallelujah.

Between and beneath the shrubs go the herbaceous plants: perennials, annuals, ferns, and groundcovers. I don't mind admitting that I blatantly copy many of my planting combinations directly from Mother Nature. When I saw a patch of white violets mingling with pale

▲ *Spicebush is delightfully aromatic—its leaves, twigs, flowers, and berries are all fragrant. It blooms in my garden at the same time that goldfinches begin to arrive during migration. The flowering branches are as pretty in a vase as they are in the garden. Flowers give way to fresh green oval leaves that are a favorite of swallowtail caterpillars. Look for curled leaves held together by a web of silk—that's where you'll find the caterpillars hiding.*

▶ *This garden is living proof that shady spots needn't lack color. Here, the plumes of pink astilbe add a splash of color among the greenery of fine-textured ferns and versatile hostas.*

Like many perennial wildflowers, Jacob's ladder is tougher than it looks. Nestle a plant against the contrasting texture of a log to show off the pretty leaves and skywashed blue flowers. Decorative seedpods follow the blossoms, and the foliage stays attractive all season.

Avoiding the Elvis Look

It happens to all shade gardeners: Before you know it, you find yourself gravitating toward variegated foliage, chartreuse plants, red leaves—anything to add some garden color other than green.

It's fun to play with colorful foliage, but don't get carried away. Used sparingly, chartreuse can light up a shady garden. But when it's taken to excess, as it seems to be in every planter at the mall these days, I find it as unappealing as those lime green stretch pants I used to wear 30 years ago. And you'll never see anything in nature like the striped, spotted, and streaked combinations that have been cropping up in some garden-catalog centerfolds.

Instead of aiming for the Elvis effect, think Jackie Kennedy. Understated is the key. The burnished metallic leaves of heuchera 'Pewter Veil', for example, will look more at home in a naturalistic shade garden than the razzle-dazzle of variegated viburnum or threadleaf golden false cypress.

blue Jacob's ladder, punctuated by spikes of blue camas lilies and surrounded by a ruff of spring green fragile ferns, I claimed the combination for my own and went home to order the plants from my stash of specialty catalogs. If it works in the wild, it will usually work in your garden, as long as you can offer the plants similar conditions.

Grow Your Own Trees

As you stroll the paths of your woodland or shade garden in spring, watch for the first unfolding leaves of baby trees. Even if there's no nearby natural woods, seedlings will sprout in your woodland garden from berries or seeds brought in by birds or on the wind or from nuts and acorns buried by squirrels.

Not only is it fascinating to watch the first tiny growth spurts of a tree, but it's also a good way to add to your garden. Try to leave the young seedling in place; it will grow faster and sturdier if its roots aren't interrupted. If you must move it, transplant as soon as possible and take a giant-size scoop of earth with the seedling to avoid disturbance.

In just four years, my woodland garden had sprouted an impromptu nursery of sugar maples, tulip trees, elms, beeches, hickories, four kinds of oaks, sassafras, wild cherries, hackberries, redbuds, dogwoods,

Limbing Up

Open your landscape to more sun and air by removing lower branches from your trees, or "limbing up." Use a pole saw to slice through any branches that are out of reach. Before you start to saw, try to imagine what your tree will look like when the selected branches are removed. When you've finished the "surgery," rub a handful of soil on the scars so they don't stand out so rawly.

A long-handled pole saw makes it easy to remove out-of-reach limbs. To operate, you pull on a rope that moves the blade. Remove the branches cleanly, close to the trunk, so as not to leave disfiguring nubs.

and even two prized hawthorns—not one of them planted by me.

It sounds like such a bonanza would overwhelm the garden, but I've found that the young trees take care of themselves. Many of them die out naturally. Others grow so vigorously you can't believe it. Did you know that a two-year-old tulip tree can reach 4 feet tall? One of my three-year-old redbuds is taller than me.

It's incredibly satisfying to watch a tree grow from a seedling sprout to a sturdy specimen. I appreciate my garden-center trees well enough, but I have a definite fondness for the trees I watched sprout their first leaves.

Foliage Favorites

Designing a garden for a shady site will quickly move your focus from flowers to foliage. Though there are plenty of flowers that bloom in shade—lamiums, hellebores, and American bellflower are three of my favorites—much of the show is carried by the foliage of the plants you choose for your garden.

Except for a cherished planting of golden hakone grass, my shade-garden colors are pretty much basic green during the growing season. Autumn brings wonderful warm colors from shrubs and perennials and long-lasting impact from the miscanthus, spodiopogon, and other ornamental grasses, which mellow to tan and

The variety of foliage effects in a shade garden can be as beautiful as flowers. Here, the twin umbrellas of may-apple mingle with sugar maple seedlings and rain-spangled twinleaf, a plant whose botanical name, <u>Jeffersonia diphylla</u>, honors plant enthusiast and American president Thomas Jefferson.

How to Saw through a Limb

The natural inclination when removing a limb is to saw straight through from top to bottom. But the results of this method can damage your tree. The weight of the branch will swing downward before you make the final cut, usually stripping off a good-sized piece of living bark from the trunk and leaving it open to diseases and insects.

Instead of sawing through the unwanted branch from the top in a single cut, make three cuts as shown here.

STEP 1: *Using a sharp handsaw, slice into the branch from the bottom, about 6 inches out from the trunk. Saw into the limb about one-third of the way through.*

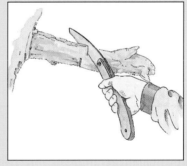

STEP 2: *Make the second cut a couple of inches outside of the first one, sawing downward from top to bottom so that the rest of the limb drops off.*

STEP 3: *Remove the nub by sawing from top to bottom near the trunk, just outside of the "branch collar," a visible thickening or wrinkling of bark that lies between branch and trunk.*

beige. Groundcover conifers acquire a tinge of red, gold, or silver with cold weather and shorter days.

I've learned that when I stick to a plain green color scheme, I can concentrate on textural effect rather than on color. My shade garden is like a needlepoint tapestry—it's rich with variations in color and texture, but they blend together into a cohesive whole.

In my shade garden, I use ground-hugging plants like bearberry and European wild ginger to add a change of height and some gloss to the planting. Because I want the shade garden to look good year-round, I use a lot of evergreen groundcovers in it.

In my woodland garden, I plant more casual groundcovers, including deciduous types. I like the spiky texture that white foamflower adds, and I choose the running type not the ones that stay in neat clumps.

I discovered one of my favorite groundcovers by accident. On one side of my woodland garden, where hardy geraniums bloom in spring, a vine of Virginia creeper sprouted from a seed probably brought in by birds. I had no place for the vine to climb, so I let it creep—and that's what it does best. Its interesting, five-part leaves provide greenery through spring and summer, but in fall they literally shine. The foliage turns brilliant red and crimson, winding through my garden like a river of fire. As a bonus, mature vines bear deep blue berries that are eagerly sought by downy woodpeckers.

Many country folk call Virginia creeper "poison oak," but this fast-growing vine, also known as woodbine, is not related to any of that itchy clan. It's a relative of Boston ivy, an old-fashioned creeper that festoons old brick houses. If you have birds visiting your yard, you'll probably have volunteer vines, thanks to the avian seed dispersal system.

Versatile ferns add something special, from the architectural oomph of tall cinnamon fern to the lacy beauty of lady fern. They do best in soil that stays moist. The Japanese maples used throughout this garden are an excellent choice for a shade or woodland garden, especially for a smaller garden where the fine texture of their foliage is perfectly in scale.

Fabulous Ferns

Ferns add a lush touch to a shady garden, even if you plant just a single clump. Beware of where you buy them, though—some unscrupulous suppliers dig them up from the wild to sell. If I'm ever tempted by the often bargain-basement prices of wild-collected stock, I think about what was destroyed so somebody could make money from it. Unless it says "nursery propagated," I don't buy it.

My friend Bill was transplanted to a new house after 70 years in the old one, and though he tried to make up for lost time, he never could re-create the gardens he'd worked on for half a century. What he missed most of all, he often said, was the fern grotto. Delicate, black-stemmed maidenhair ferns sprang from cracks in the granite, he told me, and misted like an angel's hair when the water sprayed over the rock. He planted maidenhair above a small pool at the new place, but it didn't have the same magic for Bill.

(continued on page 88)

Maidenhair fern looks so delicate that many gardeners shy away from planting it in the mistaken idea that it's hard to grow. Not true—this plant is hardy and adaptable. Press a frond in an old phone book and frame when dry for a beautiful wall decoration.

CAN'T-FAIL FERNS

The ferns listed here will thrive in the shade in rich, moist, well-drained soil. Many other species and varieties are available, but these are among the easiest to grow.

To keep your ferns happy, mulch them well with chopped leaves and let fallen autumn leaves remain in place. The emerging fronds have a lot of lift power. In spring the new fiddleheads will push up right through last year's leaves.

Beaded wood fern (*Dryopteris bissetiana*). This unusual fern has dark green, leathery, 1- to 2-foot-tall fronds that are divided into round segments, which give the plant a beaded appearance. The arching fronds stay green all winter; the plant doesn't send up new fronds until summer. USDA Plant Hardiness Zones 5 to 8.

Christmas fern (*Polystichum acrostichoides*). Common throughout eastern North America, this classic evergreen fern settles easily into the garden. The clump of deep green, leathery fronds stays fresh all winter. Early settlers supposedly used it for Christmas decoration, but I find that the fronds dry out and curl soon after picking. Zones 3 to 9.

Cinnamon fern (*Osmunda cinnamomea*). Mighty clumps of 3- to 5-foot-tall fronds surround upright spikes of bright cinnamon-color fertile fronds. This plant makes a great punctuation mark with ground-covers or among perennials, and it makes red-orange or white impatiens look new again. In autumn, cinnamon fern turns a rich, rusty brown color. Zones 2 to 10.

Fragile fern (*Cystopteris fragilis*). This little charmer usually stays under 12 inches tall and may not even clear 6 inches. It unrolls its tiny fiddleheads very early in the season and is beautiful with ephemeral spring wildflowers. The lacy fronds are a clear spring green and go dormant by summer. Fragile fern spreads into colonies but is never a pest. Zones 2 to 9.

Hay-scented fern (*Dennstaedtia punctiloba*). This airy fern grows in light shade or sun; it's a good one to plant where woodland garden meets lawn. It spreads rapidly by creeping roots to form large colonies. Brush against the delicate fronds, and you'll smell the wonderful fragrance of newly mown hay. In fall, it turns soft primrose yellow. Zones 3 to 8.

Japanese painted fern (*Athyrium goeringianum* 'Pictum'). This is the showgirl of the big lady fern genus. She comes tarted up with silver and burgundy, but it's a wonderful effect in a shady garden. The clump of 1- to 2-foot fronds can expand to bushel-basket size in moist, rich soil. Just slice through it with a spade to multiply your collection. Zones 4 to 9.

Lady fern (*Athyrium angustum*, *A. asplenioides*, and *A. filix-femina*). The first two lady fern species named are native to America; the last is from Europe. All grow in a clump of fresh, medium green, erect fronds that grow 18 to 30 inches tall. "Crested" forms of European lady fern are much in vogue among fern fanciers; their fronds are sometimes so distorted that they look like curly parsley. I prefer the species. *A. angustum*, Zones 2 to 8; *A. asplenioides*, Zones 4 to 9; *A. filix-femina*, Zones 4 to 8.

Maidenhair ferns (*Adiantum pedatum*, *A. aleuticum*). Native to eastern and western North America, these delicate ferns have fronds that radiate from a crescent-shaped axis at the top of a bare, blackish stem. Maidenhair fern gradually expands into a colony and looks beautiful on a slope, where its Rapunzel effect can be best appreciated. Zones 2 to 8.

Sensitive fern (*Onoclea sensibilis*). This was the first fern I knew, which is probably why I'm still partial to it. It is widespread in the eastern half of the country. It spreads like crazy, which can be an asset or not, depending on where you put it. Keep in mind that it will swamp all but the most stalwart plants. If you're tired of pachysandra, add this fern to the planting—they look great together. Fronds have wide segments, giving the plant a bolder appearance than the typical "ferny" fern. Sensitive fern turns brown in autumn. Zones 2 to 10.

◄ *Early spring in a woodland garden is a season of promise. Wildflowers awaken one after another, taking advantage of the sun that streams through the trees before the leafy canopy fills in.*

I thought the new planting was beautiful. Bill's ferns thrived above the water as if they'd always grown there. In my heart, I wondered what it was that he was really missing. Was it his position? His fortune? His youth?

It wasn't until years later that I found out just what Bill had given up. I was hiking along a spongy-soft trail in a stand of hemlocks when I came upon a real fern grotto. It was so beautiful that I fell to my knees without thinking, in absolute awe of such grace. Silvered with a fine mist, the rippling tresses of maidenhair fern bowed from every crevice in the wet rock wall. A fine thread of icy water dropped to a pool below, its depths so clear that I shook my head to try to clear my eyesight when a ripple spread across.

Maidenhair fern looks as ethereal as its name, but it's as tough as forsythia. Many other beautiful ferns will also adjust easily to life in a shade garden. If you've never explored the world of ferns, a shade garden is a great excuse to dig in.

Finishing Touches for Your Woodland Garden

For most gardeners, the finishing touches in a shade or woodland garden would be paths, benches, and the like. But for me, they're the first step—part of the essential bones of the garden. My finishing touches are

Long-lasting flowers and handfuls of blue berries, prized by wildlife, make Oregon grape holly a winner in the wild garden. Its leaves stay glossy fresh year-round. Keep this woodland native out of drying wind and strong sun.

Making a Bench

The right-angle seating arrangement of this design allows for easy conversation with a friend. The bench tops are made of logs sawed in half lengthwise. You won't find whole logs at the building-supply store, but a nearby sawmill will probably let you have them for a very reasonable price. Drill holes for legs at the ends of the rounded side of the logs, and insert sections of sturdy saplings for legs. To bring flowers and greenery to eye level, you can add a small section at the corner of the two benches, or just place a patio table there to support a container.

This uncomplicated design or your own version of it makes a great weekend project. Be sure the bench is sturdy; a wiggly bench is not relaxing. You can use shims to keep the legs tight in their sockets.

The fungus among us is an intriguing aspect of the natural landscape. The distinctive morel, which flourishes in woodlands or where woods once grew, is valued by wild mushroom eaters for its fine flavor.

mushrooms, moss, and other materials that make the garden seem real. But luring these humble plants into your yard isn't as easy as you might think.

The Marvel of Mushrooms

When I was a kid, I used to try to plant flowers. Literally, I mean. I'd stick dandelions and roses and whatever else I could find into the soil stem first. Naturally, lacking roots, every one died.

It's just as useless trying to transplant a mushroom. No matter how big a scoop of earth you take, you won't come close to collecting all of the many miles of the nutrient-gathering mycelial threads that keep the mushroom alive. A mushroom is only the "flower" of the fungus; it sprouts to spread spores for reproduction.

You can try collecting mushrooms for sowing spores (though I've never had any luck at it). Or you can just wait and see what comes up naturally. Shaggy mane mushrooms sprout every year in my front yard.

One of my favorite fungi sprouts liberally in my wood-chip paths. It's the tiny bird's-nest fungus, a ¼-inch cup that holds minute brown "eggs." I like to put the "nests" into plastic specimen boxes with a tight-fitting, magnifying lid as a quick gift for young friends.

A Lifelong Love of Nature

Sally Roth
New Harmony, Indiana

My favorite wild garden is the little 25-by 50-foot woodland I planted in front of our house. Looking at the garden with its bloodroot and mayapple, its spicebushes and witch hazels, I see how similar it is to the eastern Pennsylvania woods that I roamed as a kid, with the same cycle of wildflowers and the same fluting of woodthrushes at dusk and dawn. When the blue jays sweep through screaming an alarm, I remember my mother showing me how to watch those birds to see what they were hollering about—a cat, a snake, or maybe just us humans. Sauntering along the soft, humusy paths takes me back to those happy times.

Ever since I learned to toddle, I've spent most of my time outside. And I've been a gardener ever since I can remember. Planting a seed and watching it grow is a miracle I never get tired of. My earliest memories are of poking pea seeds and onion sets into the crooked rows I'd made in my own small corner of the family garden, where my mother grew enough corn, beans, tomatoes, potatoes, and squash to feed six kids all year long. Mom didn't just grow vegetables, though. She grew flowers, too—any kind she could get her hands on—and she always sent away for the penny-packet "child's garden" with her seed orders so that we kids could have the fun of growing our own marigolds, zinnias, and asters.

On Sundays, while Mom cooked dinner, the rest of the family would take a long walk in the woods beside our house. These weren't athletic hikes—they were slow, ambling, quiet times, when we looked for all sorts of treasures, from bird feathers to ladybugs to tadpoles, from pussy willows to wild plum blossoms.

I always came home with my pockets jammed full of special stones, acorns, bits of bunny fur, and all the other flotsam that I still love to collect. And we always brought back a bouquet for Mom. I remember fistfuls of violets, the big purple ones that carpeted the wet meadow like a royal cloak spread out on the grass, spring bouquets of pussy willows and red maple flowers, and bunches of colored leaves and purple asters (I can still smell their distinctive scent) in autumn. Whatever we brought, Mom gave it a place of honor, in a jelly glass on the kitchen table if it was a small bouquet, or in the big, white ironstone pitcher if it was a tall one. My mom remembered picking trailing arbutus when she herself was a kid, and she also remembered how it took only a few years for that patch to be cleared out from overpicking, so she taught us to leave the delicate spring wildflowers alone and only pick a few of whatever was most abundant in the fields.

It was my mother who instilled a lifelong love of nature in me, just by sharing her own enthusiasm. As I played in the dirt at her knee, she'd tilt her head and say, "Just listen to that woodthrush. Doesn't he have a beautiful voice?" Another time it might be, "That old blue jay! I wonder who he's scolding now?" I grew up knowing the names of the birds and their personalities as well as today's kids know the names of their favorite TV shows.

Our family outings were always to wild places—a natural spring of freezing-cold water where we collected watercress to take home and eat with fresh-baked bread, a creek where we hunted for crayfish under the rocks, a rocky wooded slope of South

Virginia bluebells have long been one of my favorite wildflowers. It's always a thrill to spot their purple spoon-shaped leaves poking up in spring.

Mountain where we found the first hepatica (we called it May flower) of the year. Mom taught me how to be observant as we drove along on those trips, pointing out wildflowers, clouds, rocks, birds, animals, barns, the colors of the fields, the shapes of the mountains, and anything else that merited a look. I'm sure that's why today I can identify a roadside wildflower or spot a fossil bed at 60 mph.

Looking back, I realize that money was scarce in our family, but I don't think that's the only reason we found our pleasure in the natural world. Even today, my own family would much rather explore a woods or the riverbank than spend hours in a shopping mall.

I believe a love of nature is the best legacy we can give our kids. Staying connected to the natural world is a great antidote to the hustle-bustle of today's world. That's why I love creating natural gardens. A garden is so much more to me than just a collection of pretty plants. It's a whole secret world, with all kinds of insects and animals interacting. All we have to do to be a part of it is to learn how to see.

Compared to the wonders of Mother Nature, my natural gardens seem a little feeble, but they are a true haven—for birds, butterflies, squirrels, mice, moles, and shrews, but most of all, for me.

◄ *I'm partial to blue and purple flowers, like this wild phlox. It looks good with everything, from wild grasses and wildflowers to perennials and spring bulbs.*

▼ *A grand finale of golden tickseed sunflowers finishes the garden year in the sunny part of my garden. These annual American wildflowers sow themselves with abandon, but I don't mind a bit because they attract clouds of butterflies.*

SCOUTING FOR DEADWOOD

Don't despair if you don't have any dead trees or stumps on your property to attract wildlife. You can always go scouting for a handsome trunk, log, or large branch to place artistically in your landscape. Here are some places to look for deadwood.

🐾 If there's a natural woods nearby, ask permission to collect a few good-size pieces of deadfall. It's best to collect soon after a storm blows down the branches, before birds and animals have a chance to move in.

🐾 Call a nearby tree service company. They are usually willing to let you have anything you can haul off, or you may be able to arrange delivery for a small fee.

🐾 Check with your local TV cable, electric, or telephone company. Trimming branches and clearing trees are routine maintenance. Like tree service companies, they will often let you have branches

or logs for the asking. Some may deliver. Make sure the truck has easy access, and look for any obstructions before you say "Dump it right here!"

🐾 Your parks department and the town or city road crew are other places to check. They maintain the public trees and often have major branches or log ends to get rid of.

🐾 Keep an eye out for possibilities in your neighborhood. If you don't mind the funny looks, your neighbors will probably be pleased to let you cart off their limbs or logs. I always explain why I want the material: It's a good way to raise consciousness about the value of deadwood.

Monkeyflowers are unfamiliar to many gardeners outside of the West, yet they are a wonderful choice for natural gardens in zones 6-9. Often found in wet areas, they adapt well to life in the shady garden.

Moss Makes Your Woods Look Old

Moss is a lot easier to move into the garden, but, like fungi, it will often appear spontaneously if conditions are right. You can move small pieces of moss from other places on your property and press them into bare soil or on moist, decaying logs. Or you can buy a bag of prepared "moss bits" from a commercial supplier and follow the instructions for sowing. (See "Resources for Natural Landscaping" on page 250 for suppliers.) Don't decimate a natural spread of moss in the wild. Mosses are slow-growing plants, and it takes them many years to recover from even one afternoon's thoughtless collecting.

The Value of Deadwood

Collecting the final finishing touch, deadwood, can become habit-forming. Deadwood may not sound too appealing at first, but it's a great way to give your woodland garden structure and make it more appealing to wildlife.

Dead trees are prized by woodpeckers, and they make a fine foundation for a feeding area. You can smear peanut butter on them, wire suet to them, or hang feeders from them. A dead tree is also a favorite perch for birds approaching the feeder.

You say you have no dead tree? No problem. You can make one.

Unless your nickname is Samson, you're probably going to have more luck erecting a dead limb than an entire dead tree. Here's how to do it:

1. Choose a limb at least 4 inches thick and at least 6 feet tall. Stab a fingernail into it to make sure the wood is firm, not decayed.
2. For a short-term, one- or two-season "tree," simply plant your limb into the soil. Dig a hole at least a foot deep (deepen the hole if the "tree" is taller), insert the thick end of the limb, and firm up the soil around it.
3. For a longer-lasting "tree," you can fill the hole with quick-setting concrete before you "plant." Mound the concrete around the limb so that it slopes downward, allowing water to drain quickly. But keep in mind that when the tree eventually falls, you'll be left with a block of concrete in the ground.

As with any dead tree, you'll want to avoid getting beaned if the thing topples. I give my dead "trees" an occasional medium-force push every now and then to make sure they're still standing firm.

Logs, stumps, and even sizable branches are heavy and awkward and hard on the back. Don't take on more than you can carry. Enlist a friend to share the labor. I sometimes amaze myself by balancing such heavy objects across my old metal wheelbarrow, holding them in place with a hoe, and finagling the barrow through the garden. But I don't recommend this procedure.

Deadwood is just as useful lying down as it is standing up, and it's often more decorative. An interesting log or branch can add a very artistic touch to a shade garden or that final bit of realism to the woodland garden. Add a good-size log (8 inches or better) to your woodland garden, and you hand an invitation to all kinds of interesting creatures. Fascinating click beetles, which pop and flip in your hand like Mexican jumping beans, will work

Last season's leaves make a beautiful background for spring wildflowers like these trilliums and mayapples. As the leaves decay, they'll add humus to the soil, keeping it light and moisture-retentive.

IT'S WOODY WOODPECKER!

If you go to the effort of lugging a rotted log into your garden, even Woody Woodpecker himself—better known to birders as a pileated woodpecker—may pay you a visit.

Pileateds (the word means "crested") are huge, crow-size woodpeckers with glossy black feathers and a vivid scarlet crest. Country folk know the bird as the "logcock" because that's where they're often digging. The bird's huge chisel of a beak gouges out rectangular holes as big as a man's fist, and it can shred wood almost as fast as a grizzly looking for grubs.

Some birders say these woodpeckers visit their feeding stations for suet, but ours never left the woods until a stump in the front yard began to decay. When it was good and ripe, almost to the point of falling apart, the pileateds began visiting regularly, pulling up strips of wood with their strong beaks like a horse tearing off a mouthful of long grass. They visited every morning for months until the stump was reduced to rubble.

Pileated woodpeckers are big birds, but they're surprisingly discreet about their comings and goings. Instead of announcing themselves with a raucous call like other woodpeckers, they often move silently. They spend a lot of time on the ground or working on stumps and logs.

on and below the bark. Engraving beetles will mark the trunk with hieroglyphics, and wood-boring beetles of all kinds will work on the wood. After bugs come birds, especially woodpeckers.

A log or stump also offers shelter for animals beneath it. When I dragged a toppled aspen into a previous garden, settling it between a couple of thickets of berry bushes, a cottontail rabbit dug a warren beneath it in less than a week. The stump in my current garden sheltered a cottontail this year, too. Actually, it sheltered six of them. If I lean down and peek at just the right angle, I can still see the soft bowl of grasses and fur that was their nursery. Mice and other small mammals will also make use of a fallen log. So will toads, salamanders, snakes, and lizards.

Another interesting character that may show up to investigate your deadwood is a skunk. Skunks are interested in the grubs that hide in the decaying wood, and like woodpeckers, they're adept at digging them out. Don't fret if a skunk turns up in your garden. If you treat it with plenty of respect and give it a wide berth, it will have no reason to spray.

I've appreciated skunks ever since one helped me out by excavating and destroying a colony of yellowjackets that had moved into my garden. I saw him sniffing near the wasps' nest-hole in the moonlight one night, and the next morning, the paper hive was strewn around the yard and nothing was left of the nest but an empty crater. I still don't know how he avoided getting stung.

Wildlife in Woodland Gardens

Deadwood isn't the only thing that will attract wildlife to your shady gardens. They'll also come to seek fruit, berries, nuts, and other foods and to seek shelter. Shrubs with berries and trees that bear nuts or acorns will draw birds and small mammals. Insects will move in to seek a niche and so will the creatures that eat them: mice, moles, voles, shrews, and other small furry types. Hawks and owls may scout your garden hoping to catch the rodents unawares.

An unexpected bonus of my woodland garden is that it swiftly became a corridor of safety for the birds that live in the real woods several hundred yards away. Towhees, rose-breasted grosbeaks, and scarlet tanagers now feel comfortable visiting my feeders, and wood thrushes and veeries scratch about in the leaf litter of my

Everybody's favorite, chickadees are welcome visitors and residents of a woodland garden. When it's nesting time, they look for soft fur and hair to line their nest in a birdhouse or tree cavity. Put out the combings from your dog or your hairbrush and they'll take it away strand by strand.

Scarlet tanagers are stunning against the green of a woodland garden. The males have resplendent plumage that almost glows, but females are dressed in dowdy yellow-green, inconspicuous at the nest. Listen for the male's buzzy, warbling carol, often sung from a treetop perch.

woodland garden. Vireos and wood warblers move from the tall sugar maples in the woods to the young redbuds and spicebushes in the garden, gleaning insects from the foliage. If there were less human and canine traffic in the garden, I have no doubt these birds would come to nest as well as dine.

Seasonal Pleasures

A shade or woodland garden is a wonderful respite from the summer sun. Even the dogs seek a haven there in summer, flopping on their sides beneath a favorite bush.

But it's a pleasure through all of the other seasons, too. In autumn, after the asters and goldenrod have finished the season in the meadow garden, my woodland garden is still a place of unexpected delights. Berries of

spicebush and hollies ripen into shining red, as polished as the bowl of apples on my kitchen table. Leaves blaze with color, then sift down from the canopy into a wonderful crunchy blanket that's as much fun to kick through now as when I was a kid.

By the time winter setttles in, chickadees, titmice, nuthatches, white-throated sparrows, and dozens of other birds have taken over the garden, gleaning the last seeds and berries, scratching aside the leaves, and scouring bark and branches for insects. Their quiet chips and call notes sound like a conversation among friends. There's always life and motion outside my window, even on the dreariest days (especially on the dreariest days— that's when the birds really come to forage). And snow in a woodland is one of nature's most beautiful sights. What a difference from a few years ago, when all I had to look out upon was a boring expanse of perfect grass.

BEST TREES FOR WOODLAND GARDENS

Trees	Description	Conditions	Comments
Flowering dogwood (*Cornus florida*)	Small tree with graceful layered habit and beautiful white or pink flowers in spring. Reaches to 10'.	Partial or light shade. Moisture-retentive, organic soil. Zones 5 to 9.	Unfortunately susceptible to fast-spreading dogwood blight; call your extension agent about the extent of the problem in your area before planting.
Oaks (*Quercus* spp.)	Many species of medium- to large-size trees, all bearing acorns. Grows 100' or more.	Partial to full shade. Zones 3 to 9, depending on species.	Many oaks are widely adaptable, but it's fun to get to know your native oaks, like white oak and red oak in the East, Midwest, and North; Gambel oak in the intermountain states; and blackjack oak in the Southeast.
Redbuds (*Cercis* spp.)	Small trees with tiny pink or white blossoms thickly studded along the branches before the leaves appear in early spring. Reaches to 40'.	Partial to light shade. Average, well-drained soil. Hardy to Zones 5 to 8, depending on species.	Redbuds are ideal for planting under tall shade trees. Eastern redbud (*C. canadensis*) is a trouble-free small tree, hardy to Zone 5. In the West, try Western redbud (*C. occidentalis*), a shrubby, multitrunked species with excellent drought tolerance, hardy to Zones 8 to 9.
Spruces (*Picea* spp.)	Large, evergreen conifers with dense, short, stiff needles. Reaches to 150'.	Sun to partial shade. Average, well-drained soil. Zones 2 to 4.	Spruces have dense branches that make excellent protection from the elements for birds. Norway spruce (*P. abies*) and Colorado spruce (*P. pungens*) are widely adaptable.
Sugar maple (*Acer saccharum*)	Large tree with graceful form and superb orange and gold fall color. Reaches to 130'.	Sun to light shade. Rich, moist, organic soil. Zones 3 to 5.	Excellent shade tree. Outstanding red, yellow, and orange fall color, even on young seedlings.

BEST SHRUBS FOR WOODLAND GARDENS

Shrubs	Description	Conditions	Comments
Flame azalea (*Rhododendron calendulaceum*) and pinxterbloom azalea (*R. periclymenoides*)	Deciduous native azaleas with loose clusters of pink or white (pinxter) or red, orange, or yellow (flame) flowers in spring reaches to 9'.	Partial to full shade. Rich, moist, acid soil. Flame azalea, Zone 5. Pinxterbloom azalea, Zones 4 to 8.	These adaptable eastern natives are like manna to hummingbirds. Pinxterbloom azalea flowers are wonderfully fragrant, while flame azalea offers vivid, unusual flower color.
Hearts-a-bustin' (*Euonymous americana*)	Deciduous shrub to 8' with intriguing fruit capsules that split open when ripe in fall, revealing the red "heart" inside. Excellent fall color. Reaches to 5'.	Partial to moderate shade. Average garden soil. Zones 6 to 9.	This relative of the common landscape shrub burning bush is a quieter presence in the garden, though it still offers brilliant crimson fall color as well as decorative fruits appreciated by birds.
Pussy willow (*Salix discolor*)	Deciduous shrubs with charming furred catkins in spring, before the leaves emerge. Reaches to 20'.	Sun to partial or moderate shade. Average soil. Also thrives in wet soil. Zones 4 to 9.	Good for early foraging honeybees. A favorite for coaxing for bouquets in late winter.
Spicebush (*Lindera benzoin*)	Graceful, open, deciduous shrub with attractive form. Dark-barked branches are studded with tiny yellow blooms in very early spring. Reaches 4–15'.	Partial to full shade. Average soil. Also thrives in wet soil. Zones 4 to 10.	An underused American native. All parts have a pleasant spicy fragrance. Red oval berries are a favorite of thrushes and don't last long on the bush.
Thimbleberry (*Rubus parviflorus*)	Deciduous shrub with maplelike leaves, white flowers in spring, and red raspberrylike fruit in summer. Reaches to 6'.	Partial to moderate shade. Humus-rich acid soil, but also adapts to average soil. Zones 4 to 9.	Shredding bark adds to winter appeal. The similar purple-flowering raspberry (*R. odoratus*) is also good for the woodland garden.

Pussy willow (*Salix discolor*)   Thimbleberry (*Rubus parviflorus*)

BEST WILDFLOWERS FOR WOODLAND GARDENS

Wildflowers	Description	Conditions	Comments
American campanula (*Campanula americana*)	Spikes of azure blue open-faced stars appear summer through fall on a branching 3–5′ plant.	Sun to full shade. Annual. Self-sows. Average, well-drained soil. All zones.	Unusual color for the shade. Scatter seed generously in fall; may not germinate until second spring. Let plants self-sow.
Bloodroot (*Sanguinaria canadensis*)	White stars and large, blue-green lobed leaves. Plants reach 8″. Blooms in early spring.	Partial to full shade. Average, well-drained soil. Zones 3 to 9.	Reliable very early spring wildflower. Naturalizes well. Roots "bleed" red sap.
Dutchman's breeches (*Dicentra cucullaria*)	Mounds of lacy gray-green foliage and arching stems of little creamy "pantaloons." Appear in spring. Plants reach 8–12″.	Partial to full shade. Humusy, well-drained soil. Zones 3 to 9.	Charming but tough. Spreads into colonies.
Fringecups (*Tellima grandiflora*)	Stems of tiny fringed green, white, or pink bells appear above rosettes of rounded, hairy leaves. Blooms in spring. Reaches 12″.	Partial to full shade. Average, well-drained soil. Appreciates humus. Zones 4 to 9.	A northwestern native that combines beautifully with other shade perennials. Foliage persists after blooming, like heuchera, which it resembles. Spreads by thick rhizomes and will form a groundcover in loose, organic soil.
Jack-in-the-pulpit (*Arisaema triphyllum*)	Unusual peek-a-boo flower with hooded spadix over erect spathe, the "Jack." Plants have two three-lobed leaves. Blooms in spring. Reaches 2–3′.	Partial to full shade. Average, well-drained soil. Zones 4 to 9.	Tight clusters of bright red berries are relished by chipmunks and other wildlife.
Mayapple (*Podophyllum peltatum*)	12″ high umbrella of usually one rounded, multipart leaf; Some plants branch into two leaves, hiding a single waxy white flower at their juncture. Blooms in spring. Reaches 1–2′.	Sun to full shade. Average, well-drained soil. Zones 3 to 9.	Watching the furled umbrellas of mayapple push through the soil and then open over a few days is a simple pleasure. Rhizomes spread freely in loose, organic soil to form colonies.
Wild sweet William (*Phlox divaricata, P. stolonifera*)	Semi-evergreen creeping perennial with beautiful blue-lavender flowers produced in great abundance in spring. Reaches to about 12″ when in bloom.	Sun to full shade. Average, well-drained soil. Zones 3 to 8.	A beautiful companion to spring bulbs. Both species spread into large, loose mats. Several cultivars in various colors are available, but the species are worthy as is.

BEST GROUNDCOVERS FOR WOODLAND GARDENS

Groundcovers	Description	Conditions	Comments
Canada mayflower (*Maianthemum canadense*)	Also known as false lily-of-the-valley, a more descriptive name, this 6″ native bears a single stem with two or three leaves topped in spring to summer by a cluster of small, white flowers.	Partial to full shade. Loose, humusy soil; also thrives in poor soils. Zones 2 to 9.	Spreads by slender, creeping roots. Slow to establish at first. Nice as a textural accent with other groundcovers.
Foamflower (*Tiarella cordifolia*)	Clumps of 1′ or taller foliage like heucheras, with feathery spikes of tiny, creamy white flowers rising above the leaves. Spreads rapidly by stolons. Blooms in spring.	Partial to full shade. Moist, humusy soil; does not tolerate drought. Zones 3 to 9.	Beautiful with wild phlox and other native wildflowers. Allow fallen leaves from overhead trees to remain in place as a mulch. Don't be fooled by the variety collina (*T. wherryi*), which looks just like the species but doesn't spread.
Green-and-gold (*Chrysogonum virginianum*)	Rosettes of triangular, dark green leaves topped with short-stemmed bouquets of bright gold daisy flowers; plants grow to 6–12″ tall. Blooms in spring.	Partial to full shade. Average garden soil; very adaptable, but not drought-tolerant. Zones 5 to 9.	Nice as an underplanting to shrubs. Long period of bloom, with sporadic flowers through summer.
Waterleaves (*Hydrophyllum* spp.)	Beautiful silver-splashed leaves grow from knotty, fast-spreading rhizomes. White or blue spring or summer flowers have fuzzy stamens. Reaches 1–1½′.	Partial sun to full shade. Widely adaptable. Zones 3 to 9.	Large-leaved (*H. macrophylla*) and broad-leaved waterleaf (*H. canadense*), shorter species with wide, silver-spangled leaves, are my favorites.

Green-and-gold (*Chrysogonum virginianum*)

Canada Mayflower (*Maianthemum canadense*)

BEST TREES FOR SHADE GARDENS

Trees	Description	Conditions	Comments
Kousa dogwood (*Cornus kousa*)	Small tree with layered branches and white bract "flowers," similar to flowering dogwood. Blooms in spring. Reaches to 20′.	Sun to moderate shade. Moist, organic soil. Zones 5 to 8.	This appealing tree and the related hybrid Stellar dogwoods (*C. × rutgersensis*) are vigorous and trouble-free. The red fruits are supposedly attractive to birds, but go ignored on my tree.
Cornelian cherry (*Cornus mas*)	Small tree with shrubby, multitrunked habit and cheerful yellow bumbles of tiny flowers along the bare branches in early spring. Reaches to 20′.	Sun to moderate shade. Average, well-drained soil. Drought-tolerant. Zones 4 to 8.	A tough little tree, undemanding and adaptable. Looks great underplanted with Virginia bluebells and muscari. Red berries follow flowers and are eagerly sought by birds.
Japanese plume cedar (*Cryptomeria japonica* 'Elegans')	An elegant evergreen conifer with soft clouds of green foliage shading to red and blue. Reaches to 150′, grows to about 50′ in a garden setting.	Sun to partial or light shade. Average, well-drained soil. Zones 6 to 9.	Adaptable and trouble-free. Needles look sharp, but are soft and springy to the touch. Foliage becomes tinged with plum purple in cold weather.
Red buckeye (*Aesculus pavia*)	Small tree or large open shrub with candelabras of tubular red flowers in spring. Foliage resembles that of horsechestnut. Reaches to 12′.	Sun to full shade. Average, well-drained soil. Zones 6 to 9.	One of the first trees to unfold its foliage in spring. Flowers are much sought by hummingbirds.
Serviceberries (*Amelanchier* spp.)	Small trees or shrubs with delicate, white, cherrylike blossoms in spring and blue-black fruits that are tasty to man and beast. Reaches to 5–20′.	Sun to moderate shade. Well-drained, acid soil. Zones 4 to 9, depending on the species.	The native serviceberries are enjoying a new popularity among gardeners, so more cultivars are appearing in catalogs and garden centers.

BEST SHRUBS FOR SHADE GARDENS

Shrubs	Description	Conditions	Comments
Korean azalea (*Rhododendron mucronulatum*)	Deciduous shrub to 8' with rose-purple flowers in early spring.	Partial to moderate shade. Acid, organic, humus-rich soil. Zones 5 to 8.	Blooms extremely early. Beautiful with emerging ferns.
Rhododendrons, evergreen (*Rhododendron* spp.)	Many cultivars. Evergreen shrubs with large, oval, glossy leaves and big trusses of flowers, often fragrant. Reaches 6–12' or taller.	Sun to full shade. Zones 4 to 8.	The sheltering leaves of evergreen rhododendrons give structure to the winter garden and offer birds protection in inclement weather. Flowers are visited by hummingbirds.
Red-flowered currant (*Ribes sanguineum*)	Deciduous shrub to 12' with very graceful form and dangling clusters of unusually fragrant deep pink or red flowers in early spring.	Partial to full shade. Humus-rich, moist, acid soil. Zones 5 to 6 (7).	This pretty shrub offers very early spring bloom for hummingbirds and berries for other wildlife.
Witch hazels (*Hamamelis* spp. and hybrids)	Deciduous shrubs or small trees with odd flowers like scraps of bright ribbons in spring or fall. Some are winter blooming.	Partial to full shade. Average soil; vernal witch hazel (*H. vernalis*) and Virginia witch hazel (*H. virginiana*) also thrive in moist soil. Zones 5 to 8.	Carefree shrubs with flowers just when you need them most—the doldrums of late winter. Vernal witch hazel (*H. vernalis*), to 10', has attractive, vase-shaped habit and blooms in very early spring. Virginia witch hazel (*H. virginiana)* is larger and blooms in fall and winter. Chinese witch hazel (*H. mollis*) is a Chinese species with yellow flowers in late winter. Hybrid witch hazel (*H. × intermedia)* has several cultivars.
Hollies, evergreen (*Ilex* spp. and hybrids)	Evergreen shrubs and small trees with prickly leaves and showy red berries. Reaches to 50'.	Partial sun to shade. Average, well-drained soil. Hardy to Zones 4 to 9, depending on species.	Good evergreens for winter interest and shelter. Abundant berries are favorites of robins and other birds.

BEST WILDFLOWERS FOR SHADE GARDENS

Wildflowers	Description	Conditions	Comments
Heucheras (*Heuchera* spp. and hybrids)	Rosettes of pretty scalloped leaves with graceful 12–18″ stems of white, pink, or red flowers. Blooms in spring or summer.	Sun to partial or moderate shade. Average, well-drained soil. Zones 3 to 9, depending on the species.	Many newer hybrids have gorgeous foliage. 'Pewter Veil' has dark-veined silvery leaves.
Trout lilies (*Erythronium* spp.)	Mottled or clear green leaves arising from a deep-set bulb, bearing a pretty, nodding, six-petaled flower in yellow, white, purple, or varied colors. 6–24″ tall, depending on the species. Blooms in spring.	Light to full shade. Moist, humusy soil. Hardy to Zones 2 to 8, depending on species.	Trout lilies get their name from the leaves, which are often speckled with brown or purple like the belly of a trout. They are long-lived and multiply, but may be slow to bloom after planting.
Virginia bluebells (*Mertensia virginica*)	An ethereal early spring beauty with light green oval leaves and 1–2′ stems of dangling bells of rain-washed blue. Buds are pink. Blooms in spring.	Partial shade. Moist, humusy soil, but will also grow in clay. Zones 3 to 9.	Dies back completely after blooming, so plant among groundcover that can later camouflage the bare spot, or overplant with other shade-loving annuals.
Wild bleeding heart (*Dicentra formosa, D. eximia*)	Lacy, gray-green foliage in shaggy 18″ clumps with arching stems of pink hearts strung along a bare stem in spring.	Partial to full shade. Moist, humusy soil. Zones 2 to 9.	Wild bleeding heart (*D. eximia*), the native eastern species, does better in humid summer heat than the western species, Western bleeding heart (*D. formosa*), which is more drought-tolerant.
Wild columbine (*Aquilegia canadensis, A. chrysantha*)	Intriguing, long-spurred blossoms above rosettes of lacy, gray-green foliage. Yellow-flowered *A. chrysantha* grows to 3½′; red and yellow *A. canadensis*, usually about 2′.	Partial sun to full shade. Average, moist garden soil. Zone 3 to 9.	Favorites of hummingbirds. Long period of bloom.

Trout lilies (*Erythronium americanum*)

Virginia bluebells (*Mertensia virginica*)

Wild columbine (*Aquilegia canadensis*)

BEST GROUNDCOVERS FOR SHADE GARDENS

Groundcovers	Description	Conditions	Comments
European wild ginger (*Asarum europaeum*)	Glossy, leathery, heart-shaped leaves appear in spring and spread in mats about 6″ high. Evergreen.	Light to full shade. Well-drained, moist soil. Zones 4 to 7.	The shiny leaves are eyecatching among other textures in the garden.
Lungwort or Bethlehem sage (*Pulmonaria saccharata*)	Pretty pointed oval leaves are generously splashed and dotted with silvery white, an effect that subtly adds light to the shade garden. The 12–18″ tall plants gradually spread to about 2 feet.	Light to full shade well-drained moist soil. Zones 3 to 8.	The spring-blooming flowers are similar to Virginia bluebells: they open pink from pink buds, then age to light blue. Pink and white cultivars are also available. If your summers are hot and humid, try long-leafed lungwort (*P. longifolia*), with extremely long, slim leaves spotted silvery gray and clusters of purple-blue spring flowers
Western beach strawberry (*Fragaria chiloensis*)	Mat-forming strawberry with very shiny, deep green leaves. White flowers and red berries shine among the foliage.	Sun to partial or light shade. Very adaptable. Does best in loose soils and thrives in sand. Hardy to at least Zones 3 to 9.	A beautiful, low-maintenance ornamental. Birds, turtles, and toads appreciate the fruits.
Wintergreen (*Gaultheria procumbens*)	Creeping, prostrate evergreen shrub with small, shiny leaves and scarlet fruits in summer and fall.	Partial to full shade. Moist, humusy, acid soil. Zones 4 to 7.	Does best in cool climates. An old favorite for glass-bowl gardens.
Yellow corydalis (*Corydalis lutea*)	Lacy, pale blue-green foliage, 8-15″ high, looks good all season. Dainty, spurred yellow blooms held on wiry stems. Most abundant in spring, the flowers show up sporadically until frost.	Light to full shade. Well-drained, moist soil. Zones 5 to 7.	Self-sows, with a charming habit of showing up in niches of rock walls or brick paths. A fine-textured companion for hostas. Tricky to start from seed; buy plants instead.

Yellow corydalis (*Corydalis lutea*)

European wild ginger (*Asarum europaeum*)

Western strawberry (*Fragaria chiloensis*)

Snuggle plants into crevices where their roots will stay cool and moist.

Water makes a garden a special place. Being around water, whether it's a pond, a brook, an ocean, or a fountain, refreshes and energizes us. Looking into water inspires both serious contemplation and idle daydreaming. And when you have water, you'll have all kinds of surprises. You may see regal great blue herons, slick-furred muskrats, iridescent dragonflies that flit about like living jewels, lotuses with flower centers that dry into huge salt-shaker pods, frogs perched on lily pads just like in cartoons—and that's just above the water.

Surface tension creates a thin film of water that is truly walkable, if you have the right equipment. Look on for water striders, which skate about like long-legged spiders, or whirligig beetles, which zip around in circles too fast for human eyes to follow. Catch one in a paper cup for a close-up look.

The submerged world holds even more curiosities. Turn over a few rocks in a streambed, and you'll get an inkling of what sorts of oddballs await in the water world. One summer, I enjoyed myself thoroughly introducing my sophisticated, well-traveled neighbor to the weirdos underwater. We crouched in the shallows, examining the primitive-looking, spike-tailed insects flattened beneath every rock. We fished out the vicious giant-jawed creatures that turn into jeweled dragonflies. And we peered at naked caddis-fly larvae hiding inside portable homes of cemented debris. Even in Rome, said my worldly neighbor, he'd never seen anything to match this gallery.

Water also brings all kinds of gardening opportunities. Now you can consider wonderful water-loving plants, from classic water lilies opening their waxen cups to the sun, to tiny white flowers of starwort (*Callitriche hermaphoditica*) spangling the water like a handful of stars, to the striking lances of golden club poking up from cool, blue-green leaves. You can plant stalwart yellow and blue flag irises that wave like French banners, or you can indulge in extravagant Japanese irises, which grow to huge, ruffled perfection in boggy places. Before you know it, you'll be wishing for more space in your water garden, just as you do in your perennial borders.

I've been lucky enough to have natural water at or near every place I've lived, so I've never had to excavate for a pond. But I've lent my back and my advice to friends putting in ponds, pools, and fountains, and I've seen the transformation that water can work on a garden. It's magic!

Water Music

A still pool offers serenity and multiplies the impact of plants and sky reflected in its mirrored surface. But it's water music that brings a garden alive. The quiet burble of a fountain, the splash as water spills over a rock ledge, a silver thread of water tinkling into a fern-lined pool—our eyes follow our ears to the sound, and we are drawn to water as instinctively as any bird or other wild creature is.

Before you reach for that shovel, though, think about what qualities of a water garden are most important to you. Start by thinking about the water itself. A quiet pool has a much different personality than a rippling brook. If the sound of water is important to you, you'll want to add a small fountain or a recirculating stream. Or you can allow one side of the pool to lead off to a short drop, where falling water will play its music. If you opt for a fountain, there's a wide variety of possible effects, from a gentle shower to an arching spray to a thin trickle.

Besides the ephemeral pleasures of water music, there are more tangible aspects to consider, too. The kinds of plants we think of as typical water-garden plants—water lilies, lotuses, pickerelweed, and many others—thrive in still waters. You'll need a pool or pond area for these to do well.

Look at the lay of your land, too, when you're planning a place for a water feature. If you have a slight slope, that's a natural beginning for a waterfall or handmade stream. A recirculating pump and buried tubing will carry the water back to the starting point.

The size of your garden or yard is another thing to keep in mind. Of course you can't dig a huge farm pond in a typical subdivision or on a city street. But a small pond can fit in any garden.

Water Garden Visitors

If you build it, they will come. Birds, animals, bugs, and butterflies, that is. The traffic at your birdbath is nothing compared to the visitors you'll see at a pond. I love to check the guest register in the soft mud at the edge of the pond. Because many of your visitors will come in the night, you'll soon want to add a field guide to animal tracks to your collection. I look for the perfect pairs of half-moon deer prints, the wide-spread stars of skunk feet, the thumbed handprints of raccoons, and the big, turkey-like marks and white-lime splashes of herons.

A small fountain enhances the appeal of a pool. Its gentle sound is especially attractive to birds, as long as it doesn't create torrential ripples. Notice how the spill of grass softens the stone edge and eases the transition to the water.

WATER GARDEN VISITORS

Water gardens are rich with wildlife. Some will come to live there, some will come to drink, and others will come to dine. Here are some you might encounter.

Beavers, mink, otters	They may move to an isolated pond or stream, or you may see them eating or fishing.
Bitterns	You'll spot them looking for food or standing with beak stretched to the sky among the reeds. Watch for the least bittern, a tiny heron the size of a robin.
Cedar waxwings	They'll be flycatching—grabbing insects while in flight over the water.
Deer	Deer visit water gardens to drink water, often at night.
Dragonflies and darners	Larvae are aquatic; adults are beauty on the wing in colors of silver, turquoise, cobalt, brilliant tropical green, and red.
Ducks	Only a big pond will draw ducks. If your pond is in the woods and away from human activity, you may be lucky enough to land a wood duck, the beauty queen of the duck world. Wood ducks are more reclusive than Howard Hughes. Unless you're very sneaky, you're more likely to see them fleeing than swimming.
Frogs	They'll move in fast and become summer-long residents.
Herons	You'll see them fishing for dinner.
Hummingbirds	Watch for hummers sipping from jewelweed near the water or collecting spider silk for nest.
Mayflies	Flat "bugs" with 3-pronged tails on submerged rocks are mayfly larvae. They hatch all at once, take to the air, and live only hours.
Minnows and other fish	Fish are brought in as eggs on bird feet.
Muskrats	They may be eating cattails or burrowing into walls.
Northern harriers (marsh hawks)	These hawks will be patrolling for mice and rodents.
Nutria	Nutrias like to nibble on reeds and vegetation. They look like giant hamsters on steroids.
Opossums and skunks	These nocturnal critters will be scouting for food or looking for a drink.
Predaceous diving beetles	Big, black, and mean, those jaws mean business to unlucky aquatic insects or larvae.
Raccoons	You may see one washing up before dinner or catching frogs and fish.
Red-winged blackbirds, swamp sparrows, song sparrows	They may nest in reeds or other vegetation.
Robins and other songbirds	Look for these busy birds bathing and drinking, as well as nesting in nearby vegetation.
Spring peepers and chorus frogs	They'll call for mates in early spring, then disappear. These are tiny, thumbnail-size guys with a voice as big as Maria Callas's.
Tadpoles	Look for them on submerged decaying vegetation or on the bottom in the shallows.
Turtles	They'll be basking on logs or swimming. Look for black dots breaking the surface of a pond, and watch to see if they suddenly disappear or move: Those are turtle heads.
Voles	Voles may set up den tunnels in the banks.
Water striders	Watch them skate on the surface film. These are resident, spiderlike insects.
Whirligig beetles	You can see them whizzing in circles on the water surface, in tight groups of dozens or hundreds. They look like tiny silvery bumper cars at high speed.
Yellow warblers	Warblers may nest in willows and other trees and shrubs near the water.

It's a toss-up between frogs and birds as to who will find your water first. When my children were toddlers, a frog often moved into their shallow inflatable swimming pool overnight! But frogs aren't nearly as plentiful today as they were ten years ago, for reasons that aren't clear yet but may have a lot to do with ozone depletion. Frogs may still move into your pond quickly, usually within a few weeks, but chances are that your first visitors will be birds. A reliable source of clean, fresh water is a powerful draw for songbirds, especially if the area is planted with sheltering grasses and shrubs.

I love to watch birds reveling in their baths. Robins, goldfinches, blackbirds, native sparrows, and bluebirds are especially fond of bathing, but I have also been privileged to spy on evening grosbeaks, cardinals, chickadees, warblers, and, once, a scarlet tanager at the bath. But even starlings and English sparrows are fun to watch as they go through the motions.

At first they duck their heads tentatively, but before long, they're thrashing about with fluttering wings, as uninhibited as a toddler in the tub. When the bird is thoroughly soaked and looking as pathetic as a wet cat, it'll look for a place to preen and perch out of harm's way while its feathers fluff and dry. On a hot, dusty summer day, you know how good that bath must feel. But they'll also bathe in weather so chilly that brittle ice decorates the water's edge. It makes me shiver just to see them, even if I'm watching through a window.

Container Water Gardens

It's amazing how satisfying even a tiny water garden can be. If you only have room for one plant, grow a water lily. They may seem pricey when you compare the cost to perennials, but even the most common types are exquisite. A single water lily, partnered with a glimpse of dark, shining water, is a delight to the soul.

When space and time (not to mention money) were really tight one summer, I made a water garden in a big plastic tub—one of those "muck buckets" sold at discount stores. I chose a black tub, which looked surprisingly good when filled with graceful rushes, a single pink water lily, and the wonderful textures of water lettuce and ferny milfoil. (I can't resist those rosettes of ruffled, pleated water-lettuce leaves.)

My tub wasn't ultraviolet (UV)-light resistant, and it only held up for three years before the UV rays

Waterlily leaves are a fine lookout if you're a frog. If your pond frogs splash into the water in alarm, stand still and watch for their heads to pop up among the lilypads.

Chipmunks, ground squirrels, and even tree squirrels will all come for a drink. Be sure to provide plenty of cover so they can make their way to the water in safety.

degraded the plastic and leaks appeared. But then again, it only cost $7. Large, sturdy, UV-resistant plastic tubs and pots are now made in appealing shapes and matte finishes and are widely available at garden centers. Or you can go the cheapskate route like I did and shop the housewares department.

Some gardeners use oak half-barrels, lined or unlined. I tried filling a half-barrel with water without using a liner, hoping the staves would swell and stop any leaks. It was a little tricky keeping the metal barrel bands evenly horizontal as the wood expanded, and the wood never became totally watertight, but the barrel did hold water. My half-barrel never did become a successful water garden, unfortunately, because my dogs claimed it as their own watering hole. After a few weeks of mourning over broken stems and damaged plants, I gave up on the water garden and let the dogs have their way. But I did get a nice bog garden out of it, thanks to the constant slopping of water over the edge of the tub and the slow leakage through the staves. Around the barrel's muddy base, moisture-loving plants, including forget-me-nots and even watercress, grew in beautiful profusion.

Tubs and pots are heavy enough even before adding water, so decide on the location of your container water garden before you move it into position. A sunny spot is good for water lilies, but a partly shaded site will cut down on evaporation and algae. You'll need to collect a few flat stones or bricks to help boost plant pots to proper height inside the tub. I like to perch a rock in my container water garden as a sipping spot for birds or a landing pad for dragonflies. I set it on top of a submerged piece of clay drainage pipe so that the surface of the rock breaks the water but the underpinnings aren't exposed.

The biggest problem with container water gardens is that they're too small. Water plants move faster than Napoleon, and their aim is the same—to expand their empire. Even if you choose well-mannered plants, you'll soon run out of room for more than a few. What to do with the rest? If you're still not ready to install a pool, try a metal horse trough. These are long and narrow, shaped like a throat lozenge with rounded corners, and they have plenty of room in which to create a good garden. You can buy them new at farm-supply stores, or check country auctions. I found an old one at a farm auction for a few dollars; I gave it a once-over with a can of black, matte-finish spray paint, and it did the job perfectly.

WATER GARDEN IN MINIATURE

Any waterproof container can become a water garden. I like to haunt thrift stores and antique shops, looking for interesting ceramic or metal pots (the bigger the better). If I use a metal container, I paint it with waterproof paint so that the metal doesn't leach out and affect the growth of plants inside.

One year, I planted a water garden for a friend's tiny patio in a Chinese fish bowl. I'd found the bowl at a discount store for less than $20. It was a fat ceramic pot about 18 inches across, finished in a simple deep blue glaze. I indulged in a containerized dwarf white water lily, then delivered the pot to my friend, telling her to go inside while I set up her surprise. I filled the pot from the hose, settled in the plant, and voilà! A summer of pleasure for a few minutes of work.

▲ *Your choice of containers is limited only by your imagination—or your shoe closet! It's fun to tuck surprises into the garden. Notice how the young water garden gains stature and grace thanks to the plumes of fountain grass next to the barrel.*

▶ *This water garden evokes memories of the old oaken bucket. A pair of variegated irises draws attention to the always-trickling pump.*

BACK-SAVERS

Consider your back and your biceps as well as your budget when you're deciding on the size of your water garden. As always when gardening, the place to start is with the soil: If your soil is good loam and free of rocks, the digging will be a lot easier than if you have to pry out or break up rocks that are in the way. Here are some other tips to make the job easier.

* Don't feel like you have to dig the hole for your water garden all in one session. Space the work out over several weekends if you need to, covering the excavation with a plastic tarp between work sessions.

* Invest in a good-quality shovel with a fiberglass-reinforced handle for extra levering strength.

* I'm a short person and I find a short-handled shovel much easier to work with. Use a shovel that fits your size. When the hole gets deeper, I switch to a long-handled spade to remove the soil from the site.

* If you're digging out a waterfall or a stream with a waterfall, start at the bottom. Dig out the area for that pool first. Then move on the next pool on the way up the hill, and so on until you finally reach the header pool at the top of the stream or waterfall.

Perennial primroses, including these easy-to-grow candelabra primroses (Primula japonica), are a staple in British landscaping but are less well known in America. They naturalize easily in moist soil, forming colonies that look lovely in a lightly shaded spot along the water's edge.

Natural Water-Garden Style

It's not difficult to put in a pond, but it takes some thinking to make it look natural. I love ponds and pools, but I wince at the unnatural stone edging I see all too often, even in the pages of the best water-garden-supply catalogs. Rubber and polyvinylchloride (PVC) liners have made it easy for pools to hold water, but the trouble is that the ponds too often end up looking artificial. They're surrounded by an edging of flat stone, laid as carefully as a flagstone walk. No matter how many water lilies grace the surface, the hand of a human is all too apparent in these gardens. I prefer my water gardens a little wilder, so they look like something that might have been there forever, not like something that was built from a kit and a truckload of stone.

For a natural look, you'll want to start with an irregularly shaped pool. Leave the rectangles and circles to formal gardens; their lines are too rigid to blend into a natural landscape. If you should happen to have a pool with a regular outline, you can disguise it with plantings that spill over its edges and merge naturally into nearby gardens. Japanese maples, which dip their weeping branches down to the water's surface, can soften almost any pool.

Pool Options

In years gone by, if you wanted a water garden, you had to mix cement and mortar and tackle an enormous project that makes me tired just thinking about it. But water gardens are getting easier every year. With the advent of PVC and butyl rubber liner sheets, installing a pool is

Water Garden Options

These days, when it's time to put in your pool, you have several choices of water garden or pond liners. Concrete is still an option, but there are better materials available, including plastic and rubber sheet liners, preformed plastic pools, and an old farm-pond standard, packed clay. Here are the pros and cons of each.

Type of Pool	Pros	Cons	Recommendations
Concrete	Long-lasting. Reasonable price.	Messy, hard work. May crack from thawing ice. Alkalinity from lime may affect water balance.	Not recommended.
Packed clay	Cheap. Good for large-size pond in area with naturally heavy soil or where water naturally accumulates.	Heavy labor. Requires pounding with a rammer or sledgehammer or by repeated rolling. Large equipment may have to be brought in, which can damage lawn and garden.	Not recommended except for very large ponds. If you have a naturally boggy site, it's easiest to plant a bog garden there and install a lined pool elsewhere.
Plastic or rubber sheet liners	Can follow any shape or contour. Less expensive than a preformed pool. Can be extended beyond pool to create bog garden. Allows quick growth of algae on bottom and sides to disguise artificial nature of pond lining. Forgiving of excavation irregularities because it drapes easily.	Must be carefully installed to avoid sharp objects and leaks. Edges must be held in place with rock, timbers, or brick. Be sure to buy a liner that resists damage from ultraviolet light (sunlight). Butyl rubber lasts up to 50 years; less-expensive PVC lasts for 5 to 15 years.	Best choice for pools and ponds. Also good for streams and waterfalls, and excellent when used in combination with preformed sections in waterfalls and streams.
Preformed	Easy to install. Small sections can be linked together to form streams or waterfalls. Rigid pools will last for up to 50 years. Often include built-in shelves for plants.	More expensive than other options. May not be size or shape desired. If you want a bog garden nearby, it will have to be created separately. Most are too small for an effective natural pond. Many are too shallow (less than 2 feet) to accommodate overwintering fish and plants. Can crack without proper soil support. Edge looks unnatural and must be disguised.	Small units are excellent for creating waterfalls and streams, either alone or combined with lined sections.

Installing a Pool

Call on a friend or two to help make the work go faster and easier when you install a preformed pool. Many preformed pools come with a stepped edge, which allows you to grow plants that like shallow water near the edges.

STEP 1: *The old carpentry adage, "Measure twice, cut once," also holds true for digging. Hold the preformed pool right side up to mark its outline with stakes and rope or string.*

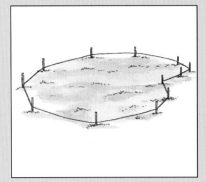

STEP 2: *When the hole is dug, insert the pool and check for levelness and fit. Be sure the preformed ledge, if there is one, is well supported by soil beneath it.*

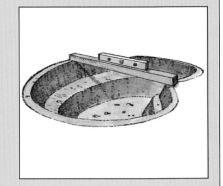

STEP 3: *Laying in a liner is easier with a helper. Lap the edges into pleats to ensure a smooth fit, but don't worry too much about wrinkles, which will be invisible once the pool fills.*

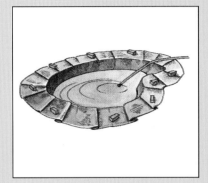

STEP 4: *Line the edge of the pool with rocks to hold the liner in place. Vary the size and shape of the stones, and pile some in groups to mimic Mother Nature's freeform arrangements.*

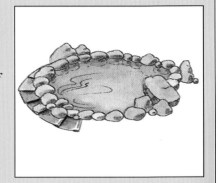

STEP 5: *Plants are the finishing touch. Lilies and other water plants can spread surprisingly fast. Be sure to keep some water clear as your plants mature; the view of water is one of the pleasures of a pond.*

MIRROR-IMAGE DIGGING: DON'T TRY IT

If you're installing an irregularly shaped, preformed pond, set it right side up and mark the outlines with bamboo plant stakes along the curves. I learned this lesson the hard way. When a friend wanted to install a kidney-shaped pool, we flipped it upside down to trace out the outline to excavate. Neither of us noticed until too late that the area we dug was a mirror image of the pool. It would have fit in perfectly upside down, but in its right-side-up position, the curves were the opposite way around. We had to start all over again, this time with the pool in its upright position. Of course, if the pool you're installing is a simple oval or circle, it won't make any difference whether you trace the pool right side up or upside down.

well within the reach of even mechanically challenged gardeners.

It's perfectly possible to install a backyard pool in one weekend of intensive labor, but I prefer to do it in three easy steps: I devote one weekend to planning and shopping, one to digging and installing, and one to planting and filling.

You'll save yourself some time and trouble if you call on your friends when it's time to put in the liner. They can help position the liner and hold the edges in place while you secure them. Liners are heavier than you'd think, and without several pairs of hands, it's easy for part of the liner you've just positioned to slip down into the hole. Also, it's a good idea to install the liner on a sunny day—let it warm up in the sun first, so it's flexible and easier to handle.

Remember that smoothing out a liner isn't as fussy as making a bed. Don't worry about pleats and wrinkles

Fish can add color that's as bright as flowers. Feed them at the same time and place every day and they'll soon be waiting for you at feeding time—a great trick for amusing children and other visitors.

in the liner; they'll soon be hidden by algae and the slight natural cloudiness of the water.

Edging Your Pool with Rocks

Liners and preformed pools are easy to install, but their plastic edges will stick out like a sore thumb unless you hide them. Rocks are the best choice for the job because soil alone will soon wash into the pool with the next good rain.

However, there's no law that says the rocks that hold the liner in place or disguise the edge of the pool must all be the same size. Incorporate several large rocks (or boulders if you can manage them) into the edging. Group them together naturally, varying the height by using rocks of different sizes or by layering them. Bury the bases of larger rocks partway into the soil to make them look natural. Extend the rocks into surrounding garden, blending them in with grasses and shrubs.

Be sure to use rocks that occur naturally in your area. Chunks of lava, for example, will look out of place in a limestone region. Keep in mind that quarried stone will also look different from weathered rock. The retaining wall of bright white quarried limestone in my garden stuck out like a spotlight until time added lichens, mosses, and natural stains to its surface.

Mottled or medium- to dark-colored rocks will blend into surrounding vegetation more easily than light-colored limestone or sandstone. But beware of a higgledy-piggledy effect of mixed colors: For a natural look, choose your rocks so that the colors blend with each other.

Sandstone will absorb water, which makes it a great place for mosses to start colonizing. Algae will colonize the rock first, giving it a green patina that makes it look like it's been part of the garden for a long time. Then mosses and lichens will move in. The drawback with sandstone is that much of the water it absorbs is lost through evaporation, so you may have to refill the pool more often.

Granite and slate don't suck up water like porous sandstone, and they're less hospitable to tiny rock plants. Their surfaces remain mostly bare until they're colonized by lichens. Use these rocks as accents or anchors around your water garden. If the rocks you're using are already weathered, remember your nature lore when you situate them: Moss grows on the north side.

This tiny water garden is tucked in near a fence, so that passersby don't literally stumble into it. Hardy geraniums weave their way across the rocks to help blend the pool with the rest of the garden. Their bloom lasts a long time.

Rocks of different shapes and sizes, jutting into the water or half-buried in the earth, give a more natural look than a rim of evenly sized flagstones. Mossy surfaces make them seem as if they've been there forever.

Consider the angles of the sides of the rocks when you position them. If your rocks slant in all different directions, your pool won't be a restful place. The clashing angles will jangle your view.

Try to include one or two substantial, flat-surface rocks near the pool as sitting spots. But keep them back from the lined edge to avoid collapsing the edge into the water when you sit on them!

A cobblestone "beach" makes an appealing approach to a small section of your pond or stream. Place rounded river stones closely together, leading from shallow water to a grassy or boggy area near the water garden. (I always wondered where cobblestones got their name until I walked the Oregon beaches, where smooth, round stones of basalt cover the sand. As the waves washed in and then receded, the stones knuckled against each other with a wonderful, low-pitched "cobble-cobble-cobble" song.) Animals and birds are quick to take to a cobbled beach, where the stones give them a feeling of safety as they drink and bathe.

Sometimes simple is best. This water-lily garden mirrors the shapes of the flat rocks that rim the pool, lending a sense of serenity to the garden. Plants in the stone crevices soften the effect without hiding the architecture of the rocks.

PLANTS FOR EVERY NICHE

Water lilies are the first plants that come to mind when we think of a water garden, but there are lots of other possibilities. In fact, there are plants that are ideally suited to every part of your water garden, from deep pools to shallow edges and boggy areas. For a large pond to look good, you'll need a mix of plants from all of the following niches. A small pool can get by with only aquatics and floating plants, if they're what you really like. A bog garden, of course, needs only bog plants.

🐦 Aquatics must have their roots submerged, so they should be planted in water that's 1 to 3 feet deep. Don't go overboard with aquatics; their big leaves can hide too much of the water. Aquatics include the familiar water lilies and lotuses, plus other less well-known plants like golden club, water hawthorn, and water violet.

🐦 Floaters are surface plants like water lettuce and duckweed, which float on top of the water. They reduce algae by blocking sunlight and competing for nutrients, but they can also conceal the water. Floaters can overwhelm a pond because they reproduce so quickly. An occasional raking to remove the extras will keep the water visible. To remove duckweed, stretch a piece of cheesecloth over the tines of your rake or use a net to gather it.

🐦 Oxygenating plants are mostly submerged, though their tops may be visible. They grow incredibly fast and help keep the water clear because they compete with algae for nutrients. They also add oxygen to the water, which is something your fish will appreciate. These plants have exotic names like cabomba, anacharis, vallisneria, and myriophyllum. But they've become familiar to

us because they're commonly sold in aquarium shops to oxygenate fish tanks. A newly planted pool will probably horrify you in a week or two, when the water turns green from algae. Be patient, though, and soon your oxygenating plants will starve out the scum.

🐦 Marginals grow in the shallower water along the pond edge or in the very wet soil nearby. They're further divided into deep marginals, which like water about 12 inches deep, and shallow marginals, which grow well in shallow water (6 inches or less) or in wet soil. They include cattails, forget-me-nots, many sedges and rushes, and my personal favorite, western skunk cabbage.

🐦 Bog plants are moisture-lovers that thrive in soggy soil. Once you see cardinal flower in full glory in a wet spot, you'll feel a little guilty about relegating it to a mixed border. Irises and sweet flag, royal fern, and astilbes also shine in boggy soil, along with a host of other interesting plants. Try button-bush, with its fuzzy globes of white flowers and persistent seedheads. Or start a collection of willows. I'm partial to pussy willows, but any of the family are glorious in winter and early spring, when their bare branches flush with color.

Scatter a few floating plants, such as water lettuce, which dangle their roots into the water instead of getting nutrients from the soil. Place the floaters where they'll look pretty and have a bit of elbow room.

Moving outward toward the pool edges, add marginals like arrowhead and pickerelweed, which thrive in shallow water. Then finish your planting with moisture-loving bog plants such as irises and marsh marigold in the wet soil around the pond's edges. You may notice in some books and catalogs that there's not a clear distinc-

tion between many bog plants and marginals. Most of these plants will flourish happily in either shallow water or boggy soil conditions—and some will adapt to life in an average garden bed!

Examine all plants for duckweed before you put them in the water. This tiny aquatic plant has leaves barely ⅛ inch long, but it can cover a pond with a film of green in no time.

Unless you live in a cold-winter area, where they grow as annuals, do not plant water hyacinth, water

(continued on page 124)

▶ *Many border perennials make beautiful plants for the water's edge. Here a billow of ladies' mantle provides contrast to the dark water. The upright form of the tree, juxtaposed with the horizontal bench, draws the eye across the water.*

Channeling Water

Jim Wulfmeyer
Fenton, Missouri

"These things just kind of evolve," Jim Wulfmeyer says in his low-key way. He's talking about his water garden, which starts with a pond, then flows over the face of giant natural limestone outcroppings and splashes into a lower pool at his home in a suburb of St. Louis, Missouri.

"The landscape just seemed like the right place for it," Jim adds. His home is on a hillside, where there's plenty of rock to work with. There are natural limestone boulders he wouldn't even dream of lifting, though he did maneuver other huge rocks by building a sturdy wooden tripod and using chains and a hoist. "You have to know where you're going to put them before you start," he points out. Much of the watercourse is formed by natural troughs in the existing rock, which channel the water into a graceful streambed.

Jim's water garden is crowned by a pool that's 26 feet long and 6 feet wide, to which he added a deck on two sides so that he and his wife can enjoy the peaceful feeling of the water. "We like to sit on chairs on the deck," he says. "You never know what you might see."

Koi, the colorful Japanese carp that look like giant goldfish, live in the upper pond, and ordinary goldfish live in the lower one. "Raccoons tend to clean 'em out periodically," he notes. The raccoons also bring their antics to his bird-feeding station, where they climb right into the feeders to dine.

Jim grew up in the Fenton area, and he's seen it change over the years. "It used to be country," he says ruefully, "but today you'd call it suburbs. I've seen a lot of changes. But we still have a big woods behind our house."

Jim's yard is full of shade, too, and that makes it easier to maintain his water garden, he says. "Algae need sun," he says. "My pond is shaded enough that it takes care of itself, with no algae problem." He notes that other water gardeners depend on their plants to shield the water from sunlight, but because of his shade, he can let more of the water remain open.

The water garden is fringed with Virginia bluebells and marsh marigolds in spring. Cardinal flower—a favorite of hummingbirds, Jim notes—raises its red spires in summer. A red Japanese maple and Japanese black pines along the water add appealing form and all-season interest.

The surface of Jim's pond is dotted with water lilies, but only one kind, the dwarf yellow-flowering species *Helvola pygmaea*, will bloom here with the minimal sunlight. Other water lilies add beautiful foliage that Jim appreciates even without flowers. Arrowheads, dwarf cattails, and parrot feathers thrive in the shallow water.

In winter, Jim brings his frost-tender water lilies and other plants into shelter. "They go into the garage," he chuckles, "and my car comes out." He's

Cardinal flower is a showstopper with its spikes of brilliant blossoms. Beloved by hummingbirds, it reaches its full glory in wet or moist soil.

found that plastic tubs make a good overwintering place for his plants.

Jim's been working on his water garden for about a dozen years, he says, "but I'm never completely satisfied." He's already planning a new addition to the garden—a small Japanese teahouse at the head of the stream.

"My greatest pleasure is sitting out there, dreaming up new ideas, creating in my mind different garden settings, different plant combinations," he says. "Helping Mother Nature and creating something more beautiful than what you started out with—that's what makes it all worthwhile."

◄ *A variety of annual and perennial flowers keep things interesting from spring through fall. This penstemon is a favorite of hummingbirds, while the candytuft at its feet is sweetly scented.*

▼ *A bridge adds an Oriental flair to the garden, and provides a special place for contemplating the water. Natural shade keeps algae growth to a minimum.*

Once your pond is planted, you'll want to watch for algae buildup, diseases or pests on pond plants, and leaks. If your winters turn cold and the water in your pond freezes, you'll have to make some allowances for tender plants and seasonal chores. If you garden in a warm-winter area, you'll need to control the growth of plants so that they don't overwhelm the water. Here are some season-by-season guidelines for good pond care.

Spring

Add marginal and aquatic plants. Rearrange plantings along the edge of the pool if needed. Clean out collected dead leaves and other debris from the bottom of the pool. Reconnect the submersible pump that was removed for winter storage. Bring aquatics out of winter storage and put them back into the pool. Collect rainwater in a wooden barrel for topping off the pool during the season; rainwater has fewer minerals than tap water, so it's less likely to cause algae growth. If snails begin devouring water-lily leaves, float some pieces of lettuce and skim them off with a net when they are full of snails. Listen for the chorus of courting frogs. Watch for migrating songbirds stopping by.

Summer

Refill the pond as water evaporates. Use collected rainwater, which won't change the chemistry in the pond. Rake or net off excess floating plants as needed to expose the water. Lift and repot any aquatic plants with stunted leaves or plants that produce lots of leaves but few flowers. Watch for green water, caused by excessive algae growth; add oxygenating plants to control. If long strands of algae form a blanket in the pond, rake them out and pile them on the compost heap. Protect fish from herons. Watch for leaks (dropping water level, wet soil) and repair with patches. Look for tadpoles and baby fish.

Fall

Put netting over the pool to block falling leaves. In cold-winter climates, remove the submersible pump. Remove yellowing foliage of water plants before it falls off into the water. Cut back oxygenating plants. Lift pots of tender water lilies and other tender plants before the weather turns cold. Overwinter tender floaters in a saucer of water in bright light, perhaps on a windowsill. For water lilies, slice off all growth to the crown and overwinter them in galvanized tubs in a cool garage. Or store the plants out of water for the winter by wrapping the pots in wet newspaper and storing in plastic bags in a cool but nonfreezing location. An old refrigerator, set to stay at about 35° to 38°F, is perfect.

Winter

Remove netting with fallen leaves. Adjust positions of rocks as needed. Check frequently to be sure water remains unfrozen if you have fish. Don't break the ice by hitting it; the shock waves can harm or kill fish. Install an electric pool heater if needed. Do not feed fish in winter in cold-winter areas; their metabolism slows as the temperature drops.

lettuce, or other aquatics that have achieved noxious weed status. If you're not sure what's welcome and what's not, call your county extension office or the Nature Conservancy.

Adding Fish

Fish in a pond are fun to watch. I prefer minnows and other small, dull-colored species to the bright ornamental goldfish or koi that populate many pools, but that's a matter of personal taste. Some gardeners become avid collectors of koi, which can cost as much as a purebred dog (or a car!). To me, koi look as out of place in a nat-ural garden as a plastic flamingo would look in a meadow. (Of course, if I lived in China, where golden carp do appear in wild waters, or in Florida, where live flamingos stalk the grassy flats, I'd have a different out-look.)

Pond fish are available at the same places where you buy plants and water-garden supplies, or you can buy goldfish at any pet store. They'll grow to amazing pro-portions once they're in a pond. Check a bait shop for live minnows and small fish.

Wait a couple of weeks after you fill your pool be-fore you add fish to allow the plants time to get rooted. Fish may dislodge even established roots as they poke around looking for food. Your mosquito population will nosedive once you have fish; wigglers (mosquito larvae) are a prime fish food. Fish also eat algae, so they'll help keep your water looking clear. And goldfish love to eat duckweed.

Even if you don't introduce them, fish may show up in your pond. I used to puzzle over this mystery—were they falling from the sky?—but then I learned that they come in as eggs on the feet of ducks, herons, and other water-visiting birds.

Great blue herons, merganser ducks, green herons, and other fish-eaters will make short work of your finny friends once they discover your pond. You can prevent predation by stretching netting across the pool or by weaving monofilament fishing line across the water at intervals and among the edging plants. Water plants and rocks will provide some protection for fish, but catching these slippery creatures is a heron's job, and they are masters at waiting for the right moment. If a determined bird finds your pond, only mechanical means can save your finny friends.

If you've stocked your water with dime-store gold-fish that you don't mind losing to birds, think of your water garden as a glorified bird feeder. (It's also a good way to avoid winter guilt when fish are trapped in ice.) It's a treat to watch herons and other birds fish. Great blues often flip their catch into the air, then swallow it head or tail first. Kingfishers take their prize to a nearby tree limb and bash it into submission by slapping it against the branch.

At Hawk Mountain, a Pennsylvania observation point on the migration route of hawks, I once saw an osprey come flapping along, its talons firmly gripping a nice, plump, bright orange and white koi. As the bird flew past the lookout, it delighted us watchers by casually reaching down and tearing off a bit of sushi on the wing.

Bringing Water to Life

A waterfall or stream can add a delightful element to your natural landscape. Water runs downhill, but that doesn't mean you need a steep hillside to create a water-fall or stream in your garden. A stretch of falling water needs only a very slight incline to be successful. Even in my flat midwestern garden, there are several good sites where water would naturally run downhill. If you can't tell the lay of your land by simply looking, lay out a gar-

Flat rocks or logs are just the ticket for basking turtles and fishing herons. Intent on dinner, this green heron waits for finny prey to swim within reach of that stabbing bill, while the cold-blooded turtle catches some warming rays.

den hose, turn on the tap, and watch where the water goes.

A streambed or waterfall can be as long and elaborate or as short and simple as you have room and muscle to build. The basic idea boils down to this: You need an upper pool, or "top pool," where the water originates, and a lower pool, or "bottom pool," which contains the hidden recirculating pump that will return the water to the top pool.

I find that a simple design with a few broad shelves of rock where water can spill over is more restful than a tumbling, complicated streambed, but in this, as in all other garden matters, suit yourself. If you have a slope with a drop of several feet, a series of rock ledges will make a wonderful, natural-looking waterfall.

Both streams and waterfalls are easiest to make by using a flexible PVC or butyl rubber liner. The liner

The look of the fall itself is a vital element of the aesthetics of a waterfall, so take time to get the look you want before you secure rocks in place. It's a lot easier to experiment during building than to try to alter the flow later.

edges are easy to hide, and you can design the twists and turns in any way you like. Preformed sections can also be joined together to make a bed. Alter the angles between them to create meandering curves like those a real stream would carve out.

Because streams are free-form, with bends and variations in width from one pool to another, it's easiest to use separate pieces of liner for each section of stream, overlapping them at the ledges. A single liner is mighty unwieldy when you're working on a stream, but if you prefer to use one piece, round up a couple of patient friends to make the work go more smoothly.

Make your streambed wide—at least 2 feet—so that you can span it with a bridge and plants can spill over the edges without totally obscuring the watercourse. A stream can be much shallower than a pond because it won't be sheltering fish and water plants that need the protection of deep water from winter cold. Six to 12 inches is a decent depth for a stream.

Making a Streambed

Create the illusion of a natural stream by piecing together several preformed ponds or stream sections. Lay out the arrangement of the stream with a pair of garden hoses or with strips of cloth ripped from an old bedsheet. Start with a pool at the highest point. Move the outline around until you have a pleasing course. For a more graceful look, end the stream in a pool that is wider than the top pool.

Plan your stream in sections. When you dig out the streambed, leave a ledge of soil between sections of the stream. That way, the water won't all drain down to the lowest pool when your pump isn't running.

Dig out a narrow trench a few inches from the streambed to carry the hose for the recirculating pump from the lowest pool back to the top pool. Remove any rocks or other sharp objects from the streambed and rake it smooth. Spread a layer of sand ½ inch deep over the bottom, or lay out a polyester padding liner in each section of stream. Lay the first piece of liner in the bottom pool, draping it over the sides and up the ledge to meet the second pool. Repeat as needed, overlapping the next liner on top of the previous one at the ledges between stream sections.

After installing the pump and pipe, Lay stone around the edges of all sections to hold the liner in place and to cover the hose trench. Allow the liner to extend outward beyond the stones. For the most permanent results, set the stones into a mortar of fast-setting concrete, like Quikrete. Build waterfalls at the ledges if desired. (See "Building a Waterfall" on page 129.) Lay the liner in the small top pool. After you've put in the liner, lay stone around the outlet pipe of the recirculating pump, which will spill into the small top pool, to hide the pipe from view.

Scoop the reserved soil onto the exposed edges of the liner, filling in between the rocks at the sides of the stream and burying the bases or the rocks partway so they look well rooted in the ground. Walk on the soil to firm it down. Add plants to the banks of the stream, planting them into the soil beyond the liner. It won't take long before they creep to the water's edge, giving your creation the look of a natural stream. Be sure to set some water plants close to the edge so they can blend with the edging plants.

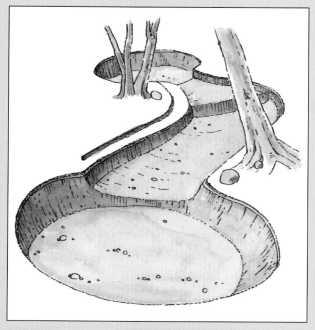

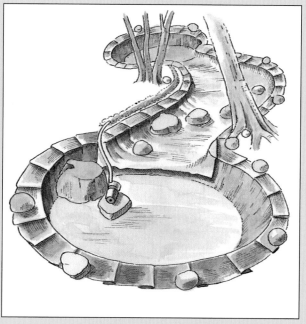

Dig out the stream, leaving a shallow ledge along the sides for anchoring the liner. Reserve the soil to cover the liner edges when your stream is complete.

Set the pump into the bottom pool on a flat stone base about 3 inches high. Site it close to the last ledge so that you don't have to run more pipe than necessary. Run the hose through the trench, along the stream, to the top pool. Fill in the trench with soil.

A leaky stream is aggravating, so check for leaks before you do the final touches. Fill the pools with water, and run the pump for about two hours to check for leaks. If water spills through the rocks and past the liner, mound soil under the liner at that point to raise it higher so that water can't escape.

If you like the look of a flowing stream but don't want to pipe water into your garden, you can mimic a natural watercourse with a bed of stones. Look for a natural depression for your stream of stone. If the area is dry all year, start by laying down a blanket of thick black landscape plastic to block weeds. Then pour sand over the plastic and set in smooth, rounded river stones.

Some gardeners put a dry stream along a swale where water already drains. If the water comes fast and furious, the stones will be dislodged, so it's best to set at least a foundation course into mortar. Landscape the edges of your "stream" with clumps of ornamental grasses that imitate the look of reeds along a natural stream, but don't obscure the water. Keep it visible from a distance.

A dry stream may fool a casual human visitor, but wildlife won't be tricked into thinking it's water. Insects and spiders, however, will love your new landscape feature. Hunting spiders that spring upon their prey, rather than orb weavers, will move into the crevices among the stones.

A rock slab serves as a bridge in this dry streambed, which mimics nature by using gravel in the middle of the course and larger stones at the edges.

A section of stream looks very odd if it ends abruptly. Disguise the terminus of your recycled stream by hiding it with shrubs or by extending the water garden into a bog. You can also stretch a streambed of dry rocks from the end of the water garden.

Falling Water Finesse

Waterfalls have impact no matter what their size. Even the narrowest sliver of water can make a big splash, figuratively speaking.

Remember that all the water channeled into the fall will be pouring over the brink. To make a thin veil of water, you can widen a stream at the point of drop with a shelf of thin rock. If the edge is fairly even, the water will fall in a single sheet of silver. A jagged, irregular front edge of the rock will break the fall into sections. You can also train the water over the face of a boulder for a whole different look.

I've always liked the surprise of delicate ferns peeking out from behind a waterfall. You can allow for a little planting like this by building a pocket of soil into the

(continued on page 131)

For a good look at birds and other wildlife, build your water garden near a room with a view or an outdoor sitting area. Keep a pair of binoculars on a hook near the window so they're in easy reach for close-ups.

Building a Waterfall

A lovely, splashing waterfall can add more to your natural landscape than any other feature. And it's not much harder to build than a water garden. Once you've selected your spot, which should of course slope downhill, dig out a top and bottom pool, as described in the directions for making a streambed on page 126. Line the pool, then take a look at your rock collection to pick out suitable pieces for the waterfall.

Choose a relatively thin, flat rock that spans the stream to serve as the waterfall rock. A piece of slate or shale will work well, but pick one that isn't too flimsy-looking. Fill in around the main rock as described in the step-by-step directions below, then install a submersible pump in the base pool. Place it on a flat rock base about 2 to 4 inches high, close to the waterfall. Lay the outlet pipe into the trench along the pools, so that it exits at the upper pool. Fill in the trench.

Finish the edges of the pools with rock. Fill the pools with water, run the pump, and check for leaks. If you've built carefully, all you should hear is the refreshing gurgle of the water as it spills over your falls.

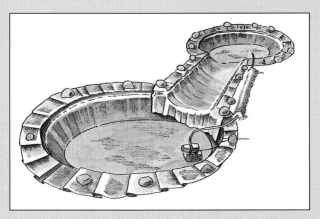

STEP 1: *After you have lined the top and bottom pools, drape another piece of liner over the face and ledge for the waterfall. This will protect the bottom liner from being cut by rocks.*

STEP 2: *Settle the rock into position so that it juts out over the supporting face of the fall and anchor it between large supporting rocks at each side. Work mortar in between the waterfall rock and the liner so that water won't sneak through underneath it.*

STEP 3: *Fill in behind and under the waterfall rock with smaller rocks, to create a seal that directs the water over the falls. Mortar these stones into place to prevent them from being dislodged by the force of the water.*

STEP 4: *Fill in soil around the edges and between the rocks. Add plants. Then pat yourself on the back and bring your friends and family to the garden to see your new waterfall.*

ledge, behind the face of the jutting shelf of rock that creates the fall. You can also fake it by setting a potted fern behind the curtain of water, hiding its container with extra rocks.

You won't have to fake it for long, though. One of the most gratifying things about creating a water garden is seeing how plants find their own niches. Places where you'd never think to plant are apt to be the spots where plants will pop up by themselves, their roots snaking into rock crevices to find the cool, moist soil below.

I love to watch mosses and lichens take hold on rocks by the water. Their textures and colors are beauti-

▲ *A simple wooden bridge makes a beautiful accent in this water garden. You can buy or build one, or even use a few planks to make a crossing. Just be sure they're sturdy enough for safe crossing.*

◄ *A moving stream is the pièce de résistance of a natural garden. Remember to consider the off-season when you plant, and include trees, shrubs, and ornamental grasses for winter interest.*

ful, but in a subtle way that demands a close-up, unhurried look to appreciate the russets and olives, the incredible chartreuse and lime green.

Add a dead branch or log beside your streambed, and you'll be surprised how quickly it becomes softened by mosses. When mosses are silvered with fine spray, I can't resist running my fingers over them—but with only the lightest touch.

Bridging the Water

Bridges are more than a way to cross the water. They're a great place for dreaming and thinking, and they add physical beauty to the natural landscape. They also let you sneak up on things you otherwise couldn't get to, like that frog in the middle of the pond or the fish that hide out in deep water.

Keep your bridge as unobtrusive as you can. If a tree won't cooperate and fall in just the right place, you can use two unfinished wooden planks, at least 2 inches thick, to span the water. If the spread is wide, brace the boards partway across with a support of rocks. You can also build or buy a graceful bow bridge or a simple flat-plank crossing, with or without a rough handrail of saplings.

Stepping stones can also get you out into and across the water. Settle them firmly so that a teetering stone doesn't surprise anyone into an unplanned dip.

The Bog Garden

I've always laughed when reading garden books that explained how to fix the drainage of a soggy spot. Shovel in sand and leaf mold, build raised beds, install drainage tile—why bother? That wet spot is a place to put in treasures that won't grow anywhere else.

My mother taught me how to turn problem sites into gorgeous gardens. When a place at the foot of a hill held water long after the rest of the yard dried out, she didn't frustrate herself by trying to grow bearded irises, dianthus, and daffodils that would have rotted in a single season. Instead, she brought in stately yellow flags (*Iris pseudacorus*) and partnered them with a clump of shorter sky blue irises (*Iris versicolor*) that swiftly grew into a wide-spreading mat. At their feet was a cloud of blue forget-me-nots (*Myosotis sylvestris*). My mother didn't know the lingo for landscaping, but her natural artist's eye told her what looked good together.

It was my mother who taught me to look at natural swampy spots and see what thrived and then to translate the best of those plants into a garden. I loved the wildness of cattails, but she knew they were rampant growers that would quickly swallow the rest of the planting. So she helped me plant their tubered roots in old galvanized buckets, where they'd stay put. Thirty years later, I'm still a cattail lover, but I've learned about other species more in keeping with the scale of my garden: a Japanese species (*Typhus minima*) that grows cute, roundish balls instead of long, thick tails, and a native American species, *T. angustifolia*, which has long, slim cattails and narrow leaves that look as graceful as an ornamental grass.

If you like Japanese irises—those exquisite, veined blooms held wide open like angel wings, in soft purples, blues, and pinks—you'll love the way they flourish and spread in wet soil. They're one of the more expensive perennials, and I never had enough to satisfy me until I planted three of them at the end of our driveway, where water always puddled. I put in a weeping willow at the same time, with thirsty roots that helped soak up a lot of the standing water but left the ground moist. The irises outdid themselves in that problem spot, and for the first time in my garden, they began to multiply at a visible speed, almost as fast as daylilies.

Another plant that will adapt to ordinary soil but which shines in wet soil is the winterberry, or deciduous holly. The berries are fatter, shinier, and more plentiful on my bushes in a boggy spot than they are on the twin plants I placed in the "normal" garden. I planted them among a stand of soft rush (*Juncus effusus*) with deep black-green color that sets off the red berries. When the rush bleaches to tan in winter, it still provides good background texture and color for the dark-stemmed, red-berried holly bushes.

Aim for diversity when you plant your moist garden. A variety of colors and textures make a garden lively and interesting. Notice how the astilbes and other flowering plants in this garden provide a splash of color along the still surface of the water and the quiet green of the wooded background.

Leave it to the British to take to heart the plants that we malign at home. Across the Atlantic, the lowly skunk cabbage is planted along water and in bog gardens, where it's valued for its unusual blooms and emphatic leaves. Skunk cabbage is a beauty, but it also has a distinctive aroma. I like musky smells, so I don't find it offensive. Besides, I think the beauty of the plant far outweighs any nasal twinges.

Most nature-lovers are familiar with eastern skunk cabbage (*Symplocarpus foetidus*), which thrusts its mottled, maroon-splotched, hooded flowers up through the soil in late winter, long before the leaves appear. The emerging buds produce so much heat that they literally melt the snow around them. This is an attractive plant for a wild bog garden, but keep in mind that it spreads enthusiastically.

I prefer western skunk cabbage (*Lysichiton americanum*) for gardens. Its flowers are shining golden yellow and look more like a calla lily than like eastern skunk cabbage. They bloom with the emergence of their spring leaves, in March or April. When I discovered this plant in Oregon, I was so enamored of the flowers that I sent a few to friends back East. I thought they smelled sweet, but evidently my nose isn't calibrated like other people's. Or maybe it's just that I've grown to like the smell of skunk.

Western skunk cabbage has waxy yellow hoods and spikes of tiny flowers pollinated by flies. The fleshy underground stems were once baked and eaten by Native Americans.

Making a Bog

Ponds and streams in nature have wet, boggy edges, where water-loving plants thrive. Gardener-built water features, however, are a different story. If you use a liner or a preformed pool, the water is kept inside so that it doesn't seep out into the surrounding soil (unless you intentionally install it that way). The plants outside the pool itself will have their roots in normal, dry soil.

Many bog plants are adaptable and will flourish even without constant moisture. You can create the effect of a bog garden beside a pool by using plants such as Japanese irises, which grow well in average soil as well as in true bogs, or by using plants with lush foliage.

But if you want a real bog, you can have a great deal of fun playing in the muck. If you're also installing a lined pool, you can make room for bog plants by leaving a stepped ledge along the top of the pool, anchoring the liner on the ledge with rocks. Then extend the liner from the ledge, allowing for a pocket of soil before slop-

Thick stands of yellow flag are favored by ducks, which take advantage of the shelter of the stems as they nibble duckweed and other water edibles. Look for ducklings hiding in the thicket of foliage in springtime.

Cross-Section of a Lined Pool

In nature, the plants you'll find at the edge of the water are bog plants that thrive in the wet or very moist soil naturally found there. But in a garden pond, the soil at water's edge is usually ordinary garden soil of average moisture, because the water is held strictly in place by the pond liner. To make bog plants happy there, you'll have to fool them by creating a mini-bog with an earthen dike and the pond liner.

Mound the soil at the edge of your pond as shown here to create a catch basin of sorts where bog plants will get the moisture they need. Rocks on the ridge help keep the liner in place.

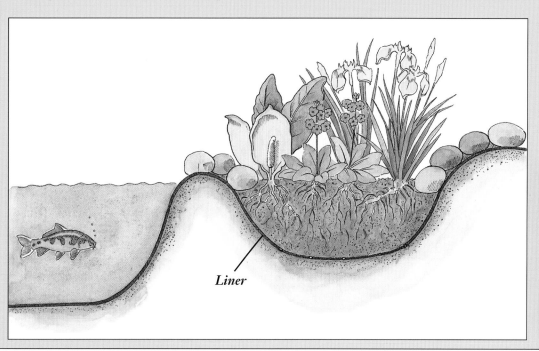

Liner

Ostrich ferns add stature as well as beauty to the bog garden or waterside planting. In England, they're known as "shuttlecock ferns," because when the fronds first emerge in spring they look just like a badminton birdie.

ing it upward above the water level. Bog plants will flourish in the saturated soil in the lined pocket.

You can create a bog garden without a pond by installing a liner at a depth of about a foot. Punch holes into the liner every 3 feet or so to provide slow drainage. A child's rigid swimming pool makes a good underpinning for a small bog garden. As with the liner, open some holes in the bottom so that you don't end up with a mud puddle. I've always loved royal ferns, but my site wasn't right for these native American bog plants. Until, that is, I dug a hole and "planted" a $10 kid's plastic swimming pool. Then I filled it with leaf mold, sand, and compost, soaked it until it was as sopping as a wet sponge, and grew fantastic ferns.

Whether it's a ferny bog garden, a stream and waterfall, a lush pond, or a simple container water garden, nothing lights up a natural landscape like water. Try it and see. And water gardening is addictive—you may not be able to stop with just one garden. That's because water—and water plants—are so delightful. Your local birds, butterflies, and other wildlife will agree.

WATER GARDEN DESIGN

A natural pond, like almost every planting in nature, is incredibly diverse. Once you start to count the types of plants that grow in, on, and around the water, you'll find you get into double digits fast. While there's something to be said for the serenity of a water garden that holds just a few kinds of plants, I like to mimic nature with a grand jumble.

Shrubs and trees anchor this four-season planting. Rushes and irises add vertical exclamation points that play against the horizontal water. Of course the garden is filled with flowers, too, from the earliest pussywillows to the glorious lotuses of high summer and the unusually shaped turtlehead that closes out the season. In fall, baldcypress adds soft russet color, and grasses hold the spotlight into winter.

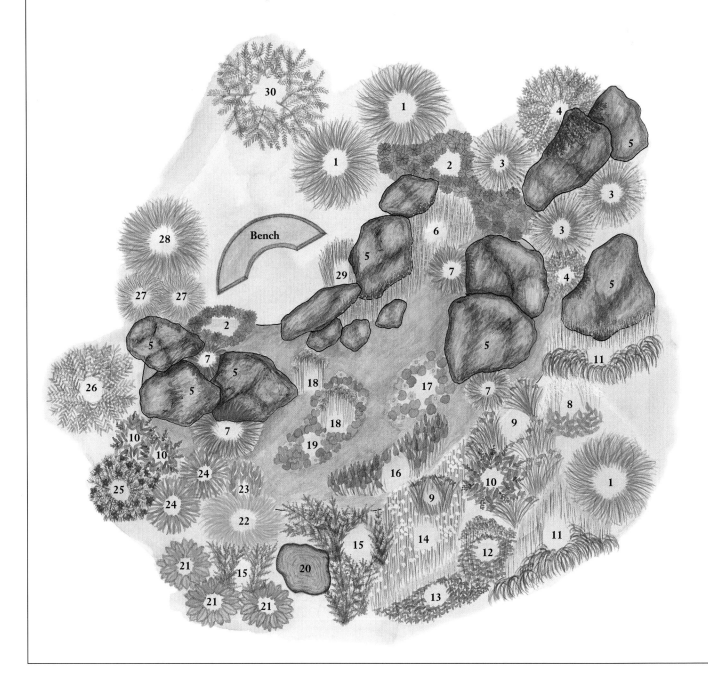

Fill in nooks and crannies between perimeter stones around a liner pond and between larger plants with spreading or creeping plants that appreciate moisture such as:

Marsh marigolds (white and yellow) (*Caltha palustris*)

Primroses (*Primula* spp.)

Forget-me-nots (*Myosotis* spp.)

Moneyworts (*Lysimachia nummularia*)

Manna grass (*Glyceria maxima*)

Horsetails (*Equisetum* spp.), including contorted horsetails (*E. scorpioides* var. *contorta*)

Youth-and-old-age (*Tolmeia menziesii*)

Sweet white violets (*Viola blanda*)

Monkey flowers (*Mimulus lutea* and other spp.)

Dwarf sedges (*Carex* spp.)

Buttercups (*Ranunculus acris, R. repens*, and other spp.)

Iris pallida and other small irises

Use small water plants to add textural contrast on water surface:

Water lettuce (*Pistia stratiotes*)

Water clovers (*Marsilea quadrifolia*)

Parrot feather (*Myriophyllum aquaticum*)

Water buttercups (*Ranunculus flabellaris*)

'Pygmaea Alba' dwarf water lilies (*Nymphaea* 'Pygmaea Alba')

Fairy moss (*Azolla caroliniana*)

Note: Integrate the pond/bog garden with other plantings; don't isolate it in the middle of a lawn. Plant outward from at least one side of the bog garden, using other plants as the soil becomes less moist.

Water and Bog Garden

1. 'Flamingo' Japanese silver grass (*Miscanthus sinensis* 'Flamingo')
2. Umbrella plant (*Peltiphyllum peltatum*)
3. Tall moor grass (*Molinia caerulea* ssp. *arundinacea*)
4. 'Flame' red willow (*Salix alba* 'Flame')
5. Rocks
6. 'Zebrinus' banded bulrush (*Schoenplectus tabernaemontana* 'Zebrinus')
7. Sweet flag (*Acorus calamus*)
8. Goatsbeard (*Aruncus dioicus*)
9. Japanese irises (*Iris ensata*)
10. Cardinal flowers (*Lobelia cardinalis*)
11. Feather reed grass (*Calamagrostis acutiflora*)
12. Joe-Pye weed (*Eupatorium fistulosum*)
13. Pink turtlehead (*Chelone lyonii*)
14. Cotton grass (*Eriophorum latifolium*)
15. Royal ferns (*Osmunda regalis*)
16. Blue pickerel weed (*Pontederia cordata*)
17. American lotus (*Nelumbo lutea*)
18. Papyrus (*Cyperus papyrus*)
19. Water lilies (*Nymphaea* spp.)
20. Large decaying stump
21. Yellow skunk cabbages (*Lysichiton americanum*)
22. 'Bowles Golden' sedge (*Carex elata* 'Bowles Golden')
23. Golden club (*Orontium aquaticum*)
24. Yellow flag (*Iris pseudacorus*)
25. Scarlet rose mallow (*Hibiscus coccineus*)
26. Hooker's pussywillow (*Salix hookeriana*)
27. New Zealand hair sedge (*Carex comans*)
28. 'Kleine Fontains' Japanese silver grass (*Miscanthus sinensis* 'Kleine Fontains')
29. Soft rush (*Juncus effusus*)
30. Baldcypress (*Taxodium distichum*)

BEST FLOWERS FOR BOG GARDENS

Flowers	Description	Conditions	Comments
Cardinal flower (*Lobelia cardinalis*)	Stunning spikes of vivid red flowers rise to 4' above a basal clump of foliage. Blooms in summer.	Sun to partial or light shade. Wet soil, but also grows well in average garden soil. Zones 2 to 9.	A hummingbird magnet. May self-sow with restraint, but more plants are always welcome.
Great blue lobelia (*Lobelia siphilitica*)	Bushy clumps of foliage topped by branching spikes of blue to blue-purple tubular flowers in summer. Reaches 2–3'.	Sun to partial shade. Wet soil or average garden conditions. Grows well in heavy clay. Zones 4 to 9.	Beautiful blue color and a long period of bloom. Cut back spent flower spikes to promote branching and rebloom until frost.
Japanese iris (*Iris ensata*, Higo strain)	The royalty of the iris clan, with 2–4' tall plants and stalks of two to four glorious, flat flowers in summer. Blue, purple, white, or reddish violet.	Sun to partial shade. Wet, rich soil. Also grows well in shallow water or in moist garden soil. Zones 5 to 9.	For best effect, plant several of a single cultivar instead of a hodge-podge. Magnificent flowers.
Marsh marigold (*Caltha palustris*)	Low-growing, mat-forming plants with glossy, round leaves and gleaming, butter yellow flowers.	Partial sun to full shade. Wet or boggy soil. Also does well in moist garden soil. Zones 3 to 10.	Fast spreading, good for disguising the edges of artificial ponds. 'Alba' has white flowers.
Western skunk cabbage (*Lysichiton americanum*)	An arum with clumps of huge oval, pointed leaves and unusual callalike waxen yellow flowers with heavy, sweet-musky scent. Blooms in spring and summer. Reaches 1-2'.	Sun to shade. Wet soil. Zones 3 to 9.	Another native beauty saddled with an unfortunate name. Treasured in British gardens. Naturalizes well.
Yellow flag (*Iris pseudacorus*)	Statuesque 5' clumps of strappy irislike foliage with fleur-de-lis-shaped yellow flowers in summer.	Sun to light shade. Moist soil to shallow water. Zones 5 to 9.	A beautiful plant for poolside. Spreads into a significant clump and may self-sow.

Marsh marigold (*Caltha palustris*)

Western skunk cabbage (*Lysichiton americanum*)

BEST FERNS FOR BOG GARDENS

Ferns	Description	Conditions	Comments
Cinnamon fern (*Osmunda cinnamomea*)	Robust clumps of erect fronds reach as tall as 5′, and sprout clusters of cinnamon-color fertile fronds in the center of the clump.	Partial sun to shade. Widely adaptable. Thrives in wet, lime-free soil but also grows well in average, humusy soil. Zones 2 to 10.	Easy to grow and statuesque. Beautiful golden color in fall.
Maidenhair ferns (*Adiantum* spp.)	Many species of delicate-looking ferns with lacy texture, from 8–30″ tall depending on species.	Partial sun to full shade. Very adaptable. Need moisture but also do best with good drainage; give them a spot on the rocks in a bog garden or create a pocket of soil among the poolside rocks. Hardy to Zones 2 to 8, depending on species.	Maidenhair ferns look beautiful near water and are worth the bit of extra trouble it takes to elevate their roots out of the wet soil. They naturally grow in woods, ravines, on waterfalls and cliffs, and at streamsides. Most have creeping roots that expand to form colonies. Although maidenhair ferns look incredibly delicate, they are tough and adaptable.
Royal fern (*Osmunda regalis*)	Airy but good-sized, forming clumps as tall as 10′.	Partial sun to light shade. Wet soil. Zones 2 to 10.	Easy to grow in the right place, and a beauty. Stays in a compact clump.
Silvery glade fern (*Athyrium thelypteroides*)	Creeping fern with erect, arching fronds to 4′ tall. Silvery undersides.	Partial sun to shade. Damp, rich soil. Zones 4 to 9.	Easy to grow. The silvery color of the frond's undersides comes from the whitish immature spore-bearing sori, which are attached in rows beneath each leaf.

Cinnamon fern (*Osmunda cinnamomea*)

Maidenhair fern (*Adiantum pedatum*)

BEST PLANTS FOR WATER GARDENS

AQUATIC PLANTS
These aquatic plants are for the deep-water part of your pond.

Plants	Description
Golden club (*Orontium aquaticum*)	Broad, strappy, velvety leaves with a showy stalk of golden flowers, 3–5′ tall. Can also be grown as a marginal plant. Zones 6 to 11.
Lotus (*Nelumbo* spp.)	Many cultivars and species with wide, round leaves held above the water's surface. Showy, water-lilylike flowers, often fragrant. Tropical species survive only in mild-winter areas. Cold-hardy species including the American lotus (*Nelumbo lutea*) grow as far north as Zone 2 or 3. Most species are hardy in Zones 4 to 11.
Water buttercup (*Ranunculus aquatilis*)	Forms large spreading mats of small, three-lobed, floating leaves (and ferny submerged leaves) dotted with small, white, yellow-centered flowers that look like buttercups. *R. flavatilis* is similar, with yellow flowers. Zone 6.
Water lilies (*Nymphaea* spp.)	Many cultivars and species with wide, flat leaves that float on the water's surface. Beautiful flowers, usually fragrant. Some night-blooming. Most are tropical species that must be taken inside in cold-winter areas. Hardy types vary in their tolerance for cold; refer to nursery catalogs to find out which will grow in your zone. Zones 3 to 11, depending on species and cultivar.

OXYGENATOR PLANTS
These plants float or grow in the water. All spread rapidly and may need occasional thinning. A rake does the trick.

Plants	Description
Hair grass (*Eleocharis acicularis*)	Very skinny leaves like fine blades of wiry grass. Actually a water rush in the Cypress family. Grows in small tufts. Zone 4.
Milfoils (*Myriophyllum* spp.) including parrot feather (*M. aquaticum*)	Several species of beautiful feathery-foliaged plants that add soft, lush texture. Hardiness varies with species; beautiful light green parrot feather, to Zone 7; others grow in Zones 3 to 11, depending on the species.
Pondweeds (*Elodea* spp.)	Familiar aquarium plant with curled whorls of small, narrow-pointed leaves. Hardiness depends on species; common *E. canadensis* and *E. nuttallii* hardy to at least Zones 5 to 11, depending on the species.
Starworts (*Callitriche* spp.)	A dense mass of small plants with fine, whorled leaves and clusters of tiny, white, star flowers. Sometimes called water chickweed, which it resembles. Several similar species. Hardiness depends on species; generally, to Zone 5.

FLOATER PLANTS

These plants aren't rooted in the ground. They float in the water, usually forming mats.

Plants	Description
Frogbit (*Hydrocharis morsus-ranae*)	Looks like small white water lilies, with leaves only one inch across. Many similar species, generally hardy to Zones 5 to 9.
Water chestnut (*Trapa natans*)	Interesting rosettes of diamond-shaped leaves with serrated edges on reddish stalks. White flowers followed by 1–1½″ hard, black fruits that can be eaten. Naturalized in America as far north as New York. Zone 5.
Water hyacinth (*Eichhornia crassipes*)	An unwelcome pest in warm areas, where you should avoid planting it. In cold-winter areas, makes an attractive accent with bulbous-stemmed glossy leaves and pretty clusters of lavender flowers. Fish appreciate the cover formed by the abundant roots and runners. Only for cold-winter areas, where it will die after frost. Zones 8 to 11.
Water lettuce (*Pistia stratiotes*)	Another nuisance plant in warm areas, this pretty floater produces rosettes of pale green, wedge-shaped leaves like a tight-packed crop of garden lettuces. Do not plant in mild climates; in cold-winter areas, it will die with hard frost. Zones 8 to 11.

Water lettuce (*Pistia stratiotes*)

BEST MARGINAL PLANTS FOR WATER GARDENS

These plants are called "marginal" because you grow them in wet soil at the water's edge or in shallow water.

Marginal Plants	Description	Conditions	Comments
Arrowheads (*Sagittaria* spp.)	Glossy, arrow-shaped leaves in dense stands with spikes of white flowers accented with a purple blotch.	Sun to light shade. Zones 4 to 11, depending on the species.	Tubers of *S. latifolia* were once used as food by Native Americans.
Banded bulrush (*Schoenplectus tabernae-montana* 'Zebrinus')	Upright, cylindrical green stems striped with horizontal yellow bands.	Sun to partial light shade. Zone 7.	This spreading rush makes striking colonies at a pond's edge and in shallow water.
Cattails (*Typha* spp.)	Strappy, erect leaves with stiff pokers of packed brown flowers, like cigars atop bare stems.	Sun. Wet soil and shallow water. Zones 2 to 11, depending on species.	Cattails are a fast-growing plant for the waterside, but they can take over small spaces in a hurry. Dwarf *T. minima*, a Japanese species hardy to Zone 4, has short, fat, brown spikes instead of long "tails," and is much less invasive.
Papyruses (*Cyperus* spp.)	Umbrellas or pompons of leafy green atop tall stems.	Sun to partial shade. Wet soil or shallow water. Zones 9 to 11.	Grow as pot plant and bring indoors for winter in cold climates.
Soft rush (*Juncus effusus*) and other rushes (*Juncus* spp.)	Upright or arching, grasslike clumps with tufts of soft brown flowers.	Wet soil or shallow water. Zones 4 to 9, depending on species.	Soft rush is a widely adaptable beauty with dark green foliage and showy flowers. Hardy to Zone 4, it turns brown in cold weather.
Sweet flags (*Acorus gramineus*)	Fans of irislike leaves that rarely bloom.	Sun to light shade. Moist soil or shallow water. Zones 4 to 11, depending on the species.	Foliage has a lovely, sweet fragrance when bruised. Once used medicinally.

★ For more marginal plants, see Best Flowers for Bog Gardens on page 138.

BEST POOLSIDE PLANTS FOR WATER GARDENS

These plants are appealing near water. They thrive in moist to wet soil.

Poolside Plants	Description	Conditions	Comments
Astilbes (*Astilbe* spp.)	Easy to grow perennial with feathery plumes, either upright or arching, in shades of pink, red, or white above ferny clumps of divided leaves.	Sun to shade. Moist soil. Zones 3 to 8, depending on species.	Most astilbes are hybrids (*A.* × *arendsii*); the cultivar selection is enormous, from diminutive 1'-tall 'Glow' to 'Purple Blaze', which can reach almost 5'.
Feather reed grass (*Calamagrostis acutiflora*)	Upright, 2–3' tall arching grass with showy panicles of flowers held well above the foliage.	Sun. Moist soil. Zones 5 to 9.	The cultivar 'Stricta' is deservedly popular.
Forget-me-nots (*Myosotis* spp.)	Annual and short-lived perennial species of low-growing, mounding habit with myriads of delicate sky blue or true blue tiny flowers.	Sun to moderate shade. *M. scorpioides* and *M. sylvatica*, two of the best, are hardy to Zones 3 to 8, depending on the species.	Longest-lived in cooler climates, but self-sow abundantly to renew and expand the planting.
Horsetails (*Equisetum* spp.)	Cylindrical, jointed, leafless stems grow in spreading colonies.	Sun to light shade. Moist to wet soil. Will also grow in average garden soil. Zones 3 to 11, depending on species.	Scouring rush (*E. hyemale*) is a common, widely adaptable species. The stems are banded with ash-color stripes.
Monkeyflowers (*Mimulus* spp.)	Several species of perennials with tubular flowers in various colors, including clear red, yellow, and blue.	Sun to part shade. Moist soil. Hardiness depends on species. Blue-lavender *M. ringens*, to Zone 3; red *M. cardinalis*, to Zone 7; yellow, often red-speckled *M. guttatus*, Zone 6.	An underused perennial with pretty and abundant bloom that lasts for a long time. Many self-sow, but never to the point of pestiness.

Common scouring rush (*Equisetum hyemale*)

Forget-me-nots (*Myosotis sylvatica*)

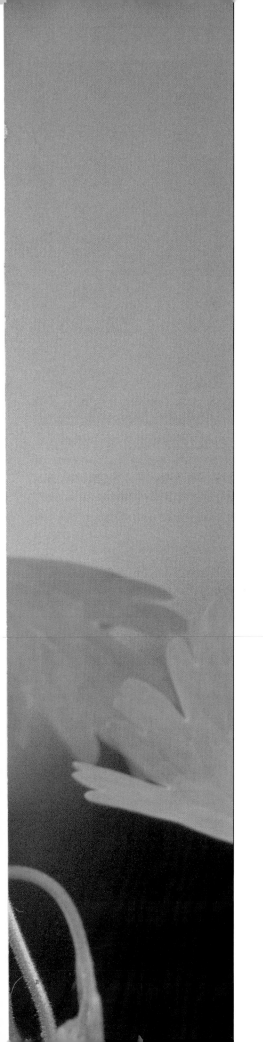

Chapter 5

BIRDSONG IN THE GARDEN
Attracting Songbirds and Hummingbirds

When you see the first red flowers bloom in your garden, hummingbirds won't be far behind. Watch for them at such early bloomers as wild columbine (shown here), flowering quince, and red flowering currant.

KNOW WHERE TO LOOK FOR BIRDS

With more than 700 species of birds visiting the United States, sorting out who's who can be frustrating at first. Narrowing down the possibilities is a big help to a novice birder. Here are the most common birds you can expect to see in various habitats.

LOCATION	BIRDS
In and around buildings and farms	Swallows, swifts, purple martin, wrens, phoebes, starling, house sparrow, robin, magpies, blackbirds, cowbird, house finch, western kingbird, rock dove
In brush or hedgerows	Cardinal, catbird, thrashers, towhees, kingbirds, Bewick's wren, scrub jay, Carolina wren, towhees, yellow-breasted chat, common yellowthroat, juncos, song sparrow, field sparrow, golden-crowned sparrow (on winter range), tree sparrow, white-throated sparrow, white-crowned sparrow, fox sparrow, indigo bunting, lazuli bunting, painted bunting, bushtit, verdin, some warblers, vireos, blue grosbeak, waxwings
On the lawn	Robin, starling, mourning dove, grackles, orioles in trees, flickers in fall or spring
In a marshy area or marginal planting along the water's edge	Red-winged blackbird, Brewer's blackbird, yellow-headed blackbird, grackles, swamp sparrow, marsh wren, prothonotary warbler, yellow warbler, cedar waxwing
In a grassy field	Field sparrow and other native sparrows, red-winged blackbird, meadowlarks, quail, swallows, swifts, horned lark, bluebirds, goldfinch, bobolink, redpoll, dicksissel
In a woodland	Wood warblers, nuthatches, chickadees, brown creeper, tanagers, woodpeckers, titmice, grosbeaks, blue jay, gray-breasted jay, great-crested flycatcher, pewees, thrushes, veery, gnatcatchers, warblers, vireos, tanagers, grosbeaks, purple finch, band-tailed pigeon, ruby-throated hummingbird
In conifers	Red-breasted nuthatches, crossbills, chickadees, western grosbeak, varied thrush, Steller's jay, gray jay, band-tailed pigeon, kinglets, red-faced warbler, Townsend's warbler, western tanager, Cassin's finch, pine grosbeak, pine siskin, crossbills, juncos, fox sparrow, nesting house finches

shrubs that let birds move safely to berry bushes or to the water garden.

Often in winter, our feeder becomes a regular stopping point for a Cooper's hawk, a slim, steel-gray songbird-eater that used to go by the old nickname "blue death." Evidently, these predators, which usually keep to the forests, have learned about the easy pickings a feeder attracts. I see them even in cities, patrolling neighborhoods for a likely feeder.

Without cover, songbirds at a feeder are sitting ducks. Cooper's hawks are swift and agile, and a chickadee is no match for them. To even the game, I always park our discarded Christmas tree on its side next to the feeders for the duration of the winter. It may not be pretty, but to the birds, it makes the difference between life and death.

More than once, I've watched the hawk perch on the Christmas tree and carefully extend a claw down into the branches to try to nab its prey. If the birds sat tight, they were safe. But sometimes a sparrow or junco became unnerved and fled in terror, becoming an instant dinner for Mr. Hawk.

Watch a flock of native sparrows or wood warblers fly across open ground, and you'll see that they don't fly in a straight line. The birds fly as fast as they can, twisting and dodging in flight. It's as difficult to follow a single bird with your eyes as it is a snowflake in a blizzard. That indirect flight is for a good reason: It's just as hard for a hawk to pick out or pick off a single individual as it is for your eyes to follow them.

The best way to provide cover for birds is to provide connected plantings so birds never need to come out in the open. Plan your garden as a series of linked sites, joined together by protective grassy or weedy patches or by brush or evergreens. Think of the corridors of plants in your garden as bird paths. They're essential to making feathered visitors feel at home.

Zigzag rail fences are a work of art, but surprisingly unobtrusive in a natural garden. You can see miles of these carefully stacked fences, some more than a hundred years old, along the Blue Ridge Parkway in the East.

Food for All Seasons

Since food is the primary attraction, the first thing you'll want to do is provide an assortment. Like us, different birds prefer different types of food. I keep my feeders well stocked year-round, but I also fill my garden with live, growing bird treats.

I grow lots of berried shrubs, but I also plant a lot of grasses and flowers for the birds. Grains and sunflowers are staples in the bird garden, just as at the feeder. In spring, I scratch up sunny ground and scatter white millet, straight from the birdseed sack. I plant extra-thick, so the millet looks like a lush bed of green grass. By midsummer, the seedheads are showing. Goldfinches and others begin nibbling long before they turn golden. Foxtail grasses, wild oats, and other natives sprinkle the garden and fill in the gaps between shrub plantings. They do double duty—no, triple duty—by supplying cover and nesting material as well as food.

(continued on page 152)

WHAT'S ON THE MENU?

I keep the menu simple at my bird feeding station: Sunflower seeds, white millet, and suet are the staples. Sunflower seeds will appeal to most of the customers, and millet will bring in the smaller seed-eaters who can't crack the big sunflower seeds. The suet takes care of woodpeckers and others that prefer soft food.

I also keep tube feeders filled with niger, the tiny black seed that used to be called thistle, but which is actually *Guitzotia abyssinica*, a sunflower relative with small yellow flowers. For high nutrition and high fat, I serve peanut butter straight from the jar, smeared on the roofs of the feeders. (Contrary to popular belief, there's no danger of suffocation from birds eating straight peanut butter, according to ornithologists at Cornell University.)

Like any good restaurateur, I offer frequent specials at the bird café. Sometimes hulled sunflower chips are on the menu. Occasionally there's expensive canary seed, a real treat for finches, or a handout of peanuts, walnuts, or pecans picked up along the road here where the trees grow wild. In winter, when the cardinal customers swell from the 10 regulars to a horde of 70 or more, I start hauling in hundred-pound sacks of cracked corn. Starlings love it, too, but it's cheap enough to share.

An Oasis of Wilderness
Dot Wiltraut
Whitehall, Pennsylvania

Like many nature lovers, Dot Wiltraut learned a love of the natural world from her parents. "I was lucky to have parents who felt that the outdoors was their life," she says.

"I remember my father taking me to watch chimney swifts flying down a chimney in the evening. And my mother threw out bread for the birds," she recalls. "I don't think they even sold birdseed back in the Great Depression."

Dot's garden in eastern Pennsylvania has undergone a transformation since she started it 47 years ago. In the beginning, her yard was mostly sunny, and she grew a lot of roses and tended more formal perennial gardens. "But I loved wildflowers," she says, "and I saw a lot disappearing from wild places. So I decided to turn half of my yard over to wildflowers."

Over the years, the young trees she planted grew tall, creating a shady woodland that's perfect for her trilliums, hepatica, and other spring wildflowers. "Violets are my favorites," Dot says. "I have yellow, pure white, white with purple...in spring, the whole yard is loaded with violets."

As her small town of Fullerton got swallowed up in the development of Whitehall Township, Dot's garden of wildflowers and trees became a haven for birds. "We're surrounded by homes now," she says, "but when people come into the backyard, they feel like they're in a wilderness."

Although she has planted some food plants for the birds, such as American cranberry bush with its bounty of red fruit, and bee balm, the nectar-rich hummingbird favorite, the abundant vegetation of Dot's garden is a big attractant all by itself. Trees and shrubs, no matter what kind, are a living smorgasbord of insects, and birds are drawn to a thickly planted garden as if to a blinking neon "Diner" sign. Dot has spotted more than 125 species of birds in or flying over her yard. A Philadelphia vireo, a northern waterthrush, and a yellow-breasted flycatcher are among her rarest sightings, and once a whippoorwill landed. "I heard him calling," she remembers, "and looked all around the yard until I found him. He puttered across the garden, paused to eat, and then kept on going."

Many birds visit her multitude of feeders year-round, feasting on black oil sunflower seed, millet, cracked corn, and suet. When a tree died, her naturalist son Rick bored holes in it, and she filled them with lard. All this bounty guarantees a yard that's full of life. Along with the finches, jays, cardinals, nuthatches, and other birds come a slew of four-footed visitors: squirrels, chipmunks, skunks, possums, groundhogs, raccoons, and flying squirrels. Screech owls and great-horned owls regularly patrol the garden, and red-tailed hawks and Cooper's hawks visit in winter. Once a rare, long-eared owl stopped by. Dot has a nature journal to keep track of the happenings in her garden.

In spring, Dot's garden is filled with migrants stopping over to rest and refuel. Many are insect eaters, and they find plenty of food in the trees and shrubs. The tiny wood warblers are among her favorites. She's seen 23 different species of warblers, including the elusive caerulean warbler, swarming through the greenery in her yard in search of insects.

Common redpolls, which breed on the tundra, are anything but common in Eastern backyards. Well-stocked feeders bring the birds to Dot's garden.

Dot added two ponds for her wild guests and intends to put in another one this year. The water has brought her some incredible visitors. "I looked out my window one morning and couldn't believe it—there was a beautiful scarlet tanager right in the waterfall. I tell people he stopped off at our roadside rest," she laughs.

Another day, she felt a tug at her hair as she worked in the garden, and when she reached up, a chickadee flew away. "Soon he was back," she says, "pulling more of my hair out!" She looked for the nest, but without success. Maybe she'll be luckier next season, since the chickadees remain in her yard all year. Robins, cardinals, house finches, and other birds also nest in the garden.

Besides enjoying her own garden, Dot volunteers her time for the Whitehall Beautification and Garden Club, and she has planted a wildflower garden at a nearby highway interchange. She spreads the word about gardening for wildlife throughout her community with slide shows and lectures, and she still finds time to write poetry.

By enjoying the outdoor world, Dot has passed on her love of nature to her five children and eleven grandchildren. "I get calls from the kids every day," she says. "Cindy will call and say, 'There's a bluebird in my yard!' Or Doug will call and tell me, 'Mom, look out the window at the sunset!' " Berry-picking in summer is a favorite family tradition, and the extended family often goes camping together in local state parks, as well as all around the country. Dot won't hear of an RV since, as she says, "That's not camping!"

But it's at home that Dot feels she has her own private refuge. "My garden is a place of complete serenity," she says. "I don't feel a need to go anywhere else. I have everything I need right here. Toward dusk, I just like to sit on the bench and drink it all in."

Dot uses groundcovers like the umbrella-like mayapples shown here beneath paper birches to give her garden a woodsy feel. Once this shady retreat was a typical suburban tract lot.

Birds can hardly wait until sunflower seeds mature—they begin pulling out the tasty morsels one by one as soon as the first outside row of seeds ripens.

Wild oats (__Chasmanthium latifolia__) grow into a lush, grassy clump of foliage, topped with flat seedheads that dangle in the breeze on delicate wiry stems. This perennial grass grows well in sun or shade.

Sunflowers are another item that's perennially on the garden menu. When I moved to the Midwest, I discovered dozens of perennial species of sunflowers, native prairie flowers that are equally at home in a naturalistic garden. Most perennial sunflowers are spreaders, but that's okay with me—and with the birds. The tasty seeds of Maximilian sunflower, sawtooth sunflower, and others attract birds well into late fall.

I tried to plan for all-year good taste when I selected berry bushes for my garden. Some fruit ripens in late summer, just in time to catch the eye of refueling migrants. Other berries are at their peak in fall, and some are ignored by birds until winter hunger drives them to search out the last fruits left on the trees and bushes.

GOLDEN BOUNTY

The best sunflower I've ever found for birds is the tickseed sunflower (*Bidens aristosa*). Despite its name, it isn't an annoyance to socks or dogs because the seeds lack the stick-tight prongs of other members of the genus.

This is an annual plant native to eastern North America, and it's a beauty. It grows into a 4-foot-tall plant, branched and bushy, with ferny leaves that look a little too much like marijuana. (Just ignore your neighbors' funny looks.) It blooms late, about August, and cloaks itself in hundreds of small golden daisies. The flowers have a delicate look and texture, more like cosmos than traditional sunflowers. They smell sweet and attract even more butterflies than butterfly bush.

But it's the abundant seeds that are the real payoff. From September through spring, my stand of tickseeds attracts sparrows, juncos, titmice, chickadees, goldfinches, and other small birds. The birds hang on the seedheads like parrots or scratch the ground beneath for dropped crumbs. The plants seed themselves with abandon, but I don't mind. Unwanted seedlings are easy to pull out or smother with mulch.

Plant tickseed sunflower where it can sow itself freely for a bounty of golden bloom, or grow it in a big pot with morning glories or cypress vine.

SONGBIRDS IN YOUR GARDEN

I didn't realize how different birdlife can be until I moved from the East to the Pacific Northwest and set up my first bird feeder. There was nary a blue jay in sight, though the elegant midnight-blue Steller's jay was a fine substitute. Cardinals, which I'd taken for granted, never managed to cross the Rockies. But I did host varied thrushes, like robins but dressed in gorgeous golden orange and blue, and a throng of ruddy brown western fox sparrows. It was an education.

The songbirds you find in your garden will depend on where you live, what kind of habitat you provide, and what kind of habitat is nearby. Here are some of the birds that may turn up in your garden.

EAST

Northern bobwhite
Mourning dove
Golden-shafted flicker
Red-bellied
  woodpecker
Downy woodpecker
Hairy woodpecker
Eastern phoebe
Blue jay
Black-capped chickadee
Tufted titmouse
White-breasted
  nuthatch
House wren
Mockingbird
Gray catbird
Brown thrasher
Robin
Veery
Eastern bluebird
Blue-gray gnatcatcher
Wood thrush
Hermit thrush
Cedar waxwing

White-eyed vireo
Red-eyed vireo
Warbling vireo
Yellow warbler
Yellow-rumped warbler
Black-throated green
  warbler
Ovenbird
Common yellowthroat
Kentucky warbler
Eastern meadowlark
Red-winged blackbird
Common grackle
Brown-headed cowbird
Baltimore oriole
Scarlet tanager
Cardinal
Rose-breasted grosbeak
Indigo bunting
House finch
Goldfinch
Rufous-sided towhee
Chipping sparrow
Field sparrow
Swamp sparrow
Song sparrow

In winter:

Red-breasted nuthatch
Brown creeper
Golden-crowned kinglet
Ruby-crowned kinglet
Purple finch
Dark-eyed junco, slate-
  colored race
White-throated sparrow
White-crowned sparrow
Tree sparrow
Fox sparrow
Evening grosbeak
Purple finch
Pine siskin

SOUTH

Northern bobwhite
Mourning dove
Golden-shafted flicker
Red-bellied woodpecker
Downy woodpecker
Hairy woodpecker
Eastern phoebe

Blue jay
Carolina chickadee
Tufted titmouse
White-breasted
  nuthatch
Brown-headed
  nuthatch
House wren
Winter wren
Carolina wren
Mockingbird
Gray catbird
Brown thrasher
Robin
Eastern bluebird
Wood thrush
Hermit thrush
Blue-gray gnatcatcher
Cedar waxwing
White-eyed vireo
Red-eyed vireo
Northern parula
  warbler
Yellow warbler
Yellow-rumped warbler
Pine warbler

Hermit thrush

Purple finch

Common yellowthroat
Kentucky warbler
Eastern meadowlark
Red-winged blackbird
Rusty blackbird
Brewer's blackbird
Common grackle
Brown-headed cowbird
Baltimore oriole
Scarlet tanager
Summer tanager
Cardinal
Blue grosbeak
Indigo bunting
Painted bunting
House finch
Goldfinch
Rufous-sided towhee
Chipping sparrow
Field sparrow
Song sparrow

In winter:

Red-breasted nuthatch
Brown creeper
Dark-eyed junco,
    slate-colored race
White-throated
    sparrow
White-crowned sparrow
Swamp sparrow
Fox sparrow
Evening grosbeak
Purple finch
Pine siskin

MIDWEST

Northern bobwhite
Mourning dove
Golden-shafted flicker
Red-shafted flicker
Red-bellied woodpecker
Downy woodpecker
Hairy woodpecker
Golden-shafted flicker
Eastern phoebe
Say's phoebe
Blue jay
Black-capped chickadee
Carolina chickadee
Tufted titmouse
White-breasted nuthatch
House wren
Bewick's wren
Carolina wren
Mockingbird
Gray catbird
Brown thrasher
Robin
Eastern bluebird
Wood thrush
Blue-gray gnatcatcher
Cedar waxwing
White-eyed vireo
Bell's vireo
Red-eyed vireo
Warbling vireo
Yellow warbler
Yellow-rumped warbler
Ovenbird
Common yellowthroat

Kentucky warbler
Eastern meadowlark
Western meadowlark
Yellow-headed blackbird
Red-winged blackbird
Rusty blackbird
Brewer's blackbird
Common grackle
Brown-headed cowbird
Baltimore oriole
Western tanager
Scarlet tanager
Summer tanager
Cardinal
Rose-breasted grosbeak
Black-headed grosbeak
Blue grosbeak
Indigo bunting
Lazuli bunting
Painted bunting
House finch
Goldfinch
Dicksissel
Rufous-sided towhee
Grasshopper sparrow
Chipping sparrow
Field sparrow
Swamp sparrow
Song sparrow

FAR NORTH

Northern bobwhite
Mourning dove
Golden-shafted flicker
Red-shafted flicker

Downy woodpecker
Hairy woodpecker
Eastern phoebe
Blue jay
Gray jay
Black-billed magpie
Black-capped
    chickadee
Boreal chickadee
White-breasted
    nuthatch
Red-breasted nuthatch
Brown creeper
House wren
Winter wren
Gray catbird
Brown thrasher
Robin
Wood thrush
Hermit thrush
Swainson's thrush
Veery
Eastern bluebird
Mountain bluebird
Golden-crowned
    kinglet
Ruby-crowned kinglet
Bohemian waxwing
Cedar waxwing
Solitary vireo
Red-eyed vireo
Warbling vireo
Orange-crowned
    warbler
Yellow warbler

Common yellowthroat

Red-bellied woodpecker

Yellow-rumped
  warbler
Black-throated green
  warbler
Blackburnian warbler
Blackpoll warbler
Ovenbird
Common yellowthroat
Wilson's warbler
American redstart
Eastern meadowlark
Western meadowlark
Red-winged blackbird
Rusty blackbird
Brewer's blackbird
Common grackle
Brown-headed cowbird
Baltimore oriole
Bullock's oriole
Scarlet tanager
Western tanager
Rose-breasted grosbeak
Evening grosbeak
Indigo bunting
Lazuli bunting
Purple finch
House finch
Pine grosbeak
Common redpoll
Pine siskin
Goldfinch
Red crossbill
White-winged crossbill
Rufous-sided towhee
Dicksissel
Dark-eyed junco

American tree sparrow
Chipping sparrow
White-crowned sparrow
White-throated sparrow
Fox sparrow
Swamp sparrow
Song sparrow

WEST

Scaled quail
California quail
Gambel's quail
Mourning dove
Red-shafted flicker
Acorn woodpecker
Downy woodpecker
Hairy woodpecker
Golden-shafted flicker
Black phoebe
Say's phoebe
Steller's jay
Scrub jay
Pinyon jay
Magpies
Black-capped chickadee
Mountain chickadee
Chestnut-backed
  chickadee
Plain titmouse
Bridled titmouse
Verdin
Bush tit
White-breasted nuthatch
Red-breasted nuthatch
Pygmy nuthatch

House wren
Bewick's wren
Winter wren
Cactus wren
Mockingbird
Gray catbird
Sage thrasher
Curve-billed thrasher
Robin
Varied thrush
Hermit thrush
Western bluebird
Mountain bluebird
Blue-gray gnatcatcher
Golden-crowned kinglet
Ruby-crowned kinglet
Bohemian waxwing
Cedar waxwing
Phainopepla
Solitary vireo
Bell's vireo
Warbling vireo
Orange-crowned warbler
Lucy's warbler
Yellow warbler
Yellow-rumped warbler
Townsend's warbler
Black-throated gray
  warbler
Common yellowthroat
Western meadowlark
Yellow-headed blackbird
Red-winged blackbird
Brewer's blackbird
Great-tailed grackle
Common grackle

Brown-headed
  cowbird
Scott's oriole
Bullock's oriole
Western tanager
Summer tanager
Cardinal
Black-headed
  grosbeak
Evening grosbeak
Blue grosbeak
Lazuli bunting
Purple finch
House finch
Pine grosbeak
Rosy finch
Pine siskin
American goldfinch
Lesser goldfinch
Rufous-sided towhee
Brown towhee
Black-throated
  sparrow
Dark-eyed junco
Chipping sparrow
Brewer's sparrow
White-crowned
  sparrow
Golden-crowned
  sparrow
Fox sparrow
Song sparrow

Dickcissel

Golden-crowned kinglet

At the Feeder

Watching birds at a feeder is a great way to spend an hour or an afternoon. It's so soothing that some institutes use it as meditative therapy for their clients. Enjoying the birds at my feeders is as much a part of my morning routine as a cup of coffee. I can't imagine starting the day without either one.

A feeding station is also a great way to learn to identify birds. Instead of a hundred or more species flitting through the leaves in a May woods, there's only a handful, and they're in plain view. Be sure to establish your station close to a window where you can easily watch sitting in your favorite chair—I can see my feeders from my kitchen table.

My first bird feeder was a simple open tray, knocked together out of scrap lumber. Twenty years later, the most-used feeder in my collection is one of that same simple design.

The more aggressive birds can monopolize a feeder, so I keep several filled. If blue jays take over one of the feeders, the shyer chickadees and titmice can visit another.

You can get as fancy as you like with feeders, from copper-roof cupolas to white-column palaces that would cost more than my birdseed budget for a year. But before you succumb to a fancy feeder, think about how you'll fill and clean it. A pretty cedar pagoda dangles from a post in my yard, but it's almost always empty. To fill it requires me to balance a cup of birdseed in my teeth while I slide open a glass door with one hand and try to keep the whole shebang from tipping over with the

---

PICTURE PERFECT

I like to snap photos of my feeder guests, but I got tired of bird-at-the-feeder shots in a hurry. So I "planted" a dead tree limb in easy view of the house. (See Chapter 3, beginning on page 68, for tips on how to set up your own dead "tree.") I spread peanut butter and suet into the knotholes on the trunk, keeping the food unobtrusive. Only I know that my woodpecker, chickadee, nuthatch, and titmouse pictures weren't the result of hours of waiting for just the right shot in the middle of a woods.

Plenty of nearby cover protects birds as they visit this feeder. Unfortunately, the vegetation also provides good hiding places for hunting cats, which will prey on ground-feeding birds that scratch for dropped seed. If cats are a problem in your neighborhood, keep an open space around your feeders.

A big, brownish woodpecker, the flicker is ordinarily a ground feeder. Watch for the "flicker" of a white rump patch and the flash of gold-lined wings when the bird flies.

A tube feeder, whether it's stocked with niger seed or sunflower, will attract finches. Here a trio of species— house finches, goldfinches, and pine siskins—dine together.

The male cardinal's crest, conical bill, and black face set it apart from any other red bird. Cardinals are fond of sunflower seeds and cracked corn. Put out melon and squash seeds for a special treat.

Evening grosbeaks have earned their nickname of "grosspigs." Their powerful beaks crack sunflower seeds so quickly that a group of feeding grosbeaks sounds like crackling flames.

FRUIT FOR ALL SEASONS

To plant a larder that will sustain birds for months, plan your fruit-bearing plantings around these seasonal treats.

Spring

Birds are looking for soft foods in spring, and they're abundant. Caterpillars and insects fill the bill nicely (and literally), with no assistance from you. A well-planted garden, full of young trees and a diversity of shrubs, will naturally attract insects, and that's what will draw the birds.

You can supplement the insect diet with strawberries. Plant a bed or a border of them just for the birds. Wild strawberries, which you can buy from one of the specialty nurseries listed in "Resources" on page 250, provide the perfect-size fruits for birds, and the plants make an appealing groundcover. The familiar wild strawberry that I gathered and made into bouquets of berries as a child is ideal. Alpine strawberries, which grow in self-contained tuffets, are a good choice, too, and so are Western beach strawberries. They're native to the West Coast, but they grow well in other regions, and their shiny leaves are as ornamental as wild ginger.

Summer

Summer kicks fruit season into high gear. Anything you like to eat, birds do, too. Sour cherries, pin cherries, and other cherry trees are great for the bird-friendly garden. Plums, apricots, and peaches are also good bird attractors. When our peach tree surprised us with a bumper crop one summer, the house finches made short work of the fruits at the top of the unpruned tree. They puncture the fruit to drink the sweet juice.

Add some raspberries and blackberries to your hedges, and plant river grapes, fox grapes, or Concords to clamber up trees and over trellises. Blueberries are superb bird fruits. Elderberries offer dinner plate–size heads of delectable, tiny berries, relished by waxwings, thrushes, robins, and other birds.

Mockingbirds thrive in areas with few trees, dense shrubbery, and lots of edible fruits like these bittersweet berries.

Try blue or red elders for a change of pace. The bushes are more substantial than common elderberry, and the crop sustains birds for weeks.

Fall

Fall is viburnum time! There are dozens of species, and the fruits of all of them are appreciated by birds. I find that the birds pick the berries off the arrowwood first; then they turn to gray dogwood and American cranberrybush viburnums. Sumacs are welcomed, too. I prefer the look of shining sumac in the garden. Its winged stems hold glossy leaves that turn fire-engine red in autumn and shine like a beacon until they drop. Bluebirds are especially fond of sumac fruits.

If you don't mind its self-sowing tendencies, and if you have birds visiting your yard, you probably already have some pokeweed. The stems turn Day-Glo purple in fall, and the clusters of black berries disappear fast when migrating birds discover them.

Winter

Now the birds turn to the last of the berry crop. They seek out the hanging, ¼-inch berries of hackberry trees, and they clean the clusters of showy orange fruits from the pyracantha that climbs the chimney. Cotoneasters also draw them in. And hollies of all kinds are eaten with relish. Roving flocks of waxwings visit the garden, searching out the last of the pokeweed and any remaining viburnum or sumac berries. Hawthorns shine like an "Eat at Joe's" sign. Crabapples, ignored by most birds until winter, become a fruit of choice. Hybrid varieties are often passed over by birds (my guess is that they just don't taste good), but the shriveled fruit that hangs from the wild crabs in my garden draws house finches, bluebirds, tufted titmice, mockingbirds, and other fruit-eaters.

RECIPE FOR BLUEBIRDS

I'm not much of a cook, but for birds, I pull out all the stops. Last winter, when deep snow hit the lower Midwest, bluebirds came in to my feeders in droves. They'd never visited the feeders before, though they had come for berries in the garden. I was stunned by their beauty—such an intense blue against the fresh snow.

Ransacking the pantry, I pulled out cornmeal, a jar of chunky peanut butter, raisins, and a bottle of corn oil. I mushed it up to crumbly cookie-dough consistency, then took it outside. The bluebirds moved off only a few feet. When I scattered the dough on the porch where it would be protected from the snow, they immediately returned, fluttering down right at my feet. What a magic day, standing in the midst of bluebirds and falling snow.

Here's my "magic bluebird" recipe:

Peanut-Butter Dough
6 cups yellow cornmeal
18-ounce jar chunky peanut butter
6 small boxes of raisins, chopped with a floured knife
  (optional)
1 cup corn oil

Mix by hand. Adjust proportions of cornmeal and peanut butter if needed until dough reaches a lumpy but crumbly consistency.

other. Pretty is as pretty does, as your grandma probably told you.

Many birds prefer an open tray, perhaps because their exits are unimpeded and they have a good view of approaching predators. You can make one easily—it's a great project for kids. Use hardware cloth for the bottom, so rainwater can drain easily. I keep the sides on mine as low as possible, so I can see the birds better. A low tray feeder that stands on the ground with short feet will serve ground-feeding birds like doves and sparrows and keep the seed off the wet ground. A tray attached to a tree trunk will attract everything from jays to juncos.

Finches, siskins, titmice, and (sometimes) chickadees visit hanging tube feeders, which offer a limited number of perches but conserve seed and protect it from moisture. Don't go the cheap route when you buy a tube feeder: You'll pay for it in spilled birdseed. Those with heavy metal bases and seed-cup holes are more stable in the wind, and that means less seed wasted on the ground. If house finches have overrun your tube feeders, buy one with perches above the holes. Acrobatic goldfinches will have no trouble reaching them, but house finches will be stymied.

The blue jay is a dashing and colorful bird, not to mention a loudmouth. In fall and winter, jays eat mainly acorns, beech nuts, and corn, but they switch to insects in summer. Peanut butter smeared on a feeder is an irresistible treat.

A BIRDSEED GARDEN

Seed-eating birds will forage for months in a garden full of naturally appealing foods. Let the stalks stand in winter—birds will continue to glean seeds and insects through the seasons, and sparrows will scratch around beneath the plants for any morsels that may have dropped. Many of the best birdseed plants are those we're used to thinking of as weeds. But if you've ever scared up a batch of sparrows from a weedy field, you know how attractive these plants are. That's because they're chock-full of seeds—and that's exactly why they're weeds. The prodigious seeds spread the plants throughout farm fields, roadsides, and other disturbed ground. As far as the birds are concerned, it's all easy pickin's. This garden uses some of the prettier self-sowing plants, and the birds should clean off the seeds well enough to keep them from being too "weedy."

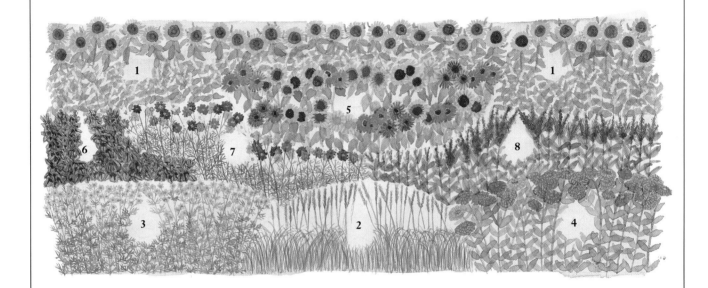

PLANT LIST

1. 'Russian Mammoth' sunflowers (*Helianthus annuus* 'Russian Mammoth') with false climbing buckwheat (*Polygonum scandens*) and grain buckwheat (*Fagopyrum esculentum*)

2. Foxtail millet (*Setaria italica*)

3. Tickseed sunflowers (*Bidens aristosa*)

4. Zinnias (*Zinnia elegans*)

5. 'Autumn Beauty' and 'Music Box' sunflowers (*Helianthus annuus* 'Autumn Beauty' and *H. annuus* 'Music Box')

6. Lamb's quarters (*Chenopodium album*)

7. 'Sensation' cosmos (*Cosmos bipinnatus* 'Sensation')

8. Amaranths (*Amaranthus* spp.)

Water—It's Essential

If you provide clean water, you'll give birds another reason to linger in your garden. Birds love a birdbath all year long, even in the coldest days of winter. It removes dust and parasites from their feathers, and it probably feels good, too—they revel in splashing as much as any two-year-old.

A shallow, rough-bottom container is a perfect choice, but birds can make do with just about anything. I keep a bucket of water filled outside for our dogs, and I've seen house finches, chickadees, and other birds using it, too. Up the road at the horse barn, bluebirds line up on the edge of a deep metal trough, sipping daintily.

The traditional birdbath is still a good design, but after two pedestals were broken by my rowdy dogs, I

A bird in the bath is a delight to watch. Be sure your bath is safe from prowling cats; wet birds are poor fliers and very vulnerable. Give your birds a nearby perch for preening, and scrub the bowl and refill with fresh water daily.

An oldie but a goodie, the pedestal-style birdbath is apparently familiar to birds. They'll take to it quickly. Such a birdbath also serves as a focal point and ornament in your garden, so buy a beauty.

Installing a Bubbling Spring for Birds

One of the prettiest birdbaths I've ever seen was a simple homemade "spring"—a collection of rounded river stones set on a bed of gravel, piped with a recirculating pump. Water bubbled up through the stones just like a real spring, spreading out between them to create shallow places for birds to sip or splash. A semicircle of larger rock surrounded the spring and sheltered ferns.

The trick to the arrangement was a small plastic trash can buried at the center of the stones, which sloped slightly downward to a center depression above the can. Topped with a sturdy metal grid, the can held the pump and the pipe that carried the water in the can to the surface. A layer of pond liner under the gravel beneath the stones collected the water and returned it to the buried can.

With the aid of a recirculating pump and some found materials, you can put together your own natural spring. If you're short on river stone, check a building supply store.

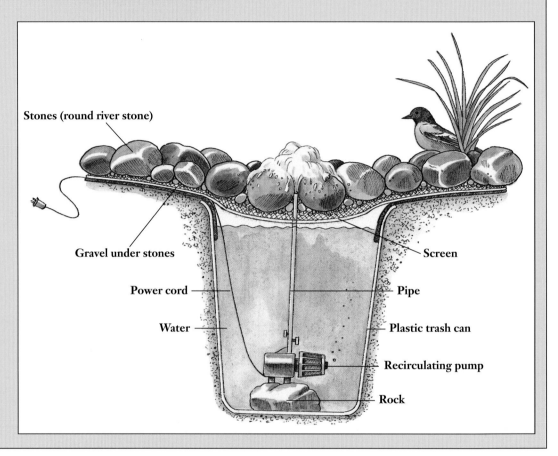

Stones (round river stone)

Gravel under stones

Power cord

Water

Screen

Pipe

Plastic trash can

Recirculating pump

Rock

switched to using only the tops. I have three basins in the garden, each set on a flat rock about 6 inches tall. The one that gets the most use is almost hidden from view, beneath an exuberant arch of boltonia stems. In spring, when the vegetation is cleared away, the birds are more wary about bathing.

A naturally hollowed-out stone that's cupped to form a shallow basin makes a good birdbath. Another birdbath alternative is a simple large clay saucer, if you set a flat, rough stone into it to provide better footing. Of course, a garden pond or stream is better yet.

Once the birds discover their bath, they'll be regulars. It's my guess that that's why pedestal-type baths at-

tract birds so quickly: Like red plastic hummingbird feeders, the birds are used to seeing them—they know what that shape means.

If you have an outdoor electrical outlet, you can use an immersible water heater to keep your birdbath in use all winter. They cost as little as $15 at pet- and pool-supply stores and are simple to install: Lay the heater in the birdbath, plug it in, and you're set. If you need an extension cord to get from outlet to birdbath, be sure to buy a heavy-duty cord suitable for outdoor use.

The sound of splashing water will catch the ear of passing migrants who might otherwise overlook your birdbath. You can rig up a slow-dripping bucket from a

A ruff of hostas makes the perfect underplanting for a sturdy column. If the top of your birdbath gets broken and you can't find a matching replacement, try a clay saucer instead.

Birds especially appreciate a source of fresh water in winter, when natural ponds and puddles are frozen over. Simply lay an electric heater in your birdbath to keep it ice-free.

branch and set your birdbath under it, or you can invest in a recirculating pump (about $50) and spend a few hours creating a gentle murmur of water.

Giving Your Birds Shelter

Shelter from the wind and weather and from predators is the last element of the bird garden. Evergreens are ideal bird shelters. An eastern red cedar that stands at the corner of my garden is home to dozens of birds every night: If you stand close to it, you can hear their sleepy twitters as they settle down for the night, safe from predators who won't risk its prickly branches.

A single evergreen will offer some shelter, but a group planting is better for cardinals and other birds that flock and roost together in winter. Many of the plants that you choose for food value will do double duty as shelter. Plant for diversity, mixing plant types and heights as they would be in nature. But remember to keep some open areas between shrub groupings so that you can still watch the birds!

Nest Boxes—Instant Homes

It's exciting to put up a nest box and watch to see who moves in. You can buy nest boxes or nest box kits, but they're also a fun project for families to build together from scratch. Birds are pretty forgiving when it comes to carpentry mistakes. They won't mind the crooked nail or the slightly off-center hole. Nest boxes also provide winter shelter. Or you can make a roost box for birds seeking shelter in winter—it looks like an elongated nest box with the entrance hole at the bottom. Birds that don't nest in cavities won't nest in your boxes, but they may turn to your trees and shrubs as a safe haven to build their nests. Try to avoid the temptation to take a peek—your scent leaves a clear trail for predators.

▲ *Robin nests may be anywhere from on the ground to the treetops, but they're usually built 5 to 15 feet above ground. A three-sided platform, mounted against a wall, makes a welcome nesting shelf. The three to five blue-green eggs are laid on a lining of fine grass inside the traditional mud cup.*

▶ *Traditional perennials and birds are great partners. Here, a pole-mounted nesting box doubles as a visual accent among hardy geraniums and catmint.*

NESTING MATERIALS

Bird-feeder traffic drops off dramatically in spring, when birds begin nesting. Instead of trying to entice birds to your yard with food, offer them some tempting nesting materials.

Scatter the items on an open area or drape them over shrubs. I like to tease the orioles by tying butcher string onto twigs. They're as adept as Boy Scouts at undoing the knots.

Here are some nest-material options, in order of their desirability:

- White duck or goose breast feathers (cannibalize an old bed pillow, ask at a farm, or check a duck pond)
- Other colors of breast feathers (breast feathers are the curled ones, wide and soft at the end)
- Goose or duck down
- Short lengths of white butcher string (no longer than 8 inches to prevent mishaps)
- Short lengths of other string or yarn
- Horsehair from mane or tail
- Rabbit and opossum fur (check a thrift shop for an old fur coat or collar, nail a strip to a board, and mount on a tree)
- Dog fur

You can also offer dried grass blades, fine twigs, bark strips (grapevines are a great source), and spaghnum moss, but birds often prefer to collect their own.

There's another trick you can use to attract nesting birds: Keep a mud puddle fresh and wet. Nest-building swallows, robins, and other birds can travel for great distances to collect mud in times of drought.

When there are nests full of hungry mouths to feed constantly during the daylight hours, the summer garden beckons with its bug-laden greenery—another good reason not to use pesticides.

Building a Bluebird Nest Box

Bluebird boxes are popular with backyard bird-watchers for one very good reason: They work. Bluebirds like open spaces, with woods or hedgerows nearby. They like farmland and suburban areas, and are partial to golf courses and cemetaries. If you have a suitable bluebird habitat in your yard or nearby, the chances of a box attracting a nesting pair are very good.

Building birdhouses is a great family activity, and you don't need to be a master carpenter to be successful at it. All you need is a saw, a drill, a hammer, and some nails. A pair of hinges and a hook and eye attached to one side will let you open the box for easy cleaning. Affix the floor 3″ from the bottom of the nest box back, and mount the box by drilling two holes through the "apron" of wood left at the bottom.

If your workshop is really minimal, you can have the boards sawed to size at a home building supply store. However, an electric saw is fairly inexpensive and worth it if you're building more than one house.

Other birds, including titmice, nuthatches, and chickadees, may also be interested in your bluebird house. Why not make several?

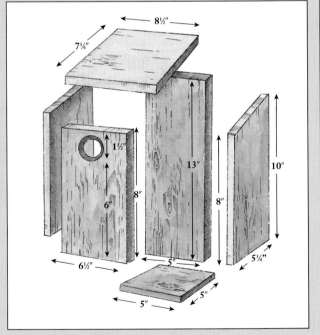

You can vary the dimensions of a bluebird box somewhat, but don't change the size of the hole. Any bigger, and it will allow entrance to starlings. Mount the box 4 – 8′ above the ground.

Hummingbirds in Your Garden

Hummingbirds are easy to bring to your garden, even if you live right in the middle of a city. These little zippers come to our yards for one big reason: to eat. It takes a lot of sugar to keep a hummingbird's energy up.

The ruby-throated hummingbird is the only species that makes its home east of the Mississippi, though strays of other species may turn up from time to time. Go west, and you'll find hummers with pink, purple, blue, and orange feathers. That iridescent flash of color comes from tiny feathers called gorgets.

If you're planning a camping trip to Texas or west of the Great Plains, take along a hummingbird feeder and a couple of packets of instant nectar. Hang it at your campground, and you're in for a treat.

I remember babbling to a ranger in the southwestern mountains about a hummingbird I'd seen in the pines. It was just gorgeous, I said, all green and purple and blue. What was it?

"That's a magnificent hummingbird," the ranger replied.

"Sure is," I agreed enthusiastically. "But what is it called?"

The ranger laughed. "That's its name," he said, "the magnificent hummingbird."

Seeing Red

Red is the key to attracting hummers. They can't resist investigating anything red or orange, from the handles of my favorite pruners to the jumpsuits worn by scientists on Mount St. Helens after the volcano. (The hummingbirds probed the grommets, trying to figure out how to get nectar out of the protective suits.)

If you haven't had hummingbirds in your garden before, start by making a big splash of red. Put out a dozen zingy geraniums and a plastic hummingbird feeder—the gaudier the better. Once you have hummers

(continued on page 171)

The ruby-throated hummingbird, which ranges across the eastern half of the country, is attracted to orange or red flowers like this trumpetvine. Its rapid wingbeats—up to 75 times per second—make it an avian helicopter.

ALL-YEAR ENTICEMENTS

Attract birds to your natural landscape year-round with these proven tactics.

AT THE FEEDER	**IN THE GARDEN**	**OTHER ACTIVITIES**
Spring		
Offer soft foods like raisins, grapes, and peanut-butter dough, as well as seed.	Plant sunflowers, cosmos, zinnias, bidens, and coneflowers.	Put out string, fur, feathers, and other nesting materials.
Keep the birdbath clean and filled.	Plant a grape arbor.	Create a mud puddle and keep it wet for swallows and robins.
If weather turns unseasonably cold, make peanut-butter dough for bluebirds, or buy mealworms from a bait shop and put them in a tray feeder.	Plant berry bushes for fall.	Protect migrants from broken necks by putting up hawk decals on windows or breaking up the deadly reflections with a drapery of camouflage netting, available at army-surplus stores.
Fill and hang hummingbird feeders; scrub them clean every time you refill, paying attention to the feeder holes.	Add sheltering evergreens to your garden.	
Empty birdseed storage containers; scrub with 10 percent bleach solution and let them air-dry before refilling with fresh seed.		
Summer		
Keep the birdbath clean and filled.	Build a pond or other water feature.	Keep a notebook of nestbox use and cowbird nest parasitism.
Offer chopped or ground suet for fledglings (ask the butcher at your supermarket's meat department).	Continue to plant annuals for birds.	Keep a journal of nesting birds.
Keep feeders stocked, but offer only a little seed at a time so it doesn't spoil when traffic is slow.	Plant shrubs, vines, trees, and perennials.	Listen to birdsong.
Put up a sugar-water feeder for orioles, and offer sliced orange halves.		Continue to offer nesting materials and mud; many birds raise more than one brood a year, and they build a new nest each time.
Renew Vaseline barrier at hummingbird feeders if needed.		Keep cats indoors; be on guard for marauding housecats at nests.

AT THE FEEDER	IN THE GARDEN	OTHER ACTIVITIES
Watch for signs of insect infestation in stored seed: visible beetles, grubs, or moths; "sawdust" excrement; or webbing that makes seeds stick together in clumps. If seed is infested, dispose of it and buy a small quantity of fresh seed.		

Fall

AT THE FEEDER	IN THE GARDEN	OTHER ACTIVITIES
Stock up on birdseed supplies.	Shop clearance sales at nurseries for shrubs and trees.	Hang camouflage netting over windows and doors to protect migrants from deadly crashes.
Keep feeders filled with seed and suet.	Let plants stand instead of clearing away foliage after frost.	Watch for fall plumage changes in goldfinches and grosbeaks.
Add cracked corn to your feeding station and offer ears of corn for squirrels.		Build or buy additional feeders.
Keep the birdbath clean and filled.		Build or buy and mount roosting boxes.
Add additional suet feeders.		

Winter

AT THE FEEDER	IN THE GARDEN	OTHER ACTIVITIES
Be generous with seed, but don't let it collect in a solid, rained-on mass in a bird feeder or on the ground.	Let foliage of flowers and grasses stand to offer cover to sparrows and ground-dwelling birds.	Build and mount nest boxes and roosting boxes.
Hang clusters of grapes on bare branches of shrubs. Keep suet feeders well stocked and offer ground or chopped suet in a tray feeder for small birds like juncos and wrens.	Note places in the garden where additional cover would be good. Write them down!	Keep track of bird visitors on a wall calendar. Kids love to do this.
Unless your weather is frigid, scrub feeders every other week with 10 percent bleach solution to keep down disease problems that can spread fast when feeder traffic is heavy.		Set out your discarded Christmas tree, laying it down on its side, for excellent winter cover.
Install a birdbath heater.		
Keep an emergency supply of suet, sunflower seed, and millet seed on hand in case of bad weather.		

A HUMMINGBIRD GARDEN

No hummingbird can resist a splashy display of brightly colored flowers and nectar-rich blossoms. This garden will bloom from spring to frost, so visiting hummers will always find something to feast upon. Wild columbine and flowering quince start the season, offering their blossoms to the first of the migrants. Rose-of-Sharon, petunias, and many other flowers are in full tilt right at nesting time, so there's plenty of high-energy food. Late-bloomers like pineapple sage make sure there's still an abundance for fall migrants.

Long-blooming annuals and tender perennials like impatiens and geraniums are a staple in the hummingbird garden, because their flowers keep going for months without letting up. Plant your favorite color of garden-center petunias the first year. Then let them self-sow. They'll revert to the species form, a vigorous plant with simple, fragrant blossoms of white, lavender, and pink-purple.

Red flowers in this garden act as a hummingbird magnet. Once the tiny birds have found your special spot, tubular blossoms will encourage them to linger.

PLANT LIST

1. White-flowering rose-of-Sharon (*Hibiscus syriacus*)
2. Cypress vine (*Ipomoea quamoclit*) with white- and blue-flowering morning glories (*Ipomoea tricolor* 'Pearly Gates' and 'Heavenly Blue')
3. Potted red-flowered geranium (*Pelargonium × hortorum*)
4. Pineapple sage (*Salvia elegans*)
5. Blue-flowered delphinium (*Delphinium × belladonna*)
6. Flowering tobacco (*Nicotiana sylvestris*)
7. Self-sown (species) petunias (*Petunia integrifolia*)
8. 'Grandview Scarlet' bee balm (*Monarda didyma* 'Grandview Scarlet')
9. Anise hyssop (*Agastache foeniculum*)
10. Salmon-rose 'Picasso' geraniums (*Pelargonium × hortorum* 'Picasso')
11. Golden columbine (*Aquilegia chrysantha*)
12. Hardy fuchsia (*Fuchsia magellanica*)
13. Red buckeye (*Aesculus pavia*)
14. White-flowered impatiens (*Impatiens wallerana*)
15. 'Homestead Purple' rose verbena (*Verbena canadensis* 'Homestead Purple')
16. California fuchsia (*Zauschneria californica*)
17. Apple-scented geraniums (*Pelargonium odoratissimum*)
18. Red- and salmon-flowered Texas sage (*Salvia coccinea* species form or 'Lady in Red' for red flowers and *S.coccinea* 'Cherry Blossom' for salmon flowers)
19. Great blue lobelia (*Lobelia syphilitica*)
20. Blue-flowered larkspur (*Consolida ambigua*)
21. Wild columbine (*Aquilegia canadensis*)
22. Coral bells (*Heuchera sanguinea*)
23. Flowering quince (*Chaenomeles speciosa*)

Tiny throat feathers of the male Anna's hummingbird glow neon pink in the sun. Like other hummers, this bird's main diet is nectar, supplemented with spiders and other small insects.

coming regularly, you can switch to a more subtle feeder design. But for starters, go for something good and tacky, like a big, red plastic strawberry.

A Hummingbird Garden

Hummingbirds are fast eaters, and they usually zip in and out pretty quickly at the feeder. To get them to linger, you can plant a hummingbird garden.

Think of that beak when you choose flowers: Hummingbirds naturally prefer flowers with long tubes, where sweet nectar awaits. Tubed blossoms (think of a trumpetvine or honeysuckle flower) or spurred flowers (think of a columbine) are great enticements. It's a win-win thing for both bird and blossom: The hummer gets

Offspring of self-sowing hybrid columbines can be as delightful as a batch of kittens: some double-flowered, some single, a variety of colors—always the unexpected. All are tops with hummingbirds.

"Lady's eardrops" is an old name for fuchsia. The abundant flowers are manna for hummingbirds, who will often stake a territorial claim and viciously defend a fuchsia shrub or hanging basket plant.

NECTAR RECIPE

Instant nectar, available wherever hummingbird feeders are sold, is fast and easy to make. But it's super-expensive when you compare it with the cost of making your own, and the red dye often used is unnecessary and unheathful. (Use red on the feeder, not in the nectar, to attract your hummers.)

Nectar is nothing more than sugar water. For every 4 parts water, add 1 part sugar. For easy refills, mix up a gallon jug and store in your fridge.

My feeders hold about 2 cups of nectar. When they need refilling, I measure out ½ cup of white granulated sugar, then pour 2 cups of boiling water over it. I stir to mix and let it cool before filling.

Don't add red food coloring, and don't use honey. Both can cause health problems for your hummers.

Superfine white sugar, which you can find at some supermarkets and at bar-supply stores, dissolves instantly even in cold water, but it costs more than granulated sugar.

the nectar, and the flower gets pollinated. Sometimes I see hummers with their heads dusted yellow with pollen. Hummers will notice tubular blossoms before you do. You've probably never thought of the herb sage as having a tubular flower, but take another look. Hummingbirds certainly do—they enjoy both culinary sage and its ornamental relatives, the salvias. Bee balm is another hummingbird favorite, and, of course, the hummers like the reddest varieties best.

Hummingbirds often make a garden their home if it includes a good-size tree where they can mount their tiny, cuplike nest of spider silk and lichens. If you see a hummer going from one spiderweb to another in your garden, watch to see whether it's picking out tiny insects or whether it's collecting silk. Then good luck trying to follow it with your eyes to a nest site!

Hummingbirds are beautiful, but they're also bullies. Not only do they claim breeding territories, but they also claim food sources—a feeder, a fuchsia, or a pot of geraniums—as their own. And they'll guard them from anybody, including humans and dogs.

CHOOSING A HUMMINGBIRD FEEDER

Hummingbird feeders have come a long way in the last ten years or so, but designers still don't have the message that form follows function. A feeder must be easy to refill and easy to clean, since you'll be doing both frequently. If your garden is graced with hummingbirds, you can count on refilling the feeder at least once a week.

Molds are unhealthy to hummers, so keeping your feeder clean is a must. I use a bottle brush to clean the main body of the feeder and an old toothbrush to get at the gook in holes and crevices.

Before you buy a hummingbird feeder, check out these features:

- Examine how the feeder comes apart. Will you be able to clean it easily, or will you have to work blindly in tight, hard-to-get-at crannies?
- Beware of feeders that require you to turn them upside down to remove and reinsert the reservoir; spilled sugar water is an annoyance on hands and clothes.
- Make sure your feeder has a decent-size reservoir that won't need refilling every day. Small feeders are cute but impractical.
- Avoid opaque feeders. You won't be able to tell if the inside needs cleaning.

Once you have chosen your feeder, you'll need to hang it up. I've found that a black iron shepherd's hook is a fine place to hang a feeder.

Hummingbird sage (<u>*Dicliptera suberecta*</u>*), a perennial from Uruguay, has the brilliant red tubular flowers that hummingbirds adore. Grow it in a hanging basket in cold-winter regions.*

I once watched a single hummingbird drive away a flock of 30-plus cedar waxwings. The waxwings were flycatching over a stream; the hummer was drinking nectar from the orange jewelweed flowers along its edge. Every time a waxwing flew out, the hummingbird zoomed to the attack, chasing the much larger bird out of sight. After several such forays, the waxwings gave up and retreated en masse.

On migration, hummingbirds follow a path of red flowers when they head north. When my flowering quince comes into bloom, I hang out the feeder. In the Pacific Northwest, it was the blossoming of the red-flowering currant, a sinuous, lovely, native shrub, that told me when to expect the first tiny guests. Of course, in mild climates such as the Southwest or southern California, hummingbirds are a year-round pleasure. I'll never forget drinking a New Year's Day toast while watching hummers zip around the flowers of a blooming bottlebrush tree in a Los Angeles backyard. It was just another part of the everyday magic that happens when you garden for the birds.

This broad-billed hummer is a male, as you can tell from its gorgeous plumage. Only 3 inches long from tip of bill to tip of tail, it breeds from southern Arizona and New Mexico into Mexico.

PLANTS THAT ATTRACT HUMMINGBIRDS

You can grow a beautiful hummingbird garden by choosing a selection of the following plants. Or plant one or a mix in a hanging basket for head-high hummingbirds.

All grow well in full sun, with average soil, unless otherwise indicated.

HARDY PERENNIALS

Bee balm (*Monarda didyma*)
Unusual whorled flowers in pink, red, white, and red-purple. Fast spreader. Zones 4 to 10.

Catmints (*Nepeta* spp.)
Loose, mounding clumps of silvery leaves with abundant, small, lavender-blue flowers. Most hardy in Zones 3 to 10.

Columbines (*Aquilegia* spp.)
Long-spurred flowers are held on bare stems above a rosette of pretty, lobed foliage. Most hardy in Zones 3 to 10.

Coral bells (*Heuchera sanguinea, H. × brizoides*)
Rosettes of scalloped leaves bear many long-blooming stems of tiny red, pink, or white blossoms. Go for the zingy colors to attract hummers. Zones 3 to 10.

Delphiniums (*Delphinium* spp.)
Beautiful spikes in all shades of blue, purple, and white rise above rosettes of foliage. Best in cooler climates. Zones 3 to 10.

Hyssops (*Agastache* spp.)
Densely packed, narrow spikes of tiny flowers, often with fragrant foliage, are more familiar to herb gardens but beloved by hummingbirds. Zones 4 to 10.

Penstemons (*Penstemon* spp.)
Midheight perennials with abundant tubular flowers in blue, white, and purple. Best in West. Many are difficult to grow and short-lived, but worth trying. Must have perfect drainage. Hardiness depends on species; varying from Zones 3 to 9.

Phlox (*Phlox paniculata*)
Old-time garden favorite with often fragrant flowers in pink, red, white, and lilac. Zones 3 to 9.

Pineapple sage (*Salvia elegans*)
Large bush with fragrant foliage and late-blooming, bright red flowers. Zones 8 to 10; grow as annual in cold regions.

Salvias (*Salvia* spp.)
Salvia coccinea (Zone 8, but grow as annual elsewhere) has brilliant red flowers. Red sage (*S. splendens*) cultivars are hummingbird magnets. Many are hardy in Zones 5 to 10, others only in Zone 9 or 10. Many of the tender salvias can be grown as annuals in all zones.

ANNUALS AND TENDER PERENNIALS
Grow in a sunny spot, in well-drained average garden soil. Many will self-sow.

Cleome (*Cleome hasslerana*)
Spidery whorls in pink, white, and purple on 4′ plants. Annual; all zones.

Four-o'clocks (*Mirabilis jalapa*)	Bushy, tuber-forming tender perennials with flowers in red, yellow, white, and pink—sometimes more than one color on a single plant! Blooms in late afternoon. Perennial in Zones 9 and 10; grow as annuals in all other zones.
Geraniums (*Pelargonium × hortorum*)	Familiar container plants with pink, salmon, red, or white flowers. Perennial in Zones 9 and 10; grow as annuals in all other zones.
Geraniums, scented (*Pelargonium* spp.)	A wonderful assortment of leaf shape and scent. Flowers are much less showy than common geraniums, but highly attractive to hummers. Perennial in Zones 9 and 10; grow as annuals in all other zones.
Impatiens (*Impatiens wallerana*)	Indefatigable bedding annual with red, white, pink, lavender, and mixed colors. Perennial in Zones 9 and 10; grow as annuals in all other zones.
Nicotianas (*Nicotiana* spp.)	Sweet-smelling tobacco relatives with tubular blossoms. Avoid 'Nikki' hybrids. Nearly all are annuals. *N. alata* is a perennial hardy in Zones 9 and 10.
Petunias (*Petunia* spp. and hybrids)	Popular annuals with sprawling plants and a variety of colorful flaring trumpet flowers. All petunias will attract hummers. Annual; all zones.
Tithonia (*Tithonia rotundifolia*)	Huge, bushy but single-stemmed branching plant, to 8′ high and 4′ wide with a multitude of brilliant orange-red daisylike flowers in late summer. Also attracts butterflies galore. Annual; all zones.

SHRUBS AND VINES

Butterfly bush (*Buddleia davidii*)	Bush with fragrant, lilac-purple flowers held in conical spires at each branch tip. Zones 5 to 9.
Flowering quince (*Chaenomeles speciosa*)	Red, pink, or salmon flowers early in spring catch the first wave of migrating hummingbirds. Use dwarf cultivars such as 'Nana' in masses, as groundcovers; taller varieties are fine shrubs for mixed borders. Zones 5 to 10.
Fuchsias (*Fuchsia* spp.)	Earring-drop flowers in fabulous color combinations of red and purple, pink and white, and others. Grow as shrubs in warm climates; annuals elsewhere. Zones 8 to 10.
Mandevilla (*Mandevilla splendens*)	Hot pink tubular flowers on a tender vine (Zone 8 or 9) that grows fast enough to be enjoyed as an annual.
Trumpetvine (*Campsis radicans*)	Fast-growing, extremely vigorous vine with rich orange tubular flowers. Give it a very sturdy support. May become a problem, but hummingbirds love it. Similar crossvine (*Bignonia capreolata*) is less aggressive. Zones 5 to 9.

PREFERRED SEEDS

Attract your favorite birds by providing their preferred seeds and other treats.

Birds	Sunflower	Millet	Suet	Others
Blackbirds (red-winged, Brewer's, rusty)		x		
Bluebirds				Raisins, grapes, dried cherries, soft dog food, peanut butter, peanuts, nut pieces, hulled sunflowers, mealworms, peanut-butter dough; suet must be chopped
Blue jay, Steller's jay, scrub jay, other jays	x		x	Peanuts, nuts
Cardinal	x		x	Safflower, cracked corn
Carolina wren		x	x	Raisins, grapes, dried cherries, soft dog food, peanut butter, peanuts, nut pieces, peanut-butter dough
Chickadees	x		x	Grapes, raisins
Evening grosbeak	x		x	
Rose-breasted grosbeak	x		x	Sunflower
Goldfinch	x		x	Niger seed
Horned lark		x		
House finch	x		x	Niger seed
Juncos		x		Suet must be finely chopped

Cardinal

Red-breasted nuthatch

Birds	Sunflower	Millet	Suet	Others
Meadowlark		x		
Mockingbird		x	x	Raisins, grapes, cherries, berries of any kind, soft dog food, peanut butter, peanuts, nut pieces
Native sparrows (song, field, tree, chipping, fox, white-throated, white-crowned, and others)	x	x		Hulled sunflower chips, small bits of peanuts and nuts
Nuthatches	x		x	Peanuts, peanut butter, nuts
Orioles				Sugar water, oranges
Pine siskin	x		x	Niger seed
Purple finch	x		x	
Quail		x		Cracked corn, buckwheat
Robin				Bread, mealworms, dried cherries, raisins, grapes; suet must be chopped
Starlings		x	x	Any soft foods, cracked corn
Towhees		x		Grapes, raisins
Western grosbeak	x		x	
Woodpeckers	x		x	Peanuts, nut pieces, peanut-butter dough

Northern mockingbird

White-crowned Sparrow

BEST FLOWERS FOR SONGBIRDS

Flowers	Description	Conditions	Comments
Cosmos (*Cosmos* spp.)	Annuals with ferny foliage and abundant blooms in shades of pink, purple, and white (*C. bipinnatus*) or yellow and orange (*C. sulphureus*) in summer reaches to 4'.	Sun. Average soil. All zones.	Grow cosmos for the pleasure of its flowers, which attract butterflies, as well as for its plenteous seeds, which bring in goldfinches and other small songbirds by the dozens.
Purple coneflower (*Echinacea purpurea*)	Rosy pink-purple daisies with drooping petals rise 2–3' above a basal rosette of foliage from midsummer to frost.	Sun. Average to dry soil. Zone 3.	Easy to grow. A favorite of goldfinches.
Sunflowers, annual and perennial (*Helianthus* spp.)	Familiar, cheerful faces with red, orange, or rusty petals and centers full of the tasty seeds that birds love. Blooms in late summer. Grows to 10' or more.	Full sun; some perennial species also in part to full shade. Adapts to almost any garden soil. Annuals, all zones; most perennials. Zones 4 to 10, depending on the species.	The top choice for birds and birdwatchers. Easy to grow.
Tickseed sunflowers (*Bidens aristosa, B. pilosa*)	Self-sowing annuals with immense mounds of lacy green foliage smothered in golden daisies in late summer. Reaches to 5'.	Sun to moderate shade. Average garden soil. All zones.	Abundant self-sowers; use mulch to control unwanted seedlings or plant where they are free to spread. Top nectar plants for many butterflies. Oil-rich seeds of these sunflower relatives are relished by birds. Lack the annoying "stick-tight" prongs of their relatives.
Tithonia (*Tithonia rotundifolia*)	Hot orange-red daisies cover this large, bushy annual in late summer. A plant can reach 8' tall and 6' wide in a single season. Leaves and stems are velvety soft.	Full sun. Average soil. All zones.	Makes a great instant privacy hedge with the bonus of butterflies, hummingbirds, and later, seed-eating songbirds. Great cut flower.
Zinnias (*Zinnia* spp.)	Old garden favorites and still worth growing for their colorful daisy flowers and bird-friendly seeds. Blooms from summer through frost. Reaches 1–3'.	Sun. Average soil. Annual species, all zones. Perennial *Z. grandiflora*, Zones 5 to 10. Drought-tolerant.	Simple to grow; great for a child's garden. Enjoy them as cut flowers, too. Finches and buntings love the seeds.

BEST GRASSES FOR SONGBIRDS

Grasses	Description	Conditions	Comments
Foxtails (*Alopecurus* spp.)	Annual, midheight grasses with upright or arching, fuzzy "tails."Reaches 2–3′.	Sun. Average, well-drained soil. All zones.	Self-sows rampantly, but seeds are beloved by birds.
Indian grass (*Sorghastrum nutans*)	Perennial 5–7′ grass with delicate panicles of golden brown.	Sun. Average, well-drained soil. Zones 4 to 9.	Small songbirds eat dropped seeds. Previous season's dead leaves collected for nest-building.
Japanese silver grass (*Miscanthus sinensis*)	Perennial grasses, usually 3–6′ tall, with fluffy plumes that persist into winter.	Sun. Average, well-drained soil. Zones 5 to 9.	Seeds are not eaten by birds, but the large clumps offer good winter shelter if planted in a group, and the previous season's dead leaves are valued for nest-building in spring.
Millets (*Milium* spp.)	Annual 1–2′ grasses with sprays of small, round seeds.	Sun. Average, well-drained soil. Grow as annual. All zones.	Sow white or red millet in thick stands and let the birds harvest it themselves.
Sorghum (*Sorghum bicolor*)	Robust annual grass, much like corn, with densely clustered erect seedheads. Reaches 3–5′.	Sun. Average, well-drained soil. Grows as annual. All zones.	A favorite of blackbirds and sparrows. Seedheads are decorative in dried arrangements.

Indian grass (*Sorghastrum nutans*)

Japanese silver grass (*Miscanthus sinensis*)

BEST SHRUBS FOR SONGBIRDS

Shrubs	Description	Conditions	Comments
Blueberries (*Vaccinium* spp.)	Deciduous shrubs ranging from 1′ lowbush types to 15′ highbush. All have waxy white flowers in spring and delicious berries favored by people and wildlife.	Sun to partial shade. Moist, fertile, acid soil. Zones 4 to 9; lowbush to Zones 3 to 9.	Easy to grow; add plenty of leaf humus to borderline soils and mulch with oak or beech leaves. Excellent red fall color.
Elderberries (*Sambucus* spp.)	Several native and European species, all worth growing for their abundant flower clusters in early summer and purple, black, red, or blue berries in midsummer. Reaches to 10′ or more, depending on species.	Sun to shade. Adaptable to most soils, but thrive best in rich, moist, humusy soils. Most are hardy in Zones 4 to 9.	A favorite of band-tailed doves, bluebirds, and other thrushes, waxwings, thrashers, and other birds.
Hollies (*Ilex* spp.)	Evergreen shrubs or trees with glossy leaves and abundant red berries in fall and winter. Reaches 3-50′, depending on species and cultivar.	Sun to shade, depending on species. Most are hardy in Zones 5 to 9.	Holly berries are much sought by wintering and migrating robins, as well as mockingbirds, waxwings, and other berry eaters. The American holly tree (*I. opaca*), which reaches 50′, is an excellent choice. Plant both male and female hollies for berry production.
Sumacs (*Rhus* spp.)	Small trees or shrubs with tropical-looking foliage and spires of densely packed, often fuzzy, small berries in fall. Most have outstanding fall color. Reaches 5–20′, depending on the species.	Sun to shade. Almost any soil. Tolerates drought. Most are hardy in Zones 4 to 9.	Shining sumac (*Rhus glabra*) is especially beautiful, with glossy foliage and knock-your-socks-off red fall color. Birds love the berries of all species. Bluebirds are particularly fond of sumac.
Viburnums (*Viburnum* spp.)	Deciduous and evergreen shrubs, with clusters of often highly fragrant flowers in spring and abundant berries in fall. Reaches 4–10′ or more, depending on the species.	Most hardy in Zones 4 to 9, depending on species.	Plant a variety of these easy-care shrubs. They mix together well in shrub borders and hedges and make good accents. The berries of arrowwood (*V. dentatum*) are especially favored by songbirds, including bluebirds and other thrushes.

BEST TREES FOR SONGBIRDS

Trees	Description	Conditions	Comments
Beeches (*Fagus* spp.)	Graceful, large trees to 60′ or more with smooth bark and glossy, tannin-rich foliage.	Sun to shade. Rich, moist, acid soil. Most species hardy in Zones 4 to 8, depending on the species.	American beech (*F. grandifolia*) bears large crops of tasty, small seeds much sought by jays, chickadees, nuthatches, woodpeckers, and other nut-eaters. Beech is slow-growing; plant for the future.
Cherries (*Prunus cerasus, P. pensylvanica, P. avium, P. virginiana*, and other fruiting spp.)	Cherry trees, to 100′ depending on species, bear masses of small-stone fruits that are beloved by birds. Clouds of white flowers in early spring add to their appeal.	Sun to shade, depending on species. Most are very cold-hardy, Zones 2 to 6, depending on the species.	Introduce a few of the native species into your wild garden. Wood warblers and other insectivorous birds are attracted by the insects drawn to the tree when it is in flower. Vireos and tanagers, among many other birds, relish the fruit.
Hackberry (*Celtis occidentalis*)	Deciduous tree, usually about 50′ but can reach 90′. Smooth gray bark studded with odd warts and growths. Light green leaves, inconspicuous flowers, and huge crops of small, hard fruits.	Sun to shade. Widely adaptable; thrives in poor conditions. Zones 3 to 8.	Easy to grow. Attracts large groups of migrating songbirds in late summer through early fall when its fruit hangs ripe for the picking. Fallen fruit sustains winter robins and other birds, as well as small mammals.
Hemlocks (*Tsuga* spp.)	Evergreen trees to 100′ with fine-textured needles and tiny cones.	Part to full shade. Cool, moist, rich soil. Best in cool climates, though Carolina hemlock (*T. caroliniana*) will grow in the humid Midwest. Zones 4 to 9, depending on the species.	Dense foliage provides good cover for birds. Cones are a source of food. Western hemlock (*T. heterophylla*), hardy to Zone 7, is a good choice in the Northwest.
Mulberries (*Morus* spp.)	Tall, deciduous trees to 100′ with multitudes of small purple, black, or white berries.	Sun to part shade. Will grow almost anywhere. Most are hardy in Zones 4 to 9.	Not a beauty, but a favorite of birds. Plant it away from walkways and driveways. Orioles, tanagers, grosbeaks, and many others feast on the berries.

Butterflies are pickier than a four-year-old when it comes to food for their larvae. They look for very specific plants. Monarch caterpillars eat only milkweed. Most others are just as selective: Hackberries lay eggs on elm; spicebush swallowtails go for (what else?) spicebush; zebra swallowtails look for pawpaws. When the eggs hatch, the first meal is right under their feet. Many caterpillars spend their entire lives on a single plant, never leaving unless the food runs out.

It's amazing how fast butterflies will find your garden if you offer suitable host plants. If you've ever grown broccoli, you've seen this in action. Those white butterflies flirting over your veggie garden are checking out a future home for their caterpillars.

The Dangers of Pesticides and Herbicides

Pesticides and herbicides are the number one enemy of beautiful butterflies. Pesticides kill off adults and caterpillars. (Ever stop to think what that creepy green caterpillar on your roses might turn into?) And herbicides take care of future generations by destroying the "weeds" that butterflies lay their eggs on. Even the nat-

▲ *Look closely at an Eastern black swallowtail to see the cloud of powdery blue and bright orange eyespot on its outer hind wing. Lure them to your garden with parsley, dill, Queen Anne's lace, or carrot plants for the caterpillars and nectar sources such as phlox and milkweed.*

◄ *A lavish spread of easy-to-grow zinnias will draw dozens of butterflies to your garden.*

SAVED BY THE COMPUTER

Black swallowtail caterpillars eat only plants in the carrot family, like dill, parsley, and Queen Anne's lace. I used to think that any particular black swallowtail caterpillar would eat all of those plants, but I learned differently when I found a group of five swallowtail caterpillars on my very last stalk of dill in the garden.

At the same time, I was also hosting a brood of swallowtails on parsley in the vegetable garden, and there was a third brood working on Queen Anne's lace near the driveway.

Wanting to raise a few butterflies, as I do every year, I took the dill stalk and its inhabitants indoors to a sunny windowsill. I filled their jar with fresh-picked parsley and waited for them to chow down. But they weren't interested. I tried Queen Anne's lace. Same deal. My caterpillars were hungry, but they wanted dill. Those caterpillars on the other plants must have come from different stock.

I made a quick trip to the supermarket and came back with a tiny $2 bunch of dill. When I put it in the jar, they fell upon it like wolves. They were hungry—much too hungry. That expensive dill wouldn't last long. I scoured friends' gardens and begged whatever dill I could find, but it was the end of summer and all I ended up with was a paltry bunch. Maybe it would hold them for the next week, I thought, and then they'll go into the chrysalis stage.

No luck. They ran through it in three days and were even bigger and more voracious. Every greengrocer for 40 miles around was out of dill. I was desperate. So I put out a message on CompuServe, the electronic communication service. The next morning, a fat package arrived by Federal Express, sent by an electronic friend. I could smell it as soon as I opened the door—fresh, fragrant dill! My caterpillars were saved. (And my very curious FedEx man felt like a hero.)

In two days, the caterpillars went into the chrysalis stage, transforming into elegant, pointed sarcophagii that hatched in another two weeks into fabulous, velvety black swallowtail butterflies. They clung to my fingertips as I carried them outside to release them, blissfully unaware of how close to oblivion they'd come.

ural control *Bacillus thuringiensis* (BT) is deadly to butterflies and moths. It kills "leaf-eating caterpillars," and that includes just about every single one. Spray BT on your young oak to protect against gypsy moths, and you wipe out future lunas, cecropias, and everything else on the leaves, along with the pests.

Our American penchant for tidiness has eliminated too much prime butterfly habitat. Every highway roadside that's mown like lawn grass could be supporting hundreds of butterflies if it were left to grow naturally.

The vivid orange-red flowers of tithonia are a standout in the garden and a favorite of butterflies and hummingbirds. Finches scour the plants for tasty seeds when the flowers have finished blooming.

BE A CATERPILLAR DETECTIVE

Once you start looking for their calling cards, you'll find caterpillars all over your garden. Check your plants for any of these three telltale signs that say a caterpillar is at home.

- Chewed leaves. Look for holes and bare ribs in leaves. Or look for totally denuded stems. When I noticed that almost every leaf was missing from a bur marigold, I thought I was too late to catch the caterpillar. Then I noticed that one of the "twigs" was actually a brown-green pillar. He was clinging with his hind feet, his body sticking out from the stem at exactly the same angle as the rest of the bare branches.

- Frass, or caterpillar droppings. Watch for collections of tiny pellets, usually dark brown or black, on leaves or in leaf axils at a stem. When a new brood of question marks hatches in the oak tree over our driveway, I follow their growth by watching the frass on the roof of our white car: At first it looks like ground pepper, then coarse ground pepper, then peppercorns.

- Web shelters. Some caterpillars, such as the red-spotted purple, draw a leaf together with webbing to make a shelter. Be careful, though—spiders do the same thing. Don't poke your finger in and get caught unawares.

Once you find a caterpillar, it's fun to figure out just what it is. Check photos or drawings in field guides. You can narrow down the possibilities by identifying the host plant it's eating—many caterpillars have favorite food plants.

A mix of colorful, long-blooming flowers is guaranteed to bring nectar-seeking butterflies to your garden. Keep them there by supplying trees, shrubs, and other host plants for caterpillar food.

Nasturtium is a sprawler, not a true climber, but you can coax it along a fence or up a trellis to bring the bright flowers, and the butterflies that visit them, into easy view.

To be a friend of the butterflies, you'll have to overcome any neatnik urges in your own garden. The easiest way to boost butterfly numbers in your garden is to let a corner get a little weedy. You don't have to grow thistles—unless you want your neighbors to be really fond of you—but you can nurture clover, asters, sandvine, milkweeds, and seedling trees. Whatever crops up is likely to become home to one kind of butterfly larvae or another.

The Fine Art of Puddle-Making

If anybody ever saw me driving down the dirt road by our house, they might put in a call to the county sheriff: I weave from one side to the other like a

drunken fool. It's not because I've been tippling, though. I'm trying to avoid the butterflies congregating at the mud puddles in the road. Yellow, white, and orange sulphurs, little blues, red-spotted purples, big, gorgeous swallowtails, and other beauties cluster around the edges of the puddles, drinking from the mud. Their delicate proboscis probes the mud, drawing up water and minerals like a portable drinking straw.

I use the same idea to draw butterflies to my garden. My installation methods are primitive: To create a mud puddle, I simply run the hose for about five minutes at about 11 A.M. each morning on a bare, somewhat gravelly patch of earth. For true puddle butterflies, it's not necessary to have standing water. Mud is what they're after.

REGIONAL BUTTERFLY CHECKLIST

Butterflies vary by region, just as birds and wildflowers do. The following species occur in all regions:

Orange sulphur
Clouded sulphur
  (yellow sulphur)
European cabbage white
Spring azure

Coral hairstreak
Gray hairstreak
Common wood nymph
Monarch
Viceroy

Mourning cloak
Red admiral
Painted lady
American painted lady
Silver-spotted skipper

Common sooty wing
Tawny-edged skipper
Checkered skipper

In addition, you might see any of those listed below, depending on where you live. I like to keep an informal checklist each year. It's my own version of the Xerces Society's annual butterfly census , and it helps me gauge population changes and new visitors.

NEW ENGLAND AND THE MID-ATLANTIC
Zebra swallowtail
Giant swallowtail
Tiger swallowtail
Black swallowtail
Spicebush swallowtail
Eastern tailed blue
Banded hairstreak
Red-spotted purple
Pearl crescent

Comma
Question mark
Great spangled fritillary
Dun skipper
Southern golden skipper

SOUTHEAST AND SOUTH
Pipevine swallowtail
Zebra swallowtail
Giant swallowtail

Tiger swallowtail
Black swallowtail
Spicebush swallowtail
Sleepy orange
Cloudless sulphur
Great purple hairstreak
Eastern tailed blue
Reakirt's blue
Banded hairstreak
Gulf fritillary
Common wood nymph

Queen
Buckeye
Snout butterfly
Red-spotted purple
Pearl crescent
Comma
Question mark
Great spangled fritillary
Dun skipper
Southern golden skipper

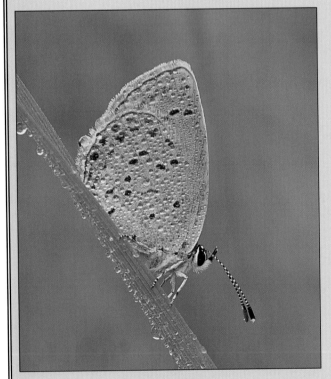

Eastern tailed blue

Question mark

MIDWEST

Zebra swallowtail
Giant swallowtail
Tiger swallowtail
Black swallowtail
Spicebush swallowtail
Eastern tailed blue
Purplish copper
Banded hairstreak
Coral hairstreak
Red-spotted purple
Pearl crescent
Comma
Question mark
Great spangled fritillary
Dun skipper
Southern golden skipper

NORTHWEST

Pale swallowtail
Two-tailed swallowtail
Western swallowtail
Anise swallowtail
Purplish copper
Lorquin's admiral
Field crescent

Great spangled fritillary
West Coast lady
Woodland skipper
Sandhill skipper

ARIZONA, CALIFORNIA, AND NEVADA

Pipevine swallowtail
Giant swallowtail
Pale swallowtail
Two-tailed swallowtail
Black swallowtail
Western swallowtail
Anise swallowtail
Sleepy orange
Cloudless sulphur
Great purple hairstreak
Eastern tailed blue
Reakirt's blue
Purplish copper
Gulf fritillary
Queen
Buckeye
Snout butterfly
Lorquin's admiral
Weidemeyer's admiral
Field crescent
Pearl crescent

Great spangled fritillary
West Coast lady
Dun skipper
Woodland skipper
Golden skipper
Sandhill skipper

MOUNTAIN WEST

Pale swallowtail
Two-tailed swallowtail
Black swallowtail
Western swallowtail
Anise swallowtail
Great purple hairstreak
Eastern tailed blue
Purplish copper
Banded hairstreak
Lorquin's admiral
Weidemeyer's admiral
Field crescent
Pearl crescent
Question mark
Great spangled fritillary
West Coast lady
Dun skipper
Woodland skipper
Golden skipper
Sandhill skipper

NEW MEXICO AND TEXAS

Pipevine swallowtail
Giant swallowtail
Tiger swallowtail
Two-tailed swallowtail
Black swallowtail
Western swallowtail
Spicebush swallowtail
Sleepy orange
Cloudless sulphur
Great purple hairstreak
Eastern tailed blue
Reakirt's blue
Banded hairstreak
Gulf fritillary
Queen
Buckeye
Snout butterfly
Red-spotted purple
Weidemeyer's admiral
Pearl crescent
Question mark
West Coast lady
Dun skipper
Golden skipper
Sandhill skipper

Lorquin's admiral

Purplish copper

Common sulphurs are found in almost any open country, including clover meadows, parks, and pastures. They also congregate at mud puddles. The male's wings have solid black borders; the female's have a spotted border.

Literate butterfly lovers appreciate the comma butterfly and its close relative, the question mark, which carry distinctive marks of punctuation on their outer hind wings. Look for commas in clearings, glades, and open woods.

If you make a mud puddle a feature of your garden, you'll attract more than butterflies. Chances are you'll also find toads if you look for them at night. They wait for earthworms to leave the saturated soil, then gulp them down. Usually a few gulps is all it takes to get a wriggler down the hatch, but once I saw a small toad using his "hands" to help shove the worm in. Robins will look for worms at your puddle, too, and they'll collect mud for nest-building. (By the way, if you see a robin with a balding breast, it has already built its nest: Smoothing out the cup of mud causes wear and tear on the feathers.)

Water in a Saucer

For the butterflies that prefer to drink water rather than mud, I fill a large, shallow, clay saucer with coarse gravel and pour in water. This stays wet all day, even in hot summer, and draws some of my favorite butterflies.

Usually the first to arrive are the fluttery brown-gold hackberry butterflies and the anglewings, mostly commas and questionmarks. Anglewings are a common type of butterfly that looks like a leaf when its wings are closed: Not only is the color right, but the edges of the folded wings are scalloped like the margin of a dead leaf. And questionmarks' closed wings boast punctuation marks that look like they've been painted on with Wite-Out. Like a bunch of impatient chickadees at the feeder,

With wings closed, the red admiral is an understated beauty. But when this butterfly opens its wings, the shocking red stripes are stunning. It's likely to alight on your head or shoulder while you stroll the garden.

the golden-brown butterflies brush against my ankles as soon as I pull out the hose.

Red admirals stop by for a drink at the saucer, too. They're bigger butterflies, with dark brown wings slashed with a brilliant red stripe and a dash of white. Like the hackberry tribe, they're completely unafraid of me. They often ride on my shoulder or my hat while I work in the garden or walk to the mailbox.

I'm always delighted when a red-spotted purple shows up at my butterfly watering saucer. These elegant creatures seem like they should be rarities, but they're as common as starlings around here. Like most butterflies, the undersides of their wings aren't as pretty as the tops. In fact, they look like two different species altogether, depending on which side you're looking at. Underneath, they're drab brownish blue spotted with Chinese red, but seen from above, they're as gorgeous as the blue morpho butterflies of the Tropics. Their velvety, matte-black wings are overlaid with a sheen of cobalt blue and powdered with vivid turquoise along the edge.

A WELL-MEANING DEATH TRAP

Commercially made butterfly feeders are big sellers, but I have yet to find one that I like. Last year I bought a yellow plastic contraption that was as poorly designed as it was ugly. It looked like a giant yellow daisy, as gaudy as a pink flamingo in the garden.

A plastic cover with grids for feeding spots covers the reservoir of sugar water. Butterflies liked the sugar water all right, and so did honeybees, yellowjackets, and bald-faced hornets. But the stinging insects weren't the real problem. The main reason I pitched the feeder was because it was a death trap.

The moat in the center is supposed to stop ants, but instead it trapped small butterflies, which managed to get in but couldn't climb out. Panicked, they battered their wings in the narrow space until they were broken wrecks. Every time I walked by the feeder, I had to free damaged butterflies or scoop dead ones out of the moat.

You can make a better, safe feeder yourself. Just put a piece of metal screening over a small saucer of sugar water. I set my sugar feeders on top of a post for easy viewing.

More Than Nectar

Nectar isn't the only thing on the menu for butterflies. Some species have truly disgusting eating habits. Roadkill and other carrion are big favorites with hackberry butterflies, red-spotted purples, and admirals. Dead snakes are a particular delicacy, and in summer, I stir up clouds of butterflies every time I drive past a flattened opossum or raccoon. Though it seems

---

CAN'T-FAIL CONCOCTIONS

When I saw how butterflies, moths, and big, interesting beetles flocked to oozing sap on the bark of our very old, very decrepit oak tree, it gave me an idea. Why not try to replicate that sap and paint a tree with it?

Actually, the idea wasn't original. I vaguely remembered reading about such concoctions in one of the old turn-of-the-century butterfly books in my collection. The first old book I checked had a guaranteed-to-work recipe, but I wasn't sure where to locate one of the crucial ingredients: "one rank-smelling snake, dead four days or longer." Fortunately, the next book suggested a mixture of beer and sugar. I mixed it up, but it was so runny it wouldn't stick, maybe because I used granulated white sugar.

Finally I came up with my own recipes, which work like a charm:

1 bottle flat beer (open the bottle and let it sit the day before you make up the recipe)
2 boxes dark brown sugar
4 mashed bananas

or:

1 bottle molasses
½ cup cheap rum
1 cup water

I slosh the stuff together with a wooden spoon in a plastic bucket, then use a big paintbrush to apply it to tree trunks, fence rails, and an old stump along the paths in my woodland garden. Butterflies gather as soon as an hour after application, and at night, moths and beetles come to feast. I reapply the bait every day for about a week, then weekly after that.

MOONLIGHT GARDEN DESIGN

Enjoy your garden in a whole new light by planting light-colored and white flowers that show up prettily at night. Delight all your senses by including flowers with fabulous evening fragrance, too.

If you like to entertain without a lot of fuss, a moonlight garden is the perfect place for a party on a balmy summer's eve. Your guests can have the fun of watching night-bloomers like the moonflower vine open their flowers, and no one will ever notice if you've been less than perfect about weeding.

Watch for night visitors in your moonlight garden. Bats may swoop down to scoop up insects at flowers, and big sphinx moths will hum at blossoms like night-flying hummingbirds.

PLANT LIST

1. Honeysuckle (*Lonicera japonica* or *L. fragrantissima*)

2. Sweet alyssum (*Lobularia maritima*)

3. Pale evening primrose (*Oenothera pallida*)

4. Night-scented stock (*Matthiola bicornis*)

5. Petunias (*Petunia integrifolia*)

6. Tobacco (*Nicotiana rupestris*)

7. Lemon lilies (*Hemerocallis flava*)

8. Moonflower vine (*Ipomoea alba*)

9. Yucca (*Yucca filamentosa*)

10. Evening primrose (*Oenothera biennis* and other spp.)

11. Madonna lilies (*Lilium candidum*)

12. White-flowered Japanese wisteria (*Wisteria floribunda*)

13. Formosa lilies (*Lilium formosanum*)

14. 'Ida Miles' daylilies (*Hemerocallis* 'Ida Miles')

15. 'Eenie Weenie' daylilies (*Hemerocallis* 'Eenie Weenie')

16. Moonflower (*Datura inoxia* ssp. *inoxia*, also sold as *D. meteloides*)

17. Flowering tobacco (*Nicotiana sylvestris*)

18. 'Mt. Fuji' phlox or other white cultivars (*Phlox paniculata* 'Mt. Fuji')

19. Flowering tobacco (*Nicotiana alata*)

20. Night phlox (*Zaluzianskya capensis*)

21. Four-o'clock (*Mirabilis jalapa*)

22. Night-blooming cereus (*Selenicereus, Hylocereus, Peniocereus,* and other genera)

Moths: Creatures of the Night

Have you ever wondered why some flowers are night-scented, saving their sweetest fragrance for the dark? Those flowers are sending a come-hither call to pollinating moths, which home in on the scent.

On languid summer evenings, when the smell of honeysuckle hangs in the heavy air, I often walk over to the hedgerow to watch the moths at work. Sometimes six or more sphinx moths will be feeding at the vine, setting the clusters of flowers quivering from the motion of their wings.

It may not warm your heart to learn that many of the moths that come to drink at the flowers in your night garden are Jekyll-and-Hyde characters: While they add grace to the night garden, their caterpillars (including

Trumpet honeysuckle is better suited to hummingbirds than butterflies, but sphinx moths, which have extra-long "drinking straws," probe the blossoms at night.

HUMMINGBIRD MOTHS

When we were kids, my sisters and I were convinced that baby hummingbirds frequented our butterfly bush. Their wings buzzed at light speed like hummers, and they had the same habit of hovering at a flower. One day, my older sister managed to capture one in a milk bottle. When we all took a close look at it, we could hardly believe our eyes: It was unmistakably an insect, not a baby hummingbird at all.

In fact, it was a clearwing moth. The common clearwing is a species of sphinx moth, related to those big, dusky, hummingbirdlike moths that hover at your moonflowers at night. But unlike the other sphinx moths, the common clearwing flies during the day, hovering at flowers to drink nectar, just like a hummingbird.

Its body can vary in color, but it is usually an almost metallic green just like a hummingbird. And the scales on its wings wear off soon after it hatches, leaving the wings transparent, with dark edges. It even has a little tuft at its hind end that looks like a hummingbird tail. No wonder this insect fools so many of us!

It's easy to mistake this sphinx moth for a hummingbird. It even flies during the day, unlike other species, which are night-fliers.

Pristine and perfect, the large blossoms of moonflower vine release a heady perfume when they unfurl at dusk. They self-sow, with restraint, even in cold-winter areas.

tomato hornworms, tobacco hornworms, sweet potato hornworms, cutworms, and armyworms) can be detested garden pests. Not to worry, though: In the well-balanced state of a natural landscape, these caterpillars rarely reach threatening numbers. Birds, mice, shrews, and other predators will soon pick them off.

Moonflowers are another night delight. I wouldn't go a summer without them. I grow the vines in a wooden half-barrel on my deck, where they climb almost to the peak of the roof, aided by a tracery of strings. These big morning-glory relatives open at dusk, unfurling their petals while you watch. Like evening primroses (another night-garden plant that I wouldn't be without), the flowers release a delicious whiff of scent when they twirl open. Sit nearby, and it smells like you've been spritzed by the atomizer of a perfume bottle.

As soon as night-blooming flowers open, moths are there to greet them. Unlike butterflies, many moths extend their proboscis while flying to suck up nectar from the flower. That tomato hornworm you despise in your garden turns into a five-spotted hawkmoth, a dusky flier with a 4- to 5-inch wingspan and an extra-long sipping straw—its proboscis may extend 6 inches or more!

HOST PLANTS FOR MOTHS

❧❧

To boost the population of moth caterpillars in your garden, and thus the adult moths (which will come to the host plants for egg-laying), nurture the native plants of your region. Many of the most common shade trees are popular host plants for pretty, harmless moths. (Pest moths usually seek out the leaves of vegetables or food crops.) Trees like acacia, alders, apple, ashes, birches, cherries, elms, fringe-tree, hickories, honey locust, maples, oaks, pawpaw, plums, poplars, sweet gum, tulip tree, walnuts, and willows are favorites for moth caterpillars. They also like shrubs like ceanothus, sassafras, and spicebush, as well as perennial plants like milkweeds, mints, and plantains.

Cecropia moths are as richly patterned as an antique paisley shawl. Look for the large red and white crescents on the hind wings. Wingspread can reach 7 inches.

Odd as it seems to us, many moths lack functioning mouthparts. Once they have wings, these insects never eat. They live only for love, emerging from their cocoons for the sole purpose of propagating the species. Their lives may be as short as a few days; at most, they live a couple of weeks. Some of the most beautiful moths meet this fate. Among them are two groups of familiar moths:

❧ Giant silk moths, which include the pink and brown cynthia moth, the Chinese-red and brown cecropia and Glover's moths, the rusty orange ceanothus and polyphemus moths, and the ethereal, celadon-green luna. Their wings can reach from 4 to 6 inches across.

❧ Tiger moths, including the dalmationlike leopard moth, the highly colored garden tiger and virgo tiger moths, and the clymene moth, whose wing markings form a fleur-de-lis when closed. The familiar brown and black woollybear caterpillar grows up to be a rather plain-Jane tiger moth, with golden-tan wings.

Moths give you a great reason to spend time in your garden at night, when you're home from work and can really enjoy it. Nectar-drinking types will visit your night-blooming or light-colored flowers, and others will seek mates and host plants in the hospitable habitats you've created. Just one glimpse of a luminous luna or a majestic cecropia will make you a moth gardener for life!

There's no mistaking a luna moth, the beauty queen of the night fliers. Delicate purple-brown traceries along the wing edges resemble twigs and buds.

Another Dimension of Beauty

Harriet Hadley Clark
West Chester, Ohio

"I love to look at what's happening in my garden," says Harriet Hadley Clark, who creates and maintains gardens for butterflies both at her home and at the Cincinnati Nature Center, where she is a staff naturalist. "I'll go out and see something I didn't anticipate at all. When I walked near the sweet rocket in bloom last May, I saw a cabbage butterfly looking funny, kind of wobbling around. When I got close, I saw it was being eaten by a crab spider. Now, crab spiders are usually yellow, but this one was lavender and white—exactly the color of the sweet rocket!"

Harriet has been fascinated by butterflies and moths since she was a child. At the age of ten or so, she found a cocoon in the huge sycamore that shaded her childhood home. She brought the cocoon onto a screened porch, and it hatched into a beautiful polyphemus moth—a female, as it happened. The next hot, humid night, more than a dozen male polyphemus moths came a-calling, rustling their velvety wings against the screen that separated them from the object of their affections.

The female moth mated and laid eggs, and Harriet raised the offspring into perfect adults. Then she branched out into cecropias and other large moths, walking around the family farm in winter to look for the cocoons. She never keeps the adults for specimen, though. "I'm very much against taking specimens for any reason. We can't afford it, with all the habitat destruction that's gone on."

Harriet encourages a diversity of plant types on her property. "I made it a point to landscape using as many larval foods as I could find," she says. Tulip tree, for instance, is a very attractive plant, even when young, and its foliage is food for the caterpillars of tiger swallowtails and promethea moths.

"It makes sense to have a wildflower garden," she points out, "since these are the plants that native butterfly species evolved with." Violets start the season, and Harriet lets them fill her beds and wander into the grass. They're the only food plant of the fritillary, she says. There's something in bloom from April to October in her half-acre back yard, including lots of purple flowers, such as purple coneflower, butterfly bush, Joe-Pye weed, and monarda 'Violet Queen', which are particularly attractive to nectar-seeking butterflies. Milkweeds are always a standard in the garden, both common milkweed and the hot-colored butterflyweed.

"Butterflies prefer an all-you-can-eat buffet to a progressive dinner," says Harriet. She gives them drifts of flowers, many plants of a single kind all blooming at once.

Sweet rocket (*Hesperis matronalis*) is a mainstay of Harriet's gardens. The sweetly fragrant, rosy-purple or white flowers are highly attractive to butterflies. The shade-tolerant sweet rocket self-sows along the woodland edge of her garden, where it now makes a long strip several feet wide that blooms for weeks.

Pink-purple, deliciously fragrant, old-fashioned phlox fills two big beds. "The fragrance is so wonderful," says Harriet. "I've had tiger swallowtails, spicebush swallowtails, great spangled fritillaries, and several kinds of skippers all visiting at once."

"I love the fragrance and the color of the garden, but even more I love the activity of butterflies, hummingbirds, and insects," Harriet says. "It adds a dimension of interest that's better than just the beauty of the flowers."

Harriet is equally intrigued by caterpillars. "You know, you can't have a butterfly population without healthy caterpillars," she explains. She includes many host plants for caterpillars among her flowers, from rue to milkweed, and even a patch of stinging nettle. She and the butterflies share the garden without conflict, even when it comes to broccoli, a favorite host plant for cabbage whites. "I have many cabbage butterflies in my garden," she says, "but I've also observed paper wasps collecting the caterpillars. It all balances out if you leave it alone."

"The garden isn't 'perfect'," says Harriet, laughing at the notion of artificial perfection. "A butterfly garden has to tolerate some wildness. If there are chrysalises on the stalks of your flowers, you don't want to cut everything down at the end of the season. My garden provides a habitat for all creatures that come. It's beneficial as well as beautiful."

◀ *This garden has the perfect combination of elements to make it appealing to butterflies. Nectar plants offer sweet bounty from early spring to frost, and trees, shrubs, and other plants feed growing caterpillars.*

▼ *Tall purple Joe-Pye weed, Queen Anne's lace, asters, and coneflowers are staples in this wild garden.*

BEST SHRUBS FOR BUTTERFLIES

Shrubs	Description	Conditions	Comments
Blue spirea (*Caryopteris* spp.)	Open, small-foliaged, gray-leaved, woody perennial or shrub with filmy clusters of light to medium blue or blue-purple flowers in late summer. Grows 3-5′ tall and 3′ wide.	Full sun. Loose soil with excellent drainage. Most species, Zones 5 to 9.	Late-blooming flowers are highly attractive to butterflies.
Butterfly bushes (*Buddleia* spp.)	Deciduous or semievergreen shrub to 10′ or more with conical spires of flowers at each branch tip in summer Grows 4–5′ wide.	Full sun. Ordinary soil. Zones 5 to 9, depending on the species.	Flowers are sweetly fragrant. Many cultivars are available.
Ceanothus (*Ceanothus* spp.)	Deciduous or evergreen shrubs with dense form and abundant clusters of tiny, usually blue or blue-purple flowers in spring and summer. Grows 1–6′ tall or more; width varies.	Full sun. Average to dry soil. Most are hardy only to Zone 8, except for white-flowered New Jersey tea (*C. americanus*) and western snowbrush (*C. velatinus*), which are hardy to Zone 4. Most thrive to Zone 10 (maximum)	Blooms last for weeks.
Privets (*Ligustrum* spp.)	Deciduous or evergreen shrubs or small trees with small leaves and highly scented, small, white flowers in summer. Grows 3–15′ tall and 4′ wide.	Full to partial sun. Average to poor soils. Hardiness depends on species; common privet (*L. vulgare*) is hardy to Zone 4. Other species, Zones 5 to 7.	An old-fashioned standard that's not often used in today's gardens. Privet is unbeatable as a dense, fast-growing hedge. The fragrant flowers attract many butterflies.

Butterfly bush (*Buddleia davidii* 'Nanho Blue')

New Jersey tea (*Ceanothus americanus*)

BEST VINES FOR BUTTERFLIES

Vines	Description	Conditions	Comments
Honeysuckles (*Lonicera* spp.)	Various species of evergreen or deciduous vines, some highly invasive, with red, yellow, white, pink, coral, or bicolor tubular flowers, usually fragrant and rich with nectar. Bloom summer through fall.	Sun to partial shade. Most soils. Most species, Zones 4 to 9.	Try coral honeysuckle (*L. sempervirens*), a beautiful, red-flowered species that attracts hummingbirds as well as nectar-seeking butterflies.
Honeyvine (*Synanchum laeve*)	Long, heart-shaped leaves and rounded clusters of extremely fragrant, small, creamy white flowers on a deciduous vine. Blooms in summer.	Full sun to partial shade. Widely adaptable. Zones 6 to 9.	This milkweed relative smells as sweet as honey and attracts nectar-seeking butterflies as well as egg-laying monarchs. Self-sows freely and can become pesty if you don't keep after seedlings.
Passionflowers (*Passiflora* spp.)	Intricate flowers of mythic religious symbolism dot these deciduous vines, followed by showy, often edible fruits. Blooms in summer.	Full sun to shade. Ordinary soil. Many are tropical; maypop (*P. incarnata*) is hardy to at least Zone 6. Most species, Zones 6 to 9.	In southern states, the Gulf fritillary lays eggs on the leaves of passionflower vines.

Coral honeysuckle (*Lonicera sempervirens*)

BEST FLOWERS FOR A NIGHT GARDEN

Flowers	Description	Conditions	Comments
Brugmansias (*Brugmannsia* spp.)	Elegant, pendant trumpets hang from the branches of these branching, tropical perennials. Blooms in summer. Reaches 3-6′ tall.	Sun. Average soil. Zones 9 and 10.	A wonderful plant for a centerpiece in a fragrant garden. Grow it in a large pot in cool climates and overwinter in a greenhouse.
Evening primroses (*Oenothera* spp.)	Perennial flowers of various height and habit, some sprawling, others erect to 5′ tall. Usually yellow, but also pink or white. Blooms in spring and summer. Most species reach 1-3′.	Full sun to light shade. Ordinary soil. Most are hardy to Zone 4 or 5 to 10.	Watch the flowers open before your eyes, with a puff of pollen and a whiff of sweet fragrance.
Impatiens (*Impatiens* × *wallerana*)	Common, tender perennial with abundant flowers in white, pink, red, or purple. To 2′, depending on the cultivar. Blooms in summer through fall.	Sun to shade. Grown as annual, all zones. Perennial only in areas without frost. Zones 9 and 10.	Common as can be, but a great flower for a night garden. White cultivars almost glow at twilight.
Moonflower vine (*Ipomoea alba*)	Tender perennial vine grown as annual in colder areas. Like a large morning glory, with heart-shaped leaves and enormous, saucer-size white flowers in summer.	Sun. Annual all zones. Perennial in frost-free areas. Zones 9 and 10.	Plan a party for early evening and watch the buds unfurl before your eyes, releasing a cloud of heavenly fragrance. Sphinx moths visit soon after the flowers open.
Nicotiana, flowering tobacco (*Nicotiana* spp.)	Annuals and perennials to 6′ tall with fragrant trumpet flowers at the top of the plant in summer.	Sun. Annuals, all zones. Perennials in Zones 9 and 10.	*N. alata* 'Fragrant Cloud' is one of the best. Avoid *N. alata* 'Nikki' series hybrids, which lack fragrance.

Evening primrose (*Oenothera speciosa*)

Impatiens (*Impatiens* × *wallerana*)

Best Food Plants for Caterpillars

You can lure your favorite butterflies into your natural landscape if you grow their caterpillars' preferred foods. Here are their favorite trees and shrubs, vines, and herbaceous plants, with the butterfly caterpillars they attract.

PLANT	CATERPILLAR ATTRACTED
Trees and Shrubs	
Birches (*Betula* spp.)	**Banded admiral, tiger swallowtail**
Chokecherry (*Prunus virginiana*)	**Tiger swallowtail, red-spotted purple, Weidemeyer's admiral**
Dogwoods (*Cornus* spp.)	**Spring azure**
Hackberry (*Celtis* spp.)	**Snout butterfly, question mark**
Hawthorns (*Crataegus* spp.)	**Pale swallowtail, Western tiger swallowtail**
Locusts (*Robinia* spp.)	**Silver-spotted skipper**
Oaks (*Quercus* spp.)	**Banded hairstreak, striped hairstreak**
Plums (*Prunus* spp.)	**Pale swallowtail, two-tailed swallowtail, western tiger swallowtail, striped hairstreak, coral hairstreak, Lorquin's admiral**
Poplars, cottonwoods (*Populus* spp.)	**Viceroy, red-spotted purple, Lorquin's admiral, Weidemeyer's admiral, mourning cloak**
Spicebush (*Lindera benzoin*)	**Tiger swallowtail, spicebush swallowtail**
Tulip tree (*Liriodendron tulipifera*)	**Tiger swallowtail**
Viburnums (*Viburnum* spp.)	**Spring azure**
Willows (*Salix* spp.)	**Western tiger swallowtail, viceroy, Lorquin's admiral, Weidemeyer's admiral, mourning cloak**
Vines	
Hops (*Humulus* spp.)	**Comma, question mark, red admiral**
Passionflowers (*Passiflora* spp.)	**Gulf fritillary**
Sandvine (*Cynanchum laeve*)	**Monarch, queen**
Wisterias (*Wisteria* spp.)	**Silver-spotted skipper**
Herbaceous Plants	
Asters (*Aster* spp.)	**Field crescent, pearl crescent**
Cleomes (*Cleome* spp.)	**European cabbage white**
Clovers (*Trifolium* spp.)**, alfalfa** (*Medicago sativa*)**, white sweet-clover** (*Melilotus alba*)	**Orange sulphur, clouded sulfur (yellow sulfur), eastern tailed blue, Reakirt's blue, marine blue, Melissa blue**
Dill (*Anethum graveolens*)**, carrot and Queen Anne's lace** (*Daucus carota*)**, parsley** (*Petroselinum crispa*)	**Black swallowtail, anise swallowtail**
Docks (*Rumex* spp.)	**Purplish copper, small copper**
Milkweeds (*Asclepias* spp.)	**Monarch, queen**
Mustard family plants (broccoli, turnips, wild mustard, etc.)	**European cabbage white, checkered white**
Nasturtium (*Tropaeolum majus*)	**European cabbage white**
Nettles (*Urtica* spp.)	**Comma, question mark, red admiral, West Coast lady, painted lady**
Pansies (*Viola* × *wittrockiana*)	**Variegated fritillary**
Pearly everlasting, pussytoes, and other everlastings (*Gnaphalium* spp., *Anaphalis* spp., and *Antennaria* spp.)	**American painted lady**
Plantains (*Plantago* spp.)	**Buckeye**
Turtlehead (*Chelone glabra*)	**Baltimore checkerspot**
Violets (*Viola* spp.)	**Meadow fritillary, variegated fritillary, Aphrodite fritillary, great spangled fritillary**
Wild petunias (*Ruellia* spp.)	**Buckeye, Texan crescentspot, Cuban crescentspot, white peacock**

Chapter 7

SPECIAL FEATURES FOR EVERY GARDEN
Paths, Walls, and Finishing Touches

Think of a stone wall as a lifetime investment. Take the time to build it right, and its architectural beauty will be around for decades. Add niches for plants, to soften the stone.

Plants that demand excellent drainage thrive in the crevices of a stone wall.

The human touches you add to your natural landscape do as much to set the mood as the plants you choose to fill your gardens. Man-made elements like fences, walls, and path materials are major attention-grabbers in a garden. If they blend in gracefully, looking like something that might have occurred naturally, they'll reinforce the relaxed attitude of the garden. But if they clash with the style of the plantings, your garden will never look right, no matter how you shift the plants around.

Natural Fence Options

When I needed to fence part of my woodland garden to keep my dogs from wandering onto the road, I started by picturing the scene in my mind. I take a seasonal approach when I do these visualizations, imagining the garden with spring wildflowers, then cloaked in summer greenery, then mellow with autumn color, and finally in the bareness of winter.

I started my imaginings with a picket fence. How would a white picket fence look around my woodland garden? Way out of place, was the instant answer: Not only would the white paint draw attention like a beacon, but it would also emphasize the rigidity of regularly spaced pickets.

But I like picket fences, so I wasn't ready to give up on the idea altogether. In my mind, I gave the fence a coat of green-gray paint—now there's a job that's much speedier in the mind's eye than it is even for Tom Sawyer!—and tried the picture again. Spring and summer were fine because the fence was hardly visible. Fall wasn't bad. But in winter, the color looked artificial.

Back to the mental paint bucket. This time I went with a deep black-green, and I modified it further by making the pickets narrower and a little more rustic in

design. In my mind, I planted shrubs against the fence here and there on both sides to create pockets of vegetation that occasionally obscured the wood. It was better, but still off.

Then I had a flash of insight: How about a weathered, unpainted fence? I kept the pickets narrow, stretched the fence a little taller, and tried it out. Perfect.

Of course, your choice of fence style is also mightily influenced by the thickness of your billfold. Luckily, compromise works well with fencing. You can use your desired, more expensive materials in short stretches, where they're most visible, and finish the job with inexpensive rolls of wire fence. Fast-growing shrubs and vines make good camouflage for the utilitarian parts of your fence. New plastic net fencing on the market, such as that sold for deer-proofing or construction, also makes a serviceable choice for fence-builders on a budget.

Make a Twig Fence

"Twig" fences are made of saplings or branches, not twigs. The name describes the style, not the materials. These fences have a rough, rustic charm that looks great in a natural landscape, and they're a good family project. Even a small section of twig fence lends immense appeal to the garden. You might use it to define the back border of your bird feeding area or to back up a bench.

To make one, you'll need a supply of branches that are about 1 to 2 inches thick and as tall as you want your fence to be. You'll also need some thicker wood, about 3 to 4 inches thick, for the horizontals and the section posts. If you don't have your own tree clippings, watch for work crews clearing utility right-of-ways or call a tree service.

Gather your branches while they're still green, and trim them to size with a hatchet. Strip off most of the smaller twigs, but leave some on to give your fence more personality. A simple picket-style fence is easy to construct. Nail the uprights to the horizontals at whatever spacing suits your fancy. Try to keep the spacing even, but don't be too rigid about it: Part of the charm of this kind of fence is its homemade imperfection. You can also lash the uprights together, using plastic twine for durability, followed by a wrapping of raffia for artsiness. If you want to experiment with a more complicated design, sketch it out on paper first. I've seen these fences done in rectangular sections, like a simple frame, with a crossed X of two pieces in each box.

Living Fences

If you're not trying to keep animals in or out, a hedgerow makes a good fence. If you want to discourage traffic from canines and others, you can plant prickly pyracantha or barberries to discourage passing through. You can also hide a simple wire fence in the bushes if needed to keep critters where they belong.

Choose plants that provide food and cover for wildlife when you plant your hedge. Viburnums, roses, brambles, and other fruiting plants are ideal candidates.

Be sure to incorporate evergreens into your hedges so that the screen is effective all year. Vary the texture by combining conifers and broadleaved types.

PLANT A LIVING FENCE

Try these plants for a living fence that attracts birds and other wildlife as well as defines boundaries. All offer superb food or shelter.

American cranberrybush (*Viburnum opulus*)
Bayberry (*Myrica pensylvanica*)
Blackberries (*Rulbus* spp.)
Evergreen hollies (*Ilex* spp.)
Hemlocks (*Tsuga* spp.)
Huckleberry and blueberry (*Vaccinium* spp.)
Japanese silver grass (*Miscanthus sinensis*)
Oregon grape hollies (*Mahonia* spp.)
Red cedar (*Juniperus virginiana*)
Red elder (*Sambucus pubens*)
Red osier dogwood (*Cornus stolonifera*)
Rhododendrons (*Rhododendron* spp.)
Serviceberries (*Amelanchier* spp.)

A FLOWERING FENCE

For a fast fence that attracts hummingbirds, butterflies, and nectar-seeking insects, try these flowering shrubs:

Blue spirea (*Caryopteris* spp.)
Bush serviceberry (*Amelanchier alnifolia*)
Butterfly bush (*Buddleia davidii*)
Chaste tree (*Vitex agnus-castus*)
Common lilac (*Syringa vulgaris*)
Privets (*Ligustrum* spp.)
Red-flowering currant (*Ribes sanguineum*)
Sand cherry (*Prunus besseyi*)

Red-flowering currant (*Ribes sanguineum*)

Simple lines and weathered wood look best in a natural garden. They set off the plants without calling undue attention to the manufactured elements in the garden.

NATURAL TOUCHES

It's always easier to play "what's wrong with this picture" than it is to decide what's right. The right garden bench can make a garden look great; the wrong furniture will stick out like a sore thumb and call attention to itself rather than to your garden. Here are some tips on choosing accessories that will match the mood of your natural garden rather than competing with it.

- Solid wood fences that create a wall seem to fade into the background.

- Fences with pickets or uprights are attention-getters. Their spaced lines create a rhythmic pattern that draws the eye. If you can't live with out a picket fence, keep the pickets taller and slimmer than usual and more closely spaced.

- Think rustic when you're choosing a fence. Roughly split rails and posts that lean a little out of kilter are better than smooth, round, sanded rails and perfectly upright posts.

- Any painted objects in the garden will shout to be noticed, unless you choose a color that blends into the greenery. Muted, grayed midrange greens, black-green, and tans or browns are possibilities.

- Unpainted, weathered wood is least distracting.

- A patina of moss or lichens helps stone and concrete hardscape become a part of the garden. Instead of faking it with spray-on recipes, let the natural process of weathering be an education in another kind of plant succession.

LEARNING FROM NATURE

To make the man-made features in your garden look like a natural part of the landscape, use nature as your inspiration.

Garden Feature	Nature	Options
Accent rocks	Stone outcropping	Groups of lichened boulders set partway into the soil—not perched on top—so they look like they've been there forever
Fences	Weathered remnants of old home-stead or farm fencing.	Fences of simple design: split rail (not round rail); tall, narrow pickets; snow fence; twig fence. Fences of natural colors—unpainted, quiet greens, gray-greens, tans, or browns
Path	Deer trail	Wood-chip path in woodland; footpath in meadow; grass or clover path. Gravel path in regions with naturally gravelly soil
Stepping stones through water or mud	Serendipitous stones or logs	Strategically placed stones or log rounds
Sitting spot	Natural objects	Flat-topped stumps; sizable, steady rocks; log bench; plank bench; unobtrusive natural wood bench
Wall	Evergreens or other natural vegetation	Wood walls planted with camouflaging vines, evergreens, and shrubs

Slope Solutions

I don't know about you, but I don't have very much mountain-goat blood in me. I'd much rather amble along level paths on a hillside than try to keep my footing on a slope. Terracing is a sensible solution that will let you get more out of your slope—not only will you be able to enjoy the garden more comfortably but you can also get a better view of it. And most important, a terraced hillside is less prone to erosion, as ancient farmers discovered millennia ago.

Making terraces is a matter of digging out soil from part of the hill and spreading it into a lower "raised bed," which you'll build out of wood or stone. I use landscape timbers, which are widely available, reasonably priced, and fairly easy to move around. Railroad ties are great, but they weigh a ton and are usually coated in creosote, which will make your whole garden smell like tar on hot days. (In addition, there is the possibility that toxins from the wood could leach into the soil.)

Like the rest of my gardens, my terraces were built in a free-form way. I didn't measure or calculate feet and

Stone terraces turn unusable space on a steep hillside into a work of art. They have their practical side, too: They prevent plants and soil on the hillside from washing away during torrential rains.

inches; I worked by eyeballing as I went. My technique went like this: "Hmmm, let's put a path along here, now another step of the terrace, a little higher, a little higher there, perfect." If this method fills you with dread, follow the formula below.

Designing Paths

I depend on my dogs, my kids, and my own feet to show me where the paths should go. If the backyard traffic takes a shortcut through a flower bed, they're trying to tell me something. Unauthorized shortcuts are a clear message that the established path misses the mark. Unless they're in the mood for aimless wandering, animals and humans want a path that's the quickest route from one place to another. If you try to force their feet onto a winding, curving detour that wastes steps, they'll outvote you and create their own switchbacks.

Build a Terrace

Before you begin digging, mark the outline of your terrace with string and stakes. Cut timbers for the sides of the beds to the length you've determined is your desired depth for each bed. Lay the first timber as shown below, then dig out the sides of the first bed, level with the bottom of the front trench and as deep as you have planned the bed. Lay in the first side timber. Repeat for the other side. Lay another front, overlapping it onto a side, then lay the sides and spike in place. Dig the soil out from the hill above to fill the bed you just made, and level it smooth. Add a back timber above the last course of sides, to form the front base of the second bed.

If this sounds like more work than you want to tackle, you might try a more informal approach. I've had good luck adding simple terraces, like a series of very broad, shallow steps, up a slope, using just a front timber or two for each step, and letting the sides of the bed roll into the natural hill. I hold the timbers in place by pounding in two stakes outside the wall. I fill in the slopes on either side of my "steps" with daylilies, butterfly bushes, and perennial hibiscus, and use the terraced steps for shorter, trailing plants, leaving a clear pathway to walk up and down.

You can also use flat, fairly thin rocks or slate or even broken pieces of paving concrete as a retaining wall for terraces. Dig a thin trench about 3 to 6 inches deep and set the stones in vertically, leaning backward, with their faces turned outward. You might think this would look artificial, but if you plant alyssum, creeping veronica, and other sprawlers to spill over the edges of the slabs, it looks almost as good as a stone wall.

Dig a shallow trench to lay the timbers for the front of the first (the lowest) bed. It only needs to be a couple of inches deep. Settle the first timber into the trench.

Lay the timbers so that their ends overlap. Spike the front and sides in place with 10-inch galvanized nails, then lay the back timber of the bed, which actually forms the bottom timber of the front of the next bed.

Continue building and filling your course of beds up the hill, measuring to make sure the depth and height are going according to plan. Dig into the hill as needed to set the sides of each bed.

Plant in the beds and along the sides, to disguise the timbers and create the illusion of a hillside of flowers. Add some low-growing plants along the front, to spill over the edge.

TERRACING: HOW MANY STEPS?

To figure out how many layers of stepped terraces you'll need, start by figuring the rise and run of the slope.

Rise is the height of the slope, the difference in height between the bottom and the top of the hill. To calculate this height, stand at the bottom of the hill with a tape measure. Stand on the end of the tape and pull it up until you can sight along it to the top of the slope. If the hill is too steep, you can do this in parts: First sight and measure to a point halfway up the slope, then walk up to that point and sight and measure the rest of it.

Run is the length of the slope, but measured as the crow flies. To calculate run, have an assistant hold the end of the tape measure at the top of the hill. Holding the tape horizontally level, walk down the slope until you can't go any farther and still keep the tape level. Note that measurement and move your assistant to that spot. Then measure the rest of the slope in the same way. Add all of the measurements together to get the run.

Once you know rise and run, you can figure out how many steps you'll need in your terrace. Decide how deep you want each step—the lateral depth, not the vertical depth, which we'll call height—then divide that depth into your run measurement. Say you want 5-foot-deep beds, and you have a run of 25 feet. You'll need five steps to accommodate your beds. If you want to add paths to your terraced slope, subtract their width before figuring the beds: Let's say we add two 3-foot-wide paths to our terraced slope. Subtract 6 feet for the paths from a run of 25 feet, and we now have 19 feet left for beds.

Rise comes into play when you're figuring the height of your beds. If you have five beds, and your rise is 10 feet, then each bed should be 2 feet high.

When I'm planning a new garden, or a new path through an old garden, I follow different guidelines for different paths. If the path is from the house to the mailbox, from the house to the driveway, or leading to any other clear destination, I plan it as a utilitarian path—an express route. If it's a path for pleasure, then I let it meander. Of course, if human or animal footprints show me that a shortcut is needed, I make sure to include a straightforward route at that point, while still giving garden visitors the alternative of a slower, less direct trail.

Utilitarian Routes

When you want to keep your paths on the straight and narrow, use these tips. They guarantee that your family and friends will stay on the path and out of your gardens.

- Keep them straight, avoiding curves if possible.
- Make the path at least 3 feet wide for easy travel when carrying packages.
- Keep the surface level and "fast," as they say at the racecourse: Don't use loose gravel that will be hard to tread; instead, use packed material that will spur your steps. Wood chips will soon pack into a dense layer that makes solid footing.
- Be sure the path is easy to see, both during the day and at night.

Garden Paths

When it's not necessary to get quickly from point A to point B, plan your paths so that you get the most you can out of your garden. You can weave your paths in curves and cross them back and forth over each other to make the stroll a longer one.

One continuous loop through the garden is the minimum when it comes to paths. A single, dead-end path that makes you retrace your footsteps coming and going isn't nearly as much fun as a path that loops around and lets you keep going without doing an about-face. I avoid dead ends unless there's a sitting area at the end of the path.

(continued on page 222)

The flat cap of stone on the bottom wall of this terrace makes an inviting sitting spot. Be sure the stones are solidly in place—not wiggly or precariously balanced, as you lay each course so that they don't shift unexpectedly.

Creative Solutions

Tom Chakas
Berkeley, California

Tom Chakas was studying art at Yale when he fell in love with gardening. "I got a job on Nantucket, working for a Portuguese gardener," he remembers. "He was a real master. Two days a week we tended these beautiful gardens. I felt really fortunate to work with him."

That love of plants and gardens infuses all of Tom's work, both in his home garden in Berkeley, California, and in the intimate gardens he creates for others through his business, Nut Hill Garden Design, named after the creative, eclectic neighborhood in which he lives.

Tom favors Mediterranean and native western plants that are naturally well-suited to the rigors of the climate. He likes to include artemisias, thymes, dwarf teucriums, and other gray-leaved plants. "I try to stay with drought-tolerant plants with interesting foliage effects, in unconventional plantings," he says.

Deer were a problem in Tom's garden, he says, "but I pretty much weeded out everything they eat. I had to eliminate deer magnets like red valerian—*Centranthus ruber*. They devoured it in one night." Raccoons, however, are welcome. "They pick out the snails and eat them," says Tom with satisfaction.

A view of San Francisco and the Bay is part of the romance of Tom's garden. "The garden is especially beautiful on foggy days," he says, "when you can really see the form of the garden and the plants. The gray-leaved plants stand out on those kind of days."

He's also entranced by fragrant plants. "I distinctly remember the first time someone held a santolina under my nose," he says. "Then I became really intrigued by strongly scented foliage—plants like artemisias and rosemary, and thymes of course. I like to be in my garden on a hot, sunny day, when the fragrances really stand out, like the spicy perfume of *Cistus ladanifera*, the crimson-spot rock rose. It just pumps out fragrance on a sunny day."

Botanical names are like a native tongue to Tom, and they roll out effortlessly as he extols the glories of his favorites. "Hummingbirds love the chaparral currant—*Ribes malvaceum*," he says, noting how well native plants like this pink-flowered shrub can fit into gardens. "If I'm watering, a hummingbird will always come around. They like to fly through the spray."

The stairway that goes up the hill at Tom's house is built of reclaimed redwood, and the path that gracefully makes its way through the abundant plantings is made of broken pieces of concrete sidewalk. "There's always some kind of sidewalk demolition going on," he notes, "and the pieces are always free for the asking." The concrete has a naturalistic appeal when laid in pieces—a completely different look than its earlier incarnation as sidewalk.

It took Tom a while to collect enough concrete pieces to make his path, but it took only a few days to lay the stones. The path traverses the hill, following a gentle rise. It's a series of terraced steps, with a sec-

These plants are desert dwellers, but the gardener has included a bit of precious water for a delightful surprise. Recirculating pumps prevent waste of water.

Tom uses artful combinations of foliage to achieve a richly textured effect throughout his garden. Smooth stone and masonry provide contrast to the plants, setting them off as specimens.

tion of path perhaps 6 feet long followed by a step up, then another stretch of path, and so on.

Tom learned quickly that it was easiest to start at the bottom and work up, not to work from the top down. "If you start at the top," he points out, "you'll be sticking pieces of concrete under the last piece when you get to the steps."

The concrete pieces are closely fitted together in a random jigsaw, but Tom purposely left gaps where things can grow. "Woolly thyme is happiest there," he says, "and perennial chamomile. They're so fragrant when you walk on them." On the steps, he planted caraway thyme for another delicious scent.

"I like to be in my garden any time of day," says Tom. "It's always different. The light in late afternoon is particularly beautiful, when the sun is setting over San Francisco and the Bay."

An overhead view of the garden shows how it makes the house a part of the landscape. Every inch is jam-packed with Tom's favorite plants for a wonderfully lush effect.

To guide family, friends, and visitors to the main paths through the garden, mark these paths with a simple ornament. Anything that draws attention to the beginning of the path will work. These are great spots to use special favorites from your own collection or any of the garden ornaments sold in shops and catalogs. Here are a few suggestions:

- A pair of rocks flanking the entrance.
- A metal ornament with black, brass, or verdigris finish. I like to use a metal stick hummingbird, butterfly, or other natural subject. Many artists are beginning to turn out wonderful, whimsical designs, like oversize praying mantids and dragonflies, made of copper that will weather beautifully.
- A small metal or concrete frog, turtle, or other animal, perched on a rock or settled in mulch.
- A special rock or a small grouping of specimens: agate, crystal, volcanic lava, or whatever you've collected.
- A cast stone or concrete Japanese lantern straddling a thick, flat rock.

NIGHT LIGHTS

If your garden gets nighttime visitors, you might add the following night lights to mark the paths:

- a solar path light
- a black iron shepherd's crook holding a hurricane chimney with candle
- a concrete or ceramic Japanese lantern with votive candle
- luminarias

For a special occasion, try handmade luminaria accents. They're fast and simple to make. The easiest way is to pour 2 inches of sand into paper lunch sacks and settle a tea candle in each. Rice paper and twig luminaria are not fast to make, but they're beautiful and elegant enough for a garden wedding: Make a four-sided framework of twigs with a glue gun, then fold heavy rice paper (from an art supply store) into a four-sided rectangle and slip it inside the twig framework. Add a tea candle in a heat-proof glass holder inside.

Stepping stones accent pathways and entice young and not-so-young visitors into striding with giant steps. For a less obvious look, you can embed the stones into the soil so that their surfaces are flush rather than raised.

Simple steps made of railroad ties make it easy to climb a hill, and they provide a showcase for plants that tumble along the edges. The vertical line and color of variegated iris foliage help mark the entrance to the steps.

Installing Low-Level Walkway Lights

A series of restrained, low-level pathway lights will make your steps surefooted after dark and show off your plants, too. Strands of electric path lights are available at any discount store. They're easy for even a novice to install, but you'll need an outdoor electric outlet within easy reach for plugging them in.

STEP 1: *Dig a shallow trench along the path where you want to install the lights.*

STEP 2: *Measure the distance to the outlet, then lay in the cord and insert the lights at appropriate spacings. Cover the trench with soil and walk on it to firm it.*

STEP 3: *Add plants around lights, being very careful not to dig into the trench where the wire is laid. Be sure the lights are unplugged until the planting is finished, so that you don't get a jolting surprise.*

The beckoning path leads the way into this woodland garden with an air of mystery. You can't help being drawn around the bend to see what lies ahead.

The width and shape of your paths have great psychological effect. A narrow path flanked by shrubbery will make passersby hurry through. Though we may not realize it consciously, our animal instincts sense danger in such close quarters. Widen a path, and footsteps slow like magic.

To make your garden seem larger, curve the paths. Sketch your plan on paper first, and you'll be surprised at how much mileage you can get out of a curving trail.

I like to allow plenty of options as to which way to go, so I include intersecting paths to give a choice of direction. Human feet don't turn corners easily, so instead of making paths meet at right or sharp angles, I widen the inside corners at intersections into curves to allow easy travel in either direction. Curved corners can be useful, too, if you want to turn traffic in a certain direction: By curving just one inside corner, you encourage travelers to move in that direction.

When I have a plant I want to show off, I widen the path into a bulge at that point. That's an effective way to slow feet, and it lets my special plant get more attention. Intersections also get a lot of attention, so they're a good place to plant your favorite specimens. Of course, I look at every plant in my garden every morning, so these machinations are more for visitors than they are for me.

I find a path of carefully laid stone a distraction, but I like to keep a sense of fun in my garden by using log rounds or stepping stones to leapfrog short distances. Stepping from one to the other makes me remember my days in the woods as a kid, when I'd squeak through bushes and undergrowth by stepping from one rock or log to another. These types of stepping stone paths are often less obtrusive than full-scale trails, so they don't interrupt the integrity of the planting design or affect the mood of the garden.

Path Materials

Some years back, a friend brought two natives of Hong Kong to visit us. The girls were high school teenagers who'd lived in the city all their lives. As we led our guests out to the table in our shady yard, they began giggling and talking excitedly to each other, meanwhile walking very oddly, with high, bouncing steps.

Was something wrong? We wanted to know. They were extremely shy, but finally they explained. Never before, they said, had they walked on grass. All they knew beneath their feet was the concrete of city life.

I tried to give them a word to describe what they were feeling, but everything I thought of—springy, spongy, firm but with a give—failed miserably. What English word can convey that delicious feeling of walking on natural grass? For that matter, how could you describe all of the sensations of walking a forest path, or a river trail, or a sandy beach? You can't come close to summing up all of the things that make an ordinary day in nature such an incredible experience. It's not just the feel of humus or turf beneath your feet, but the scents in the air, the sounds of birdsong, the play of sun and shadow.

Why surface a path at all? You may not need to. *Au naturel* paths of fallen leaves, pine needles, softly packed earth, or sand are perfectly suitable. But in my area, rains can turn an earthen path or fallen leaves into slippery city. I like sure footing beneath my feet, so I use wood

(continued on page 228)

REGIONAL PATH MATERIALS

Wood chips are usually widely available, and they make an excellent, all-purpose, low-cost path material. But regional specialties are other possibilities. Do a little research before you buy, though, to make sure you are actually using a regional resource and not encouraging the growth of an industry that decimates natural habitat. Think about your choice: Is it a by-product from a manufacturing process (such as bark chips)? Or has it been created specifically for garden use? Pine needles, for instance, are a good choice only if your pine trees shed them in quantity. Otherwise, they've probably been collected from stands of native trees, where their absence will have a negative impact on the local ecology. Here are some of my favorite path materials:

- bark chips
- cocoa-bean shells
- crushed volcanic stone (tufa)
- pine needles you collect yourself
- river pebbles
- shredded cypress bark

A few young trees, a quiet path, and a dense underplanting of wildflowers and ornamentals gives this small garden the feel of a much larger woodland. A wood-chip path quickly weathers to a soft color.

GARDEN PATHS DESIGN

Multiply the pleasure of your garden by letting paths meander wherever there's room. Include a few intersections so that garden visitors can have choices of where to go next. Use shrubs to create a sense of mystery and anticipation of what's around the next bend.

You can adapt the ideas in this design to fit your own yard and your own plants. Work the paths around the existing trees and shrubs that anchor your garden. You can start with a basic framework of paths to get you to the mailbox, house, and car, and then add others as the garden evolves. I find that paths often suggest themselves—if I keep stepping into the groundcover to get a closer look at the caterpillars on the spicebushes, I add some stepping stones up to and around the shrubs so that I have easy access.

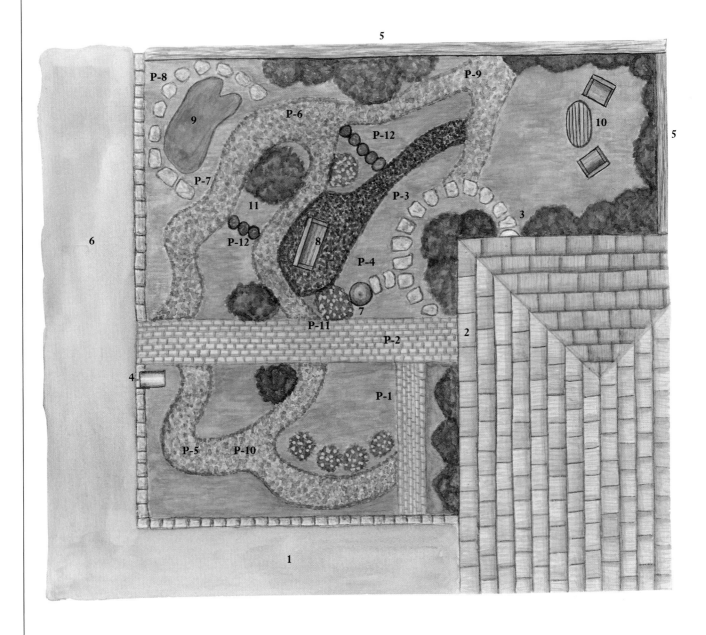

PATH DESIGN KEY

Landscape Elements

1. Driveway

2. Front door

3. Utility meter

4. Mailbox/newspaper box

5. Privacy fence

6. Street

7. Bird feeding area

8. Sitting area

9. Water garden

10. Small tea table with two chairs

11. Shrub

PATHS

Often-Used Routes:

P-1 Path from driveway to front door: Should be as direct as possible for fast, sure-footed route.

P-2 Path from front door to mailbox: Should be straight and direct for those occasions when a quick route is desired.

P-3 Connecting route from P-1 path to utility meter: Should be clearly defined for meter readers.

P-4 Connecting route from front door to bird feeding station: Should be simple and direct with good footing and wide enough to haul supplies as needed.

Optional Paths:

P-5 Alternate route back to house from mailbox: A curving path makes the garden seem larger.

P-6 Curve the path around shrubs to create a sense of mystery and anticipation.

P-7 Widen the path to slow footsteps; a narrow path makes people walk faster.

P-8 Vary materials for different feeling: Flagstones around a water garden mimic stepping stones in a pond for a casual, fun approach.

P-9 Avoid dead ends unless there is a sitting area at the end of the path. Plan paths so that there are plenty of options as to which way to go.

P-10 Instead of making paths meet at right or sharp angles, curve the corners widely to allow easy travel in either direction. Curve only one corner if you want to direct traffic toward that side.

P-11 Place a particularly interesting specimen plant at wide intersections in the path. Wide places naturally invite lingering, so spice them up with something neat to look at.

P-12 Log rounds can bridge a short distance between paths—without interfering with garden planting design. They unobtrusively guide visitors to "squeak through" a place.

chips on my paths. In a meadow garden or other sunny area, you can use wide mown grass trails as paths, or you can plant traffic-tolerant groundcovers like clover or chamomile.

Natural materials are best for natural landscapes. Wood chips are my path surface of choice for a woodland or shade garden. In these settings, they look as natural as a deer trail. They're low-cost (or free), and they only need to be renewed once every couple of years in most cases. Installation is simple: Just rake them into a layer 4 to 6 inches deep. They'll pack down under foot traffic. And maintenance couldn't be easier: Just renew them as needed—usually once or twice a year.

If you're not fond of wood chips, or if you live where trees are scarce, turn to other natural materials. Your choices will vary depending on where you live and what the terrain is like.

The Fragrant Path

Forgiveness, an old saying goes, is the scent of the violet that clings to the heel that crushed it. I find walking on flowers a little sadistic but I don't have any compunction about walking on fragrant herbs.

Creeping thyme is hardy and easy to grow, and it spreads like mad. Roman chamomile is almost as obliging. (Don't confuse the mat-forming perennial Roman chamomile with German chamomile, a kneehigh, airy annual.) Both plants are great to work into an existing grass path. Or you can put down a wood-chip path and transplant starts of the herbs here and there along it. Walk carefully for a season, and the herbs will fill in nicely. Both release a delicious fragrance when you tread on them, and they quickly bounce back if traffic isn't too heavy.

Let plants crowd the path, so that the edges of the pathway are obscured. But be sure to keep the path wide enough so that you don't feel like you need a machete to get through the jungle.

Don't try herbs on the main path to your house because their leaves will quickly get worn off. But even on the busiest thoroughfare, you can plant chamomile, thyme, or creeping pennyroyal at the edges, where they can send aromatic tendrils out into the traffic.

Building a Stone Wall

Having grown up in the Northeast, where stones are a natural harvest every time you turn the soil, my attitude toward them was as objects of annoyance rather than objects of beauty. I remember reading a national columnist's advice for naturalizing a yard full of daffodils: Loosen the soil to a depth of 2 feet, she advised, so that you could plunge your arm into the soil up to the elbow. Right, I scoffed, thinking of the skinned knuckles and broken wrist that would result if I tried to do that. Planting bulbs for me was more likely to be a matter of working with a dandelion digger and making narrow slits into the earth to nestle the bulbs into.

I admired stone walls, of course, but it never occurred to me to try to make one until we bought the old quarrymaster's house at a former slate quarry. Suddenly I had tons of rock to play with, big slabs of charcoal-colored slate 6 inches thick or better.

With such a ready supply just a short wheelbarrow's drive from my garden, I planned my first stone wall, a 30-inch-high, curved retaining wall for a raised bed of herbs and perennials.

Plants that seed themselves in unexpected places, like these California poppies, are a great choice for growing on a stone wall because the progeny are likely to spring up in the crevices of the rock. Seeds are determined to grow, and roots are incredibly adept at finding soil.

I couldn't believe how easy it was to make. Though I boned up by reading step-by-step how-to books, the actual process was as instinctive as building with my then-two-year-old's set of wooden blocks.

Before You Begin

If you're not blessed (or cursed) with an abundance of natural stone on your own place, you'll have to order it. Check the Yellow Pages under "Stone—Natural" to find

---

BACK-SAVER

You've heard it before, and it's still good advice: Lift with your legs, not your back. Bend your knees and crouch to pick up stone, boosting its weight with your heavy-duty thigh muscles when you lift. Don't bend at the waist, even though that seems easier, unless you want a long vacation at the chiropractor's office.

STONE-BUILDING BASICS

Stone walls are one of the nicest features of any landscape, but most people are afraid to build one themselves. The work is heavy but not hard, and you'll end up with attractive walls if you follow a few simple rules. Just remember to use your legs to power your lift. (See "Back-Saver" above.) And choose local stone for the most natural look.

- To make a stable wall, lay one over two: The stone on an upper layer covers the junction between two stones on the lower layer.
- If your wall will have soil behind it, angle the face so that it slants slightly backward from bottom to top. You can figure this slant before you start: 2 inches for each foot of height is recommended.
- The bottom layer of stone, or foundation layer, should be wider than the top layers. Allow about 24 inches of foundation width for a 3-foot-tall wall; if your wall is higher, figure another 4 inches of foundation width for each 6 inches of height.

---

dealers. Before you order, plan a visit to the dealer's yard to see samples of the rock. You can expect to pay about $100 or more a ton for natural stone. You'll want flat stones for easy stacking.

I was lucky to have my own rock quarry because I seriously underestimated how much rock I'd need. A couple of formulas from professionals will make it easy for you to get a handle on how much stone you need.

Use these formulas to get a ballpark estimate to see if the project fits your budget, then double-check your needs with your stone supplier. The final amount will vary somewhat depending on the type and size of the stone you select.

If your dealer sells stone by weight, your figuring is simple. Allow a ton of stone for every 25 square feet of the wall's face. To figure square feet, multiply the height of the wall times its length. A 20-foot-long wall that's 3 feet tall equals 60 square feet of face (60 ÷ 25 = 2.4 tons of stone). Allow a little extra for waste, and order 2.5 tons of stone.

If your rock yard sells by the cubic yard, you'll need to do a bit more calculating:

1. Measure the length of your intended wall in feet. Let's say 20 feet, as an example.
2. Multiply by the intended height and width. We'll make our imaginary wall 3 feet high and 12 inches wide, so 20 feet × 3 feet × 1 foot = 60 feet.
3. Divide by 27 to get the number of cubic yards, which is the measure by which stone is often sold by the truckload. In our case, 60 ÷ 27 = 2.222.
4. Add 5 percent to your cubic yard total to allow for waste—those stones that you can't gracefully fit into the wall. 2.222 × 0.05 = 0.111.
5. Add your totals from Steps 3 and 4 together: 2.222 + 0.111 = 2.333, or rounded up, 2.5 cubic yards of stone.

Garden Accents

Along with the gardening renaissance has come an explosion in art for the garden. No longer do you have to search out sornaments from antique shops. Now anybody with a phone can order all kinds of finishing touches, from Victorian gazing globes to resin gargoyles that look like they just dropped in from Notre Dame.

Remember that garden ornaments are like jewelry: It's better to have one great piece than it is to pin a

Build a Hundred-Year Wall

Building a stone wall can sound more intimidating than it really is. Keep in mind that even a petite wall can carry a lot of weight, both visually and literally. But it's really not hard to build. I revamped my mother's always-eroding front garden one year by carving a path at the bottom of her steep bank and setting in a stone wall about 18 inches high to hold the soil. I added a second retaining wall about halfway up the slope, making it just two stones high and one stone thick. The whole project took only an afternoon, and the stone "walls" set off her collection of ferns and wildflowers beautifully.

Take your time when building—you want this to last forever. The only tools you'll need are a chisel and a stonemason's hammer to whack off occasional protruding bumps that keep the stones from lying smoothly. A level is optional, but don't forget safety goggles and a long-sleeved shirt and pants so that you don't get nicked by flying chips.

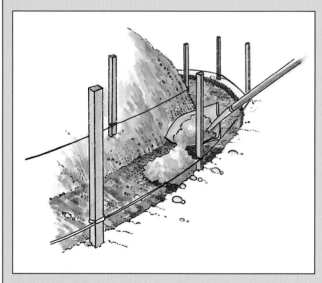

STEP 1: Mark off the area for the wall with stakes and string, then dig out existing soil and turf to a depth of 6 to 12 inches. If your wall will have soil behind it, angle the back edge of this foundation so that it slants backward. Fill with coarse gravel.

STEP 2: *Pick out some of your biggest, most level stones, and lay them on the gravel. If your stones are rectangular, lay them endwise so that the short ends are at the face. Make sure they're solid and level. You can eyeball the horizontal lay of your wall by using a piece of string tied to two stakes, raising it after each course of stone. Or you can use a carpenter's level. You're not aiming for perfect flatness, just a general impression of horizontal trueness. In other words, you don't want your wall to look like it's crooked. Fill in chinks between stones with small broken pieces or gravel. Ram them in with the end of a hoe. Pour 2 inches of soil over the base layer of stone so that it's easier to level the next layer.*

Set the next course of stone, working by the one-over-two rule. (See "Stone-Building Basics" on page 229.) This time, you can set rectangular stones so that their longest side is toward the face, except at the ends of the wall. At both ends of the wall, set a rectangular stone with the short end facing front, as on the bottom layer, digging it into the earth behind the wall for extra stability. It also adds strength to set in a stone this way about every 6 feet along the wall. If your stones are wobbly, shim them with small pieces of rock until they feel solid.

STEP 3: *If your wall is built against a slope, fill in behind the wall after each layer with broken stone and soil, packing it in solidly with your trusty hoe handle. Continue laying courses in this manner. Put aside pretty, flat, large stones as you find them to save for the top layer.*

STEP 4: *For the top layer, lay the stones as you did for the foundation, with their short ends facing the front. Finish packing the space behind the wall, and fill in with soil around the wall as you like.*

You'll want to avoid the vertical when you're choosing plants for atop the wall. Tall, upright growers look awkward; a waterfall effect is much more appealing. Rock cress, or aubrieta, is a colorful choice and an early bloomer.

Garden ornaments carry tremendous weight in the landscape. Notice how the urn in this garden immediately draws the eye. Only after we satisfy ourselves with a look at it do we turn to the plants and other parts of the garden.

This old mortar and pestle is heavy and serious, but the ceramic frog perched on the edge of the bowl instantly changes the mood to whimsical. Private garden jokes like these make a garden your own.

dozen cheap sparklers to your bosom (though there are times, I admit, when I'm in the mood for flash). Instead of lining the edges of your pond with a dozen facsimile frogs, turtles, and bunny rabbits, why not invest in a statuesque, life-size heron?

Of course, part of the fun of a natural garden is that you can hide ornaments for visitors to come upon unawares. A concealing curve in the path is a great approach to a special piece of garden art. I have a small collection of concrete frogs (some not in the best of health) that I like to move around during the season. My son likes to discover their new hiding places. Sometimes I lose track of one or another of them myself, and then it's fun to come upon them again.

Keep in mind that any object made by human hands is automatically an attention-getter in the garden. Birdhouses, butterfly shelters, and bat houses are often focal points in the natural landscape. So use them sparingly but well—you, your visitors, and wildlife will all enjoy them.

Fuchsia and impatiens do best in shade and fertile soil. Plant them where they belong and you'll be rewarded with lush growth and abundant flowers. Force them to grow in hot sun or tight-packed soil and the plants will be stunted and prone to disease.

REGIONAL GARDENING GUIDES

Invest in a regional gardening guide for your area before you begin to make wish lists of plants. With so many vagaries of climate, soil, and conditions in this huge country of ours, an all-purpose book can leave a lot of gaps. You can read between the lines in catalogs and encyclopedias when it comes to matching soil conditions, but most won't tell you if a plant needs snow cover or constant cold or other special conditions to do its best.

I also depend on catalogs from nurseries in my general area. Spend an hour or so finding nearby sources by using Gardening by Mail (see "Recommended Reading" on page 250), which lists and describes hundreds of catalogs from specialty and regional growers. You'll find woodland wildflowers for Northeast gardens, desert natives for the Southwest, prairie plants for Midwest gardens, fruiting plants that are impervious to cold, and dozens of other possibilities tailor-made to your garden.

Your county extension service or agricultural office may also be able to help, especially when it comes to suitable trees and shrubs. These offices are paid for with your taxes, so don't feel shy about calling. You'll find the phone number in the blue pages of your phone book.

farming. That's because decaying leaves and grass create wonderful soil.

In a natural landscape, you don't need to strive for that epitome of soil perfection unless your soil has been altered. If you live in a subdivision or other area where topsoil is commonly scraped off, your soil may actually be subsoil—the layer of clay or other less-than-desirable soil that underlies the rich layer of stuff that should be on top. If your house was built on farmland, years of heavy tractors and combines may have compacted it. If you have a suspicion that your soil is not all it could be, then it will be well worth your while to spend a few weekends improving it before you plant.

The easiest way to make better soil is to add organic matter, like humus, well-rotted leaves, compost, and aged manure. These readily available materials will improve your soil's texture, keeping it well aerated and helping it to hold water and nutrients so that they don't wash away with the rain. Even good soils can benefit from an inch of organic matter worked into the surface of the soil every year.

Here's my simple method to improve the soil.

1. In fall, rake a 4-inch layer of organic material onto the bare soil of your garden bed.
2. Using a spade, hoe, or fork, work the material into the top 6 inches of your soil, mixing it together well.

By late spring, the soil should be ready to plant.

Plant Matters

The most important thing you can do for your natural landscape is to choose the right plants. Be sure your selections fit the conditions of your garden—the soil, the amount of sun or shade, and the seasonal variations, as well as the USDA Plant Hardiness Zone, which is based strictly on minimum temperatures. (See page 252 for the USDA Plant Hardiness Zone Map.) I'm pleased to see that many recently published catalogs and garden references are including a range of zones in which plants can

BARGAIN TREE AND SHRUB SEEDLINGS

One of the best sources for low-cost plants I have found is the Department of Natural Resources (DNR). Many states offer packages of tree and shrub seedlings, which you order in fall and have delivered for spring planting. The plants are grown at state DNR nurseries and usually include a terrific selection of the best natives for wildlife, as well as adaptable, well-suited, non-native types.

The prices are incredibly low. In 1995, one of the DNR offerings for Indiana was a "wildlife packet" that included 25 pecan trees, 25 spruces, 10 hawthorns, 10 dogwoods, 10 river birches, 10 black gums, and 19 other species—a total of 130 plants of 25 species—for $25! Another possibility was an "outdoor lab packet" of three to four plants of each of 40 different species—90 to 120 young, healthy trees and shrubs—for $40. Other states have comparable offers.

What's the catch? The plants are sold only in large quantities, usually 50 or 100 of a single kind unless you buy the mixed packet. That sounds like a lot, but if you're landscaping a good-size property, you'll use them up fast. If you can't fit all the plants in, split the cost and the plants with a friend.

The plants are usually one- to four-year-olds, depending on the species. But young trees and shrubs grow much faster than you'd expect because they don't take as long to get established after planting. (Older nursery stock may sit in a holding pattern, showing little growth above ground for a year or longer, while the roots recover from transplanting.) In two years in the garden, these young shrubs make a decent showing, and in five years, even the trees will look substantial.

You can't beat this deal! Just be sure to schedule a weekend to plant as soon as the stock arrives. It's shipped bareroot, so you'll want to get it into the ground in a hurry. The seedlings are wrapped in brown paper, with no packing material, so put them in a bucket of water if you're planting within 24 hours. If you can't plant them that quickly, keep the roots moist in a bucket filled with wet, shredded newspaper about as moist as a lightly squeezed-out sponge. Plant within 2 days or you'll lose them.

Because these are bareroot plants, you'll need to pay attention to watering the first year. A bucket of water per plant per week is about right; the soil should never dry out completely. If your soil is fast-draining, water your plants more often.

be expected to do well, rather than including only the coldest region, for example, "hardy to Zone 6." Many plants do not take well to extremes of summer heat and humidity, and including information such as "for Zones 4 to 8" saves gardeners in mild-winter areas a lot of disappointments.

Of course, we gardeners are well known for trying to bend the rules. I still haven't given up on growing hardy fuchsia (*Fuchsia magellanica*), though it freezes to the ground every winter. It's supposedly hardy only to Zone 7, yet it flourishes in my mother's Zone 6 garden in Pennsylvania. Our winter temperatures in southwest Indiana don't get much colder than hers, but here those occasional blasts of frigid air usually come on the heels of a week of warm Gulf Stream breezes, and that does in my plant every year. Yet I keep trying, just as I do with certain cryptomerias and heathers that would also be much happier elsewhere. I know it's a gamble, but I go into it with my eyes open.

Such malcontents aren't the backbone of my gardens, though. While I don't mind babying a few of my favorites, treating the whole garden that way would get old in a hurry. So I depend on reliable performers that I know will do well here.

Starting from Seed

When it comes to ordering from catalogs, I always bite off more than I can chew. It's hard to keep a rein on my good intentions when it's wintertime and all the promise of spring is in the pages on my lap. That's why I, like most gardeners, have a treasure chest filled with packets of seed that never made it into the ground.

But even when I factor in the overload, starting plants from seed is still the cheapest way to fill a garden. A packet of seeds will give me at least 20 healthy plants for only a dollar or two. With perennials costing upwards of $3 apiece these days, that's definitely a bargain.

I usually sow annuals in place in the garden because they sprout and grow to a decent size rapidly. But I sow my perennials in pots. I've learned that by the time they sprout in the garden, the perennials will be facing competition from zillions of weed seedlings that got a head start in the bed. Starting slower-growing plants in pots saves me hours of painstaking weeding around tiny seedlings.

I used to start my seeds in peat pots, but I don't use peat anymore because of concern for the decimation of

THE RAINMAKER

❧❧

One of the best investments I've ever made was a $15 watering wand for my hose. The rigid plastic extension screws onto the end of the hose, and a valve lets me adjust the flow, just as I do on my indoor shower head. To water seedbeds, I use a fine, drizzly mist. To drench established plants, I prefer a stronger flow like summer rain.

Several companies market this kind of device. I found mine at a large discount chain store.

peat bogs. Instead, I use plastic pots. They take less watering because there's no evaporation through the pot walls, and the plants slip out easily when it's time to move them into the garden.

I've found that the depth of the pot is more important than the size at the top. A slim, very deep pot works much better than the standard 2¼-inch pot. Roots have more room to grow, and when it's time to transplant, they're not coiled around the pot in a tangled mass.

Perennials take a year to mature before they'll bloom, and sometimes I run out of garden space for tending a row of young plants. So I often start seed-

It's an education to see just how many plants a single packet of seed produces. Put some thought into your seed-starting space so that the multitude of pots you're sure to end up with are easy to care for. A shady area open to breezes will help keep plants healthy and vigorous.

Starting from Seed

grown perennials in large, black plastic pots, eliminating the step of transplanting from small pots. They grow almost as well in the pots as they do in the garden, and I can keep them potted until the following spring. I over-winter them in a cold frame, nestled into an insulating layer of straw, or park them in my unheated garage.

I don't fuss too much when I plant seeds in the garden. I scratch up a patch of bare soil with a handheld claw digger, scatter the seeds across it, and crumble a couple of handfuls of fine soil on top. Then I moisten the spot with a soft spray from a hose.

Seed-Starting Indoors

I'm always champing at the bit long before the spring thaw, so I start many seeds indoors. I press every sunny windowsill into service, and park the overflow under lights in the basement.

A pair of low-tech, low-cost fluorescent shop lights, suspended by chains from eye screws in the ceiling, will provide enough light to grow hundreds of healthy seedlings. Keep the lights close to the plants, about 3 to 4 inches above their tops, and raise the chains as the plants grow. Plug your lights into a timer, and run them for 16 hours a day. Your plants will grow as if it's summer in Alaska.

I place my individual seed-starting pots in plastic foam trays that I get at the supermarket with meat or vegetables (or fresh pasta), and set those trays on metal cookie sheets for easier handling. Local thrift shops provide a ready source of cookie trays. Too discolored or rusted for baking, they're perfect for raising plants. My "plant table" is nothing more than a simple sheet of plywood supported by sawhorses. It's easy to put up during seed-starting season and just as easy to dismantle and store once my seedlings have been transplanted into the garden.

I use professional seed-starting mix, sold by the bag at discount stores and garden centers, for filling my pots. Garden soil makes my plants fall victim to damp-ing-off disease, and pure vermiculite or perlite falls apart at transplanting time, damaging fragile roots. After the plants have their second set of true leaves, I start watering them with a soluble organic fertilizer like compost or manure tea at weak strength. I pour the water into my foam trays and let the plant pots soak it up from the bottom.

THE NURSERY BED

Starting perennials from seed means you'll have to forgo instant gratification. Except for coreopis and a few other sorts, most perennials need to have at least one full year under their belts before they're established well enough to bloom. If you're growing plants from cuttings, you'll also need to give them extra coddling until they root and become strong enough to fend for themselves.

Instead of putting these plants in your garden helter-skelter, then trying to keep track of them, I find it easier to set aside a corner of my garden as a nursery bed. With all of my young plants gathered in one place, it's easy to give them the extra watering and weeding they need. I also add aged manure to that bed to encourage fast vegetative growth. In spring, it's tremendously gratifying to move healthy young perennials out of the nursery and into my garden.

Buying Plants

I use mail-order catalogs a lot for buying perennials and grasses. Over the years, I've ordered from many different companies, starting with the big guns of mail order, who inundate my mailbox with catalogs until I lose all resistance. I've ended up with my share of flops and dis-appointments, and in the process, I've weeded out my mail-order suppliers to those that I know are reputable. When I buy plants through the mail, I want them to be true to species and cultivar and in good health—and (of course!) the bigger, the better. I hate waiting for a $50 order and ripping it open to find a handful of puny plants. Any mail-order nurseries or seed sources listed in "Resources for Natural Landscaping" on page 250 are companies that I've dealt with personally and have been happily satisfied with.

When it comes to trees and shrubs, I shop in person. I can spend an hour picking out the cream of the crop—the biggest, best-shaped, and most healthy of the available plant selection. (Of course, I often snap a twig getting it home in my compact car, but then I have no-body to blame but me.) Prices for larger plants are usu-ally better at local garden centers, too, because no shipping fees are involved.

Sometimes the plants I want just aren't available lo-cally, though, and then I turn to mail order. I prefer to

If you're within driving distance of a native plant nursery, make the trip. Catalog descriptions and even color photos can't compare with seeing the real thing. You're sure to get all kinds of ideas.

BUYING HEALTHY PLANTS

Here are a few dos and don'ts to make sure the plants you buy are vigorous and both pest- and disease-free.

- Do choose plants with fresh, vigorously growing leaves.
- Don't buy plants with wilted leaves, discolored foliage, or visible signs of insects or disease. Examine both sides of the leaves for insects or webbing, which can indicate the presence of spider mites. Look for circular lesions or discoloration patterns on leaves. Watch for oozing sap or odd growths on a plant's branches and trunk.
- Do choose plants with new growth pushing out from the tips of branches or the crown.
- Don't buy plants that look as if they're static or barely clinging to life.
- Do choose plants in bud rather than in bloom—anticipation of bloom is more fun than fast-fading instant gratification.
- Don't buy plants that look thin or malnourished or plants that are lanky and falling over from weak stems.
- Do choose stocky, densely branched plants (unless the variety is naturally spindly).
- Don't buy trees with tight crotch angles, crossed or rubbing branches, or other imperfections that can possibly lead to weak wood and disease problems later.
- Do choose trees and shrubs with attractive branching patterns. Well-spaced branches on a young plant are the foundation for its mature silhouette.

order from companies that state clearly the size and/or age of the stock they sell. That way, I avoid those "Oh-my-gosh-is-this-little-stick-my-$30-tree?!" surprises. If I know I'm getting a seedling, I'm prepared for its unimpressive size.

Putting Plants on Hold

If you buy containerized stock, you can be lazy about planting. They'll sit safely in their containers for weeks or even months, as long as you keep them watered. More than once I've stocked up on orphans at year-end clearance sales at my local nursery, then kept the plants in

their pots until the following spring. I group them tightly together in a sheltered spot behind the garage, and blanket them with 2 feet of oak leaves to keep them insulated during the winter.

Bareroot stock is another matter. Most mail-order companies will let you specify a delivery date, so you can plan to be home to receive the package and plant immediately. If you'll be at work when the plants are delivered, have them delivered to your workplace if possible. They'll be better off in an office than sitting in the hot sun on your doorstep.

When you open a package of bareroot plants, plunge them into a bucket of water while you dig the holes. They'll be fine in water for up to 24 hours, but

Easy Layering

The lazy gardener's way to propagate plants, simple layering requires nothing more than a handful of soil and a rock. Bend a low-growing stem of a favorite shrub to the ground, scoop some dirt over it, weigh it down to avoid disturbing it while it's rooting, and come back in a few months to a year to transplant your new shrub.

STEP 1: Gently bend a flexible branch of forsythia, privet, rose-of-Sharon, or other shrub to ground level, being careful not to snap the branch.

STEP 2: Strip the leaves from an area about a foot long and pile several handfuls of soil over the bare branch, patting it firmly into a mound.

STEP 3: Weigh the earthbound branch down with a brick or heavy stone to keep it from springing out of the mounded soil.

STEP 4: When erect new growth sprouts, it means the branch has rooted. Wait until the following spring, then sever the branch and transplant your new shrub.

don't leave them in any longer. It's a horrible feeling to fish your plants out of the bucket and discover that the roots have turned to smelly mush.

Perfect Planting

I use a simple six-step method for planting trees, shrubs, and perennials and it works every time. This method doesn't require a great deal of work, and it gives every type of plant a good start. Here's what I do:

1. Dig a hole.
2. Fill it with water.
3. Let it drain.
4. Pop in the plant.
5. Refill the hole with the soil I dug out of it.
6. Give the plant a good drink.

Conventional gardening wisdom to the contrary, I don't make ten-dollar holes. I dig only as deep and as wide as the plant's roots need to spread comfortably at the size they are now. Research now backs up my instinctive method of refilling the hole with the same soil I dug out. It seems you can indeed kill with kindness: If you fill a planting hole with perfect, fertile soil, the roots will be reluctant to reach out into the real world beyond (reminds me of some twenty-somethings I know). I used to scratch up the sides of the hole to make it easier for growing roots to penetrate, but I haven't bothered with that for the past ten years. Having seen how even a young plant can crack a paved road, I realized plant roots have more power than I'd been giving them credit for. Judging from my own experience, even a wall of Indiana clay isn't going to slow them down.

My bare-bones method works so well that I can transplant almost anything, almost any time of year. In July one summer, when the thermometer seemed to be perpetually stuck at 100°F, I dug up three 10-foot-tall golden raintrees (*Koelreuteria paniculata*) and moved them to a more serendipitous site in my garden. They never lost a leaf. I frequently move perennials in full bloom. (Are those shastas too far from the pink roses? No problem—just move 'em over a couple of feet.) I've even relocated clumps of blooming daffodils and tulips.

I credit my success to plenty of water (see "Muddying Plants In" on page 247) and to digging extra deep whenever I'm transplanting. I try to get beneath the roots instead of slicing through them. I'd rather struggle with a 20-pound ball of earth than risk shearing off the roots.

Propagating Your Plants

With plants, making more of what you have is a cinch. Dividing an established plant is the fastest route: You slice off a section with a spade, replant it, and in a year or two, have a plant as big as its parent. Cuttings take longer to grow into good-size plants, but they're a lot of fun to fool around with. When I began trying my hand at cuttings, I was dubious about the results, but now my nursery bed and my gardens are full of plants started with a snip of the pruning shears. Most plants will root easily from cuttings. Once you discover how simple it is to start plants from cuttings, you'll soon be digging up more ground to expand your garden.

Taking Cuttings

Many plants will grow from cuttings of roots, stems, or twigs and sometimes from leaves. This is how (and when) to go about it.

- Take cuttings of herbaceous plants like perennials and groundcovers in late spring to early summer, when they're growing vigorously. Insert the cuttings into moist soil. Try the perennials on the list in "Making Stem Cuttings" on page 246, as well as dahlias, mums, thymes and other herbs, or anything else in your garden. (If the cuttings don't root, you're out only a few minutes' time.)

- Take softwood cuttings of woody plants in late spring to early summer, when the wood is green and pliable. Insert cuttings into moist soil. Try forsythia, junipers, viburnums, blue spirea, pussy willows, willows, and butterfly bush.

- Take leaf cuttings any time of year. Place the base of the leaf with a bit of petiole (stem) attached in moist soil. Try hens-and-chicks, begonias, sedums, and foamflower (*Tiarella cordifolia*). The common house plant known as piggyback plant (*Tolmiea menziesii*) is actually a Pacific Northwest native that makes a good garden plant where winter temperatures stay above 20°F. It's so easily propagated from leaf cuttings that you can use it as a filler in the garden in any zone. I prefer the Northwest name of "youth-on-old-age" for this pretty plant.

- Take root cuttings after plants are dormant. Insert 2-inch sections of root (keep top up and bottom down!) in moist soil. Try Oriental poppies, bear's-breeches (*Acanthus* spp.), Japanese anemones (*Anemone* × *hybrida* and *A. tomentosa* 'Robustissima'), and globe thistle (*Echinops ritro*).

Pest and Disease Control

I can count on one hand the pest and disease problems I've had in my natural gardens: moles and other small burrowing varmints; rabbits; groundhogs; canker on cherry trees; and occasional mildew. That's pretty much it.

Making Stem Cuttings

Multiply your perennials by rooting cuttings of the stems. By the end of summer, you'll have dozens of new plants to put in your gardens.

STEP 1: *In spring or early summer, when the plant is growing vigorously, snip off a 4- to 6-inch length of stem that includes at least two stem joints.*

STEP 2: *Using your hand, strip off the leaves from the bottom of the stem, exposing at least one joint on the stem.*

STEP 3: *Push the cutting into a pot of very moist sand or potting soil. Firm the soil around the cutting and keep it well-watered until it sprouts vigorous new growth. Then transplant it to your garden.*

Here are some of the easiest perennials to root:

1. **Asters** (*Aster* spp.)
2. **Bee balm** (*Monarda didyma*)
3. **Blue marguerite** (*Felicia amelloides*)
4. **Candytuft** (*Iberis sempervirens*)
5. **Fleabanes** (*Erigeron* spp.)
6. **Leadworts** (*Plumbago* spp.)
7. **Salvias, perennial species** (*Salvia* spp.)
8. **Sedums** (*Sedum* spp.)
9. **Sneezeweeds** (*Helenium* spp.)
10. **Spurges** (*Euphorbia* spp.)
11. **Yarrows** (*Achillea* spp.)

My approach to all of these was the same: I did nothing. The results? The autumn-flowering cherry is still oozing sap, but it keeps growing healthy new branches to make up for those that die off. I learned to watch my step to avoid twisting my ankle in mole tunnels. A couple of summers' harvests of strawberries and tomatoes went to furred creatures instead of into our bellies. The mildewed plants looked ugly but grew back vigorously the following year.

Only you can determine your plant-care comfort level. If you get nervous seeing signs of trouble, then you'll want to take preventive measures.

A Natural Balance

A natural landscape operates by keeping pests and problems in balance, so they don't become overwhelming. Since I'm not trying to keep a showplace, I don't mind occasional outbreaks of leaf spot or caterpillars. Besides, any bugs that show up in quantity are apt to be interesting to watch. When I spot aphids on my goldenrod, I don't panic. Instead, I anticipate the almost certain arrival of ladybugs and their spiny larvae, which will make short work of the aphids. If ladybugs don't show up, ants certainly will. They tend the aphids like cows, milking them for the sweet honeydew.

Crab spiders make themselves at home among flower petals, awaiting unwary butterflies that drop in for a sip of nectar. A litter of wings beneath a plant is a clue to this predator's presence.

Hanging head down is an easy trick for the agile praying mantis, who waits motionless on plants for an unsuspecting insect to wander by. If traffic is heavy, a well-fed mantis may stay on the same plant for weeks at a time.

MUDDYING PLANTS IN

Water is the magic ingredient for successful planting or transplanting. My mother taught me the trick of muddying in perennials and trees and shrubs many years ago. After you dig the planting hole, fill it to the brim with water and let it drain. If it drains quickly (as it will if your soil is sandy or high in organic matter), fill it again and let it drain once more. This process saturates the soil around the planting hole so that it stays moist for several days and doesn't draw water away from the soil in the hole.

After you're through playing in the mud, set in your plant and fill the hole with the soil you dug out of it. I tamp the soil in the hole pretty firmly, using my foot. But I don't tamp it so strongly that it would totally compact, which would force all of the air out of the hole. The hole should be slightly depressed from the surrounding ground. Water again, but be careful not to wash the soil away from the roots. I usually turn the hose on to just above a trickle, using a thumb-valve connector, and let it run for 20 minutes or so, until the soil is thoroughly soaked around the plant. This slow soaking will penetrate the soil quite a distance from your new plant. With all this moistness, you won't have to worry about watering your new transplant for several days, and its roots will have plenty of time to get established, undisturbed.

Other predators stalk my garden constantly. Praying mantids—both the familiar, big green Chinese type and the smaller, native species—take up residence on my plants. I've learned that a mantis will often spend the entire summer on a single plant, if the pickings are good. Mantids are more catholic in their diet than I'd prefer—they eat the good along with the bad. When a mantis moved in on a plant of small-flowered black-eyed Susan (*Rudbeckia triloba*), I was puzzled at first as to what she was doing there. I soon found out the mantis was lying in wait for the small butterflies that visited the flowers. One grab with a foreleg, and another butterfly was history.

My favorite garden predator is the assassin bug, a weird, spiky-legged critter that looks like it carries a toothed gear ring on its back. Although their gait is odd, the bugs' methods are effective, and assassin bugs make short work of many types of smaller fry. They can also give a human a nasty bite, but only if forced into it. They're big enough to spot easily, and I treat them with the respect they deserve.

This care calendar starts in December rather than in January because that's when I like to place my catalog orders.

December: Order seeds and plants for next year's garden. Ordering early avoids disappointments when items are sold out. Prune grapevines as needed and make wreaths from the trimmings. (Or make mini-trees: Take your tomato cages, turn them upside down on top of a large clay pot, tie the legs of the cage together, and wrap with vines and white Christmas lights.) Prune or limb up trees as needed; construct a rustic twig fence or trellis from the clippings.

January: Start seeds indoors for geraniums, impatiens, and other annuals that take a long time to reach blooming size. Fill in the gaps if you've overlooked anything on your seed orders. Order garden tools if you need them; the best-quality tools are available from distributors who sell to professionals, such as those listed in "Resources for Natural Landscaping" on page 250.

February: Start more seeds under lights. Remove any plants that are still standing in your garden if they look ratty after winter. Cut back ornamental grasses to the ground. Watch for snowdrops, winter aconite, and the first of the wildflowers in protected places. Begin a notebook of garden changes to make next year—where you need a few more daffodils, where to add a star magnolia. Listen for the love songs of titmice and chickadees.

March: Look for emerging seedlings in the garden. Plant shrubs, perennials, trees, and vines. Divide daylilies and other perennials as they emerge. Look for migrating birds at the feeder. Set out hummingbird feeders.

April: Plant, plant, plant! Transplant hardened-off seedlings into the garden; sow seeds; plant perennials and other new additions. Start cuttings of perennials

Lamb's ears, gayfeather, and ornamental grasses glow in late summer sun.

and shrubs. Spread compost, aged manure, and other organic materials. Renew paths if needed with fresh wood chips or other improvements.

May: Prune spring-flowering shrubs if needed. Continue April activities. Take a census of nesting birds.

June: Keep young plants well watered if rains are scant. Continue planting. Apply or renew mulches to retain water and keep down weeds. Pull noxious weeds at first sight; pull rampant weeds like beggar's-ticks before they seed themselves out of control.

July: Mulch deeply to hold moisture. Be alert for dry spells—trees and shrubs in the ground for two years or less will need supplemental watering. Order irises and daylilies. Take a count of butterflies.

August: Begin collecting seed as flowers mature. Sow the seeds wherever you want more plants next year, or dry and save them for spring sowing. Water as needed. Spread a fresh layer of wood chips or other path materials.

September: Order daffodils and other spring bulbs early, while stocks are at their peak. Plant shrubs and trees. This is a great time to add some berry bushes and evergreens. Continue collecting seed.

October: Plant bulbs. Rake leaves off paths. Neaten up your garden if desired by cutting back some of the spent perennials. But keep in mind that birds and wildlife like a wilder garden better—more places to hide and more things to eat.

November: Continue planting bulbs. Mulch the garden with chopped leaves. Water deeply, especially broad-leaved evergreens, if rain has been scarce. Look for bird nests in the garden, and examine them to see how they're made, but don't remove them—small mammals find shelter in them in the cold season.

Multitudes of spiders also fill my gardens. I like to go out with a flashlight and a kid on a summer night and look for the red eyes of wolf spiders foraging in the meadow. All spiders are superb predators that help keep the zillions of insects in balance.

Birds, of course, are also your allies in keeping a healthy garden. The more birds you entice into sticking around, the fewer pest problems you'll have. (For more on the role of birds, see Chapter 5, beginning on page 144.)

A natural garden is a healthy one. Diseases may occur, but they won't affect every plant. If a plant dies back inexplicably, cut off and destroy the affected parts. If it doesn't recover, take a closer look at your garden. A sickly garden is an indication that something basic is wrong. Maybe you're trying to grow plants unsuited to your soil type or climate. Maybe the shade is too deep for the sun-loving plants you've selected. Perhaps tree roots are competing for moisture and nutrients. Instead of reaching for a cure, take a closer look at the cause.

Year-Round Maintenance

The beauty of the natural landscape is that it doesn't require a lot of intervention. In fact, the less you fuss with the garden, the more wildlife you'll attract. Plantings flow into one another, and the garden has an informal, casual look where you'll hardly notice the occasional weed. Your natural landscape will get along fine with as much or as little care as you enjoy giving it.

The fan-shaped leaves of the gingko turn yellow in the fall, then drop all at once when the temeprature dips below 25°F. The gingko, introduced from China in the 1700s, is now rare or extinct in the wild.

Recommended Reading

The following books have great ideas for planting and plants for a natural landscape.

Adams, George. *Birdscaping Your Garden.* Emmaus, Pa.: Rodale Press, 1994.

Cox, Jeff. *Landscaping with Nature.* Emmaus, Pa.: Rodale Press, 1991.

Daniels, Stevie. *The Wild Lawn Handbook.* New York: Macmillan Publishing Co., 1995.

Editors of Sunset Books and Sunset Magazine. *An Illustrated Guide to Attracting Birds.* Menlo Park, Calif.: Sunset Publishing Corporation, 1990.

Ellis, Barbara W., Joan Benjamin, and Deborah L. Martin. *Rodale's Low-Maintenance Gardening Techniques.* Emmaus, Pa.: Rodale Press, 1995.

Heriteau, Jacqueline, and Charles B. Thomas. *Water Gardens.* Boston: Houghton Mifflin Co., 1994.

Mickel, John. *Ferns for American Gardens.* NewYork: Macmillan Publishing Co., 1994.

National Wildlife Federation. *Planting an Oasis for Wildlife.* National Wildlife Federation, 1986.

Phillips, Harry R., et al. *Growing and Propagating Wild Flowers.* Chapel Hill, N.C.: University of North Carolina Press, 1985.

Schneck, Marcus. *Your Backyard Wildlife Year.* Emmaus, Pa.: Rodale Press, 1996.

Tripp, Kim E., and J. C. Raulston. *The Year in Trees: Superb Woody Plants for Four-Season Gardens.* Portland, Ore.: Timber Press, 1995.

Tufts, Craig and Peter Loewer. *The National Wildlife Federation's Guide to Gardening for Wildlife.* Emmaus, Pa.: Rodale Press, 1995.

Guides to Identification

BIRDS

My favorite field guide is *A Guide to Field Identification: Birds of North America* (New York: Golden Press). *The Peterson Field Guide* series (Boston: Houghton Mifflin Co.) is also top-notch. Start with one of these, then add *The Audubon Society Field Guide* series (New York: Alfred A. Knopf) as a good backup, with lots of interesting text. One caveat on the Audubon guides: They fall apart quickly if you use them a lot.

PLANTS

Peterson's wildflower guides (regional) are a must. My second choice is *A Guide to Field Identification: Wildflowers of North America* (New York: Golden Press); the illustrations aren't as true-to-life as Peterson's, but this includes more plants. Audubon's photographic field guides are also excellent, but limited in the plants included.

WILDLIFE AND INSECTS

The books I learned the most from and find easiest to use are the small-size *Golden Guide* series (retailing for about $5 each), with separate volumes on spiders, reptiles and amphibians, mammals, butterflies and moths, and other natural history topics. Concise, fact-packed text, extensive coverage, and excellent pictures.

The Audubon Society Field Guides series is also good for identification and learning. Other field guides are worthwhile for filling in the gaps.

The Fieldbook of Natural History (Palmer and Fowler, New York: McGraw-Hill, 1975) is packed with esoteric facts, though it's not as useful a field guide the other books are. It's a hefty volume of almost 800 pages, good to read once you've identified the subject in question.

Sources of Seeds and Plants

If you are looking for a particular plant, check *The Andersen Horticultural Library's Source list of Plants and Seeds* (Minneapolis: University of Minnesota, 1996). It lists tens of thousands of plants—perennials, annuals, shrubs, trees, vines—in alphabetical order by botanical name and cultivar, and it tells you exactly where to mail-order them. It will save you hours of flipping through catalogs.

Bear Creek Nursery
P.O. Box 411
Northport, WA 99157
Specializes in cold-hardy fruit trees, shrubs, and berries, many of them ideal for wildlife.

Busse Gardens
5873 Oliver Avenue SW
Cokato, MN 55321
(612) 286-2654
Fabulous hardy perennial plants, including wildflowers, hostas, and heucheras.

Comstock Seed
8520 W. 4th Street
Reno, NV 89523
(702) 746-3681
Top-notch seed supplier for drought-tolerant native grasses and other plants of the Great Basin. Extremely helpful owners.

Edible Landscaping
P.O. Box 77
Afton, VA 22920
(804) 361-9134
A selection of food-bearing plants for you and the birds and other wildlife—many fruiting trees and shrubs.

Finch Blueberry Nursery
P.O. Box 699
Bailey, NC 27807
(919) 235-4664
Excellent selection of blueberries for your wildlife garden.

Forestfarm
990 Tetherow Road
Williams, OR 97544
(541) 846-7269
Unbelievable catalog of more than 2,000 plants, including Western natives, perennials, and an outstanding variety of trees and shrubs. A must!

The Fragrant Path
P.O. Box 328
Ft. Calhoun, NE 68023
Seeds for fragrant annuals, perennials, shrubs, and vines, many of them old-fashioned favorites.

Niche Gardens
1111 Dawson Road
Chapel Hill, NC 27516
(919) 967-0078
Good, healthy plants including grasses, nursery-propagated wildflowers, perennials, and herbs.

Pen Y Bryn Nursery
1 Box 1313
Forksville, PA 18616
(717) 924-3377
Primarily a bonsai nursery, but also sells mosses mail-order.

Plant Delights Nursery, Inc.
9241 Sauls Road
Raleigh, NC 27603
(919) 772-4794
A wide plant selection and a delightful catalog.

Plants of the Southwest
930 Baca St.
Santa Fe, NM 87501
(505) 983-1548
Specializes in plants and seeds for arid southwestern climates.

Prairie Moon Nursery
Route 3, Box 163
Winona, MN 55987
(507) 452-1362
Generously sized plants and seeds of native prairie grasses and wildflowers.

Prairie Nursery
P.O. Box 306
Westfield, WI 53964
(608) 296-3679
Educational catalog of prairie grasses and native wildflowers.

Shady Oaks Nursery
112 10th Avenue SE
Waseca, MN 56093
(507) 835-5033
Specializes in plants for shade, including wildflowers, ferns, perennials, and shrubs.

Southwestern Native Seeds
P.O. Box 50503
Tucson, AZ 85703
Responsibly collected wildflower seed from the Southwest, the West, and Mexico.

Sunlight Gardens
174 Golden Lane
Andersonville, TN 37705
(423) 494-8237
Wonderful selection of wildflowers, all nursery propagated, of southeastern and northeastern North America.

Tripple Brook Farm
37 Middle Road
Southampton, MA 01073
(413) 527-4626
Fun catalog with wildflowers, mosses, and other Northeastern native plants, along with fruits and shrubs.

Vermont Wildflower Farm
Route 7
Charlotte, VT 05445
(802) 425-3500
Excellent wildflower seed and seed mixes, regionally adapted for all areas of the U.S.

We-Du Nurseries
Route 5, Box 724
Marion, NC 28752
(704) 738-8300
Incredible variety of wildflowers and native perennials from several continents; many woodland plants.

Wildlife Nurseries
P.O. Box 2724
Oshkosh, WI 54903
(414) 231-3780
Plants and seeds of native grasses, annuals, and perennials for wildlife. Also water garden plants and supplies.

Woodlanders, Inc.
1128 Colleton Avenue
Aiken, SC 29801
(803) 648-7522
Mouth-watering selection of native trees, shrubs, ferns, vines, and perennials, plus other good garden plants.

Yucca Do Nursery
P.O. Box 655
Waller, TX 77484
(409) 826-6363
Unbelievable selection of trees, shrubs, and perennial plants, including many natives (wait until you see the list of salvias!).

Sources of Water Garden Liners, Plants, and Supplies

Lilypons Water Gardens
6800 Lilypons Road
P.O. Box 10
Buckeystown, MD 21717
(800) 999-5459
Extensive list of plants, fish, and supplies for water gardens.

Van Ness Water Gardens
2460 N. Euclid Avenue
Upland, CA 91786
(909) 982-2425
Everything you could possibly need for a water garden, from plants to pools to supplies.

Sources of Bird Feeders, Nest Boxes, and Other Supplies

Bird feeders and nest boxes are widely available in wild bird supply stores, discount stores, and lawn-and-garden centers. I like to see mine before I buy, but if you prefer mail-order, here is a reliable source:

Duncraft, Inc.
102 Fisherville Road
Penacook, NH 03303
(603) 224-0200
Bird feeders, birdhouses, birdbaths, and other bird-related items, including hummingbird feeders and supplies.

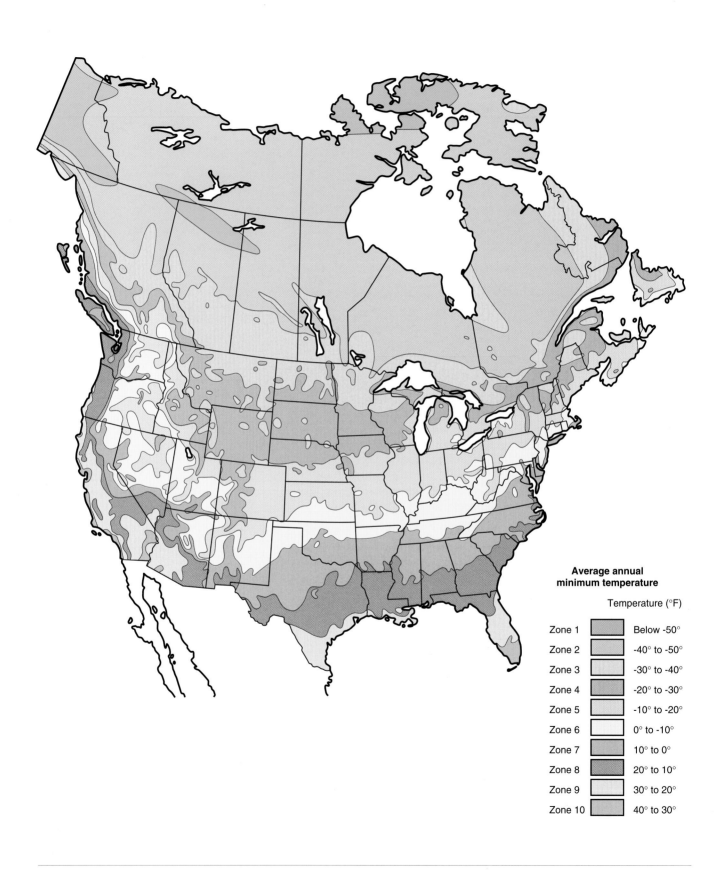

**Average annual
minimum temperature**

Temperature (°F)

Zone 1		Below -50°
Zone 2		-40° to -50°
Zone 3		-30° to -40°
Zone 4		-20° to -30°
Zone 5		-10° to -20°
Zone 6		0° to -10°
Zone 7		10° to 0°
Zone 8		20° to 10°
Zone 9		30° to 20°
Zone 10		40° to 30°

Index

Italicized page numbers refer to photographs and illustrations.

A

Acanthus, 77
Accents, 230, *232,* 233, *233*
Acer, 96, 119
Achillea, 59
Acorus, 137, 142
Adiantum, 87, 119, 139, *139*
Aesculus, 100
Agastache, 171, 174
Agropyron, 67
Agrostemma githago, 41, 51
Ajuga, 119
Alopecurus, 42
Amarantha, 160
Amelanchier, 78, 100, 213
Andropogon, 67
Anemones, 79
Annuals, 20, 80, 123, *123,* 174–75
 fast-blooming, 184
 meadow garden, 38, 43, 44
Aquilegia, 171, 174
Arbors, 21, 22, 25
Arisaema, 98
Arrowheads, 120, 142
Aruncus, 137
Asclepias, 42, 59, 63, *63,* 197
Aster, 24, 26, 30, 33, *33,* 35, 36, 42, 43, *43,* 51, 53, *53,* 59, 64, 197
Astilbes, 77, 80, *81,* 119, 120, 132, *133,* 143
Athyrium, 79, 87
Azaleas, 24, *24,* 70, 73, 79, 97, 101
Azolla, 137

B

Baby blue eyes, 41
Bachelor's-buttons, 41, 184
Baldcypress, 136, 137
Bamboo, 119
Bearberry, 84
Bear's breeches, 77
Bee balm, 59, 171, 172, 174
Bees, 13, 48, 70
Bellflowers, 77, 79, 83
Benches, 21, 62, 79, 88, 89, *89*
Bergamot, 42, 63, *63*
Bidens, 152, *152,* 160, 178
Biennial plants, 36
Birdbaths, 21, 161, *161,* 162, *162,* 163, *163*
Birdfeeders, 21, 94, 146, 148, 156, *156,* 157, *157,* 159, *159,* 173
 supply sources, 251
Birdhouses, 13
Birds, 13, 107
 attracting, 47, 144–81
 baths for, 79, 109
 blackbirds, 109, 154, 155
 bluebirds, 13, *13,* 24, 30, 31, 47, 109, 146
 bobwhites, 153, 154
 buntings, 46, 154
 cardinals, 46, 109
 catbirds, 155

chickadees, 30, 70, 95, *95,* 109, 146, 147, 148, 154, 155, 156
 cowbirds, 154, 155
 creepers, 147
 dicksissel, 47, 154
 doves, 153, 154
 ducks, 125, 134
 finches, 26, 46, 47, *47,* 109, 146, 157, *157*
 flickers, 153, 154, 155
 food for, 13, 73–74, 84, 149, 152, 158, 159, 172
 gnatcatchers, 153
 grackles, 153
 grasses for, 179, *179*
 grosbeaks, 76, 94, 109, 154, 157, *157*
 hawks, 30
 herons, 106, 125
 hummingbirds, 20, *20,* 122, *144,* 145, 167, *167,* 170–71, *171,* 172, *172,* 173, *173,* 220
 indigo bunting, *6, 16*
 jays, 155
 juncos, 46, 155
 kingfishers, 125
 kinglets, 155
 looking for, 148
 magpies, 47, 155
 in meadow gardens, 46–47
 meadowlarks, 47, 155
 mockingbirds, 155, 158, *158*
 nuthatches, 95, 146, 147, 155
 orioles, 153, 155
 ospreys, 125
 ovenbirds, 154, 155
 in prairie gardens, 46–47
 quail, 155
 red-wing blackbirds, 47
 regional, 153, *153,* 154, *154,* 155, *155*
 robins, 109
 safety for, 94, 95
 scarlet tanagers, 94, 95, *95,* 109
 seasonal, 153, *153,* 154, *154,* 155, *155*
 shelter for, 13, 26, 61, *61,* 73–74, 146, 148–49, 163–64, *164,* 165, *166,* 166, *166*
 shrikes, 47
 shrubs for, 180
 siskins, 153
 sparrows, 26, 30, 46, *46,* 95, 109, 147, 148, 149, 154, 155
 starlings, 109
 tanagers, 154
 thrashers, 153
 thrushes, 24, 80, 94, 155
 titmice, *95,* 153
 towhees, 94, 155
 trees for, 181
 veeries, 80, 94
 vireos, 95, 154
 warblers, 76, 95, 109, 147, 154, 155
 waxwings, 154, 155
 woodcocks, 47
 woodpeckers, 30, 94, *94,* 146, 147, *147,* 154, 155, 157, *157*

 wrens, 26, 149, 155
 yellowthroats, 154, 155
Black-bearded wheat, 41
Black-eyed Susans, 32, *32,* 42, 43, *43,* 51, 59, 64, 197
Blanketflowers, 27, *27,* 66
Blazing stars, *28,* 29, 35, 66
Bleeding heart, 77
Bloodroot, 70, 76, 79, 98
Blueberries, 78, *78*
Bluets, 42, 51
Boltonia, 59
Bridges, 123, *123*
Brooklime, 119
Buddleia, 197
Bugle, 119
Butter-and-eggs, 42
Buttercups, 119, 137
Butterflies, 13, 30, 31, *31,* 48, *48,* 49, *49,* 50, *50,* 80, 107
 attracting, 58, 91, 182–207
 feeding, 193, 195, 197
 flowers for, 184
 herbs for, 184–85
 looking for, 188
 puddles for, 189, 192
 raising, 198–99, *198–99*
 regional, 190–91, *190–91*
 shelter for, 194, *194*
 shrubs for, 206, *206*
 vines for, 207, *207*
Butterfly bush, *182,* 183, 197, 206, *206*
Butterfly weed, 42, 63
Button-bushes, 120

C

Calamagrostis, 137, 143
Calendars
 for garden care, 248
 meadow care, 60
 for pond care, 124
Calliopsis, 41, *41*
Callitriche, 106, 140
Calluna, 79
Caltha, 137, 138, *138*
Campanula, 77, 79, 98
Candytufts, 246
Cardinal flowers, 120, 122, *122,* 137, 138
Carex, 137
Catchfly, 44
Catmint, 174, 197
Cattails, 120, 122, 132, 142
Cedrus, 78
Centaurea cyanus, 41, 51
Cercis, 96
Chakas, Tom, 220, *220,* 221
Chamomile, 184
Chenoposium, 160
Chicory, 34, *34,* 43
Chrysanthemum, 42, 51, 59, 63, *63*
Chrysogonum, 99, *99*
Cinquefoil, 57
Clark, Harriet Hadley, 204, *204,* 205
Clematis, 26, *26*
Cleome, 174
Columbines, 26, 77, *144,* 145, 171, 172, *172,* 174

Compass plant, 35, 52
Compost, 237–38, *238*
Coneflowers, 32, *32,* 35, 36, 53, *53,* 54, 66, 178, 197
Consolida, 171
Coral bells, 26
Coreopsis tinctoria, 41, *41*
Corn cockles, 41, 51
Cornflowers, 51
Cornus, 78, 96, 100
Cosmos, 41, 43, 160, 178, 184
Coyotes, 30
Crayfish, 30
Cryptomeria, 100
Cup plant, 52
Curly dock, 59
Cymbalaria, 119
Cystopteris, 87

D

Daisies, 32, *32,* 42, *42,* 43, 51, 54, 57, 59, 63, *63*
Dame's rocket, 51
Deadwood, 92–94
Delphiniums, 52, 76, 171, 174, 236
Dennstaedtia, 87
Dicentra, 77, 79, 98
Dragonflies, 48, 110, 118
Dryopteris, 79, 87
Duckweed, 120, 125, 134
Dutchman's breeches, 24, 76, 79, 98

E

Echinacea, 66, 178, 197
Eichhornia, 141
Eleocharis, 140
Elodea, 140
Elymus, 59
Equisetum, 137, 143
Erica, 79
Erigeron, 246
Eriophorum, 137
Eschscholzia, 41, *41*
Euonymus, 79, 97
Eupatorium, 59, 66, 137, 197
Euphorbia, 44, 246

F

Fagus, 181
Fairybells, 74
Fairy moss, 137
Felicia, 246
Fences, 22, 54, 62, 149, *149, 214*
 flowering, 213, *213*
 natural, 212–14
 twig, 212–13
Ferns, 71, 76, *76,* 80, *81,* 85, *85,* 86, 87, 88, 128
 beaded wood, 87
 for bog gardens, 139, *139*
 Christmas, 79, 87
 cinnamon, 85, *85,* 87, 139, *139*
 fragile, 87
 grottoes, 88
 hay-scented, 87
 Japanese painted, 70, 79, 87
 lady, 85, *85,* 87
 maidenhair, 85, *85,* 87, 119, 139, *139*

ostrich, 135, *135*
royal, 120, 135, 137, 139
sensitive, 87
shuttlecock, 135, *135*
silvery glade, 139
woodferns, 79
Filipendula, 119
Fish, 115, *115*, 122, 124–25
Fleabanes, 246
Foamflowers, 84, 99
Foliage, 21, 22, *23*, 73, *73*, 82, *83*, 83–84, *84*, 220
Food chain, 17
Forget-me-nots, 119, 120, 137, 143, *143*
Fountains, 106–7, *107*
Foxes, 30
Foxgloves, 36, *36*
Fringecups, 98
Frogbit, 141
Frogs, 6, *16*
Fumitory, 74
Fungus, 89, *89*

G
Gaillardia, 66
Garden designs
  birdseed garden, 160, *160*
  butterfly garden, 196–97, *196*
  garden paths, 226–27, *226*
  meadow gardens, 50, 51, *51*, 54, *55*, 56
  moonlight garden, 200, *200*
  prairie gardens, 50, 51, *51*, 54, *55*, 56
  shade garden, *78*, 78–79
  water garden, *136*, 136
  woodland gardens, *78*, 78–79
Garden ornaments, 230, *232*, 233, *233*
Gardens, bog, 134, *134*, 135, *135*
  ferns for, 139, *139*
  plants for, 138, *138*
Gardens, butterfly, 26, 182–207
Gardens, hummingbird, 170, *170*
Gardens, meadow, 28–67
  designs for, 50, 51, *51*, 54, *55*, 56
  grasses for, 65, *65*
  maintenance, 60–62
  mowing, 33, 38, *39*
  planting, 56–59
  plants for, 41, 42
  site preparation, 56–59
  starting, 38
  wildflowers for, *63*, 63–64
  wildlife in, 46–50
Gardens, moonlight, 200, *200*, 201
Gardens, natural
  maintenance, 235–49
  planning, 22
  structure of, 21
  transition to woods, 19, *19*, 40, *40*
Gardens, prairie, 28–67
  burning, 61–62
  designs for, 50, 51, *51*, 54, *55*, 56
  grasses for, 67
  maintenance, 60–62
  planting, 56–59
  site preparation, 56–59
  wildflowers for, 66
Gardens, shade, 26, 36, *36*, 68–101

characteristics of, 72, 73–74
designs for, *78*, 78–79
hardscape elements, 77
shade depths, 74, 76–77
shade quality, 76
shrubs for, 101
trees for, 100

Gardens, water, 22, *23*, 104–43
  container, 109–10, *110*
  designs for, 136, *136*
  marginal plants for, 142
  miniature, 110
  natural, 112
  plants for, *136*, 136–37, 140, *140*, 141, *141*
  poolside plants for, 143, *143*
  supply sources, 251
Gardens, woodland, *68*, 68–101
  characteristics of, 72, 73–74
  designs for, 78–79, *78*
  groundcovers for, 98
  paths in, 224, *224*
  shrubs for, 97
  trees for, 96
  wildflowers for, 98
  wildlife in, 94–95
Gayfeather, 59, *59*
Geraniums, 116, *116*, 171, 175
Ginger, wild, 84
Glyceria, 137
Goatsbeard, 137
Golden club, 106, 120, 137, 140
Goldenrod, 24, 33, *33*, 35, 42, 51, 53, *53*, 59, 64
Grasses, *28*, 29, 30, 31, 33, 34, 36, 38, 52, 136
  bluebunch wheatgrass, 45
  Blue Lyme, 59
  bluestem, 30, 33, 35, 42, 45, *45*, 53, *53*, 57, 59, 65, *65*, 67
  bottlebrush, 79
  buffalo, 33, 54
  cheatgrass, 45
  cord, 67
  cotton, 137
  feather reed, 137, 143
  fountain, 110, *110*
  foxtail, 42
  foxtail barley, 65
  frama, 33
  hair, 140
  hakone, 79, 83
  Indian, 35, 45, *45*, 67, 179, *179*
  Japanese silver, 137, 179, *179*
  low-growing, 33
  mail-order, 242
  manna, 137
  for meadow gardens, 65, *65*
  moor, 137
  needlegrass, 45
  orchard, 44
  ornamental, 83, 119
  perennial, 33
  for prairie gardens, 67
  purpletop, 51, 65
  for songbirds, 179, *179*
  stipa, 67
  sweet vernal, 65, *65*
  switch, 59, 67
  wheatgrass, 67
Green-and-gold, 99, *99*

Groundcovers, 19, 80, 84, 151, *151*
  coltsfoot, 73
  for woodland gardens, 98

H
Hamamelis, 79, 101
Hearts-a-bustin', 79, 97
Heathers, 79
Heaths, 79
Hedera, 119
Hedyotis, 42
Helianthus, 59, 66, 160, 178
Heliopsis, 42, 197
Hellebores, 77, *77*
Hemerocallis, 201
Hepatica, 70
Herbicides, 187–89
Herbs, 184–85, 220
Hesperis, 51
Hibiscus, 171
Holly, 24, 78, 101, 132
Honeysuckle, 201, 207, *207*
Horsetails, 137, 143
Hostas, 73, *73*, 77, 80, *81*, 163, *163*
Houstonia, 51
Hydrangeas, 70
Hydrocharis, 141
Hydrophyllum, 78, 99
Hyssop, 171, 174
Hystrix, 79

I
Iberis, 246
Ilex, 78, 79, 101, 180
Impatiens, 77, 171, 175, 239, *239*
Indian paintbrush, 35
Insects, 48, *48*, 70, 93, 94, 95, 106, 247, *247*
Irises, 120, 136
  flag, 106
  Japanese, 106, 132, 137, 138
  variegated, 110, *111*
Ironweed, 30, 36, 59, 66, 197
Ivy, 119

J
Jack-in-the-pulpit, 98
Jacob's ladder, 82, *82*
Joe-Pye weed, 30, 58, *58*, 59, 66, 137, 197
Johnsongrass, 59, 62
Juncus, 119, 132, 142

K
Knapweed, 57

L
Lady's mantle, 120, *121*
Lamb's quarters, 160
Larkspur, 171
Leadworts, 246
Liatris, 66
Lichens, 116
Lightning bugs, 48
Lilies
  camas, 82
  lemon, 201
  Madonna, 201
Linaria, 42
Lindera, 78, 80, *80*, 97, *97*
Linum, 41
Lizards, 14, *14*, 31, 94
Lobelia, 137, 138, 171

Lonicera, 201
Lotus, 118, 120, 136, 137, 140
Lupinus, 63
Lysichiton, 134, *134*, 137, 138, *138*
Lysimachia, 137

M
Macleaya, 77
Maianthemum, 99, *99*
Marguerites, 246
Marsh marigolds, 119, 120, 122, 137, 138, *138*
Marsilea, 137
Mayapples, 76, 83, *83*, 93, *93*, 98, 151, *151*
Mayflowers, 99, *99*
Meadowsweets, 119
Mentha, 59
Mice, 31, 94
Milfoils, 109, 137, 140
Milkweed, 34, *34*
  common, 197
  swamp, 30, 59, 63, *63*, 197
Mimulus, 137, 143
Mint, 59
Miscanthus, 137, 179, *179*
Mistflower, 30, 59, 197
Molinia, 137
Monarda, 36, 59, 63, *63*, 171, 174
Moneyworts, 137
Monkeyflowers, 92, *92*, 137, 143
Moonflowers, 201, 202, *202*
Morels, 89, *89*
Mosquitoes, 124–25
Moss, 17, 89, 92, 116
Moth mullein, 42, 57, 64
Moths, 199, *199*, 201, *201*, 202–03
  hummingbird, 202, *202*
  plants for, 203
Mowing, 60
Mulch, 59, 87, 147, *147*, 237
Mushrooms, 89, *89*
Myosotis, 119, 137, 143, *143*
Myriophyllum, 137, 140

N
Nandina, 119
Nasturtium, 119, 189, *189*
Nelumbo, 137, 140
Nemophila, 41
Nepeta, 174, 197
Nettles, 30
Nicotiana, 175
None-so-pretty, 184
Nymphaea, 137, 140

O
Oenothera, 64, 201
Onoclea, 87
Oregon grape holly, 88, *88*, 213
Orontium, 137, 140
Osmunda, 87, 137, 139, *139*
Owls, 30

P
Panicum, 59, 67
Papaver, 41, 51
Parrot feathers, 122
Parthenocissus, 79
Paths, 21, 22, 37, *37*, 54, *54–55*, 77, 88
  designing, 216, 219
  fragrant, 228–29

garden, 219, 222, *222*
lighting, 222, 223, *223*
materials for, 225, 228
woodland, 224, *224*
Pelargonium, 171, 175
Peltiphyllum, 137
Penstemon, 32, *32*, 59, 123, *123*, 174
Perennials, 20, 80, 123, *123*
aggressive, 59
border, 120
hardy, 174
meadow garden, 30, 36, 38, 43, 44
shade garden, 82
tender, 174–75
woodland garden, 82
Persimmons, 79
Pesticides, 187–89
Phacelia, 70
Phlox, 24, 26, 76, 91, *91*, 174, 197, 201, 205, *205*
Picea, 96
Pickerelweeds, 107, 120, 137
Pigweed, 30
Pistia, 137, 141, *141*
Plants
aquatic, 118, 120, 140
bareroot, 243–44
for bog gardens, 120, 134, *134*, 135, *135*, 138, *138*
buying, 242–43
choosing, 26–27
communities, 27
compatible, 57
container, 118, 243
cuttings, 245, 246, *246*
easy-care, 236
floating, 120, 141, *141*
fragrant, 220, 228–29
hardiness zone map, 252
healthy, 243
for hummingbirds, 174–75
layering, 244, *244*
for living fences, 213
mail-order, 242–43
marginal, 120, 142
for meadow gardens, 41, 42
for moonlight gardens, 201
for moths, 203
overlapping bloom, 54
oxygenating, 118, 120, 140
pest and disease control, 245–46
poolside, 143, *143*
propagating, 244, *244*, 245
from seeds, 42, 43, 45, 57, 58, 240–42, *241*
self-sowing, 32, *32*, 44
for songbirds, 178
spring ephemerals, 76
succession, 33
supply sources, 250
for water gardens, 106, 118–21, 136–37, *136*
Plumbago, 246
Podophyllum, 98
Pokeweed, 30
Polystichum, 79, 87
Ponds, 112. *See also* Pools
edging, 20
fish in, 124–25
Pondweeds, 140
Pontederia, 137

Pools, 22, 112–21. *See also* Ponds
algae in, 116, 122, 125
edging, 116–18
installing, 114, *114*
planting, 118–21
types, 113
Poppies
California, 41, *41*, 44
field, 41, 51
plume, 77
Shirley, 41
Predators, 14, 47, 125, 247
Primroses, 64, 112, *112*, 137
evening, 201
Primula, 112, *112*, 137
Prunella, 59
Pussywillows, 79, 97, *97*, 120, 136, 137

Q

Queen Anne's lace, 43
Quercus, 96

R

Ranunculus, 119, 137, 140
Rattlebox, 30
Rhododendrons, 74, *75*, 79, 97, 101
Rhus, 180
Rocks, 17, 19, 21, 116–18
Rose-of-Sharon, 171
Roses
Lenten, 77, *77*
pasture, 42
Roth, Sally, 90, *90*, 91
Rubus, 78, 97, *97*
Rudbeckia, 42, 51, 59, 64, 197
Rushes, 119, 120, 132, 136, 142

S

Sagittaria, 142
Salal, 71
Salix, 79, 97, *97*, 137
Salvias, 246
Sanguinaria, 79, 98
Sargent, Mary Lee, 52, *52*, 53
Scarlet flax, 41
Schizachyrium, 59, 65, *65*, 67
Sedges, 119, 120, 137
Sedum, 246
Self-heal, 59
Serviceberry, 78, 100, 213
Shrubs, 20, *20*
berried, 70
for butterflies, 206, *206*
flowering, 72, *72*
fringetree, 80
hazel, 78, *78*
for hummingbirds, 175
planting, 22
seedlings, 240
for shade gardens, 101
for songbirds, 180
for woodland gardens, 97
Silene, 44
Silphium, 52, 66
Skunk cabbage, 120, 134, *134*, 137, 138, *138*
Skunks, 94
Snakes, 94
Sneezeweeds, 246
Snow-on-the-mountain, 44
Sod stripping, 57, *57*
Solidago, 42, 51, 59, 64

Sorghastrum, 67, 179, *179*
Spartina, 67
Spicebushes, 70, 78, 80, *80*, 95, 97, *97*, 197
Spurges, 30, 246
Squirrels, 14, 31, 109
Starworts, 106, 140
Stipa, 67
Streams, 125–27, *127*, 128, *128*
dry, 128, *128*
Sumac, 42, 180
Sunflowers, 26, 30, 35, 41, 44, 46, 59, 66, 91, *91*, 152, *152*, 160, 178, 197
Sweet flag, 120, 137, 142
Sweet William, 98
Switchgrass, 30
Symplocarpus, 134, *134*

T

Taxodium, 137
Tellima, 98
Terracing, 215–16, *216*, 217, *217*, *218*, 218–19
Thimbleberry, 78, 97, *97*
Thistles, 59, 62
Tiarella, 99
Tickseed, 41, 91, *91*, 160, 178
Tithonia, 197
Tolmeia, 137
Toothwort, 76
Trapa, 141
Trees
beeches, 181
birches, 71, *71*, 79
cedars, 78, 100
coniferous, 71
Cornelian cherry, 100
deciduous, 70
dogwoods, 78, 80, 96, 100
elms, 70
flowering cherry, 74, *75*
hardwood, 71
hemlocks, 70, 78
Japanese maples, 15, *15*, 21
limbing up, 82, *82*
magnolias, 79
maples, 70, 79, 85, *85*, 95, 96, 112, 119, 122
oaks, 70, 96
persimmons, 79
pines, 70, 78
planting, 22
red buckeyes, 100
redbuds, 96
seedlings, 240
for shade gardens, 100
softwood, 70
spruces, 70, 71, 96
understory, 77, 79, 80, 82
for woodland gardens, 96
Trela, Mark, 36, *36*, 37
Trellises, 21
Tridens flavus, 51
Trilliums, 24, 93, *93*
Triticum turgidum, 41
Tsuga, 78
Typha, 142

U

Umbrella plant, 137

V

Vanilla leaf, 74
Verbascum, 42, 64
Vermonia, 66
Vernonia, 59, 197
Veronica, 119
Viburnum, 70, 180
Vines, 26
for butterflies, 207, *207*
for hummingbirds, 175
Viola pedata, 42
Violets, 42
Viper's bufloss, 57
Virginia bluebells, 90, *90*, 122
Virginia creeper, 79, 84, *84*
Virgin's bower vine, 24

W

Walls, 22, 54, 62, *210*, 211, 215
building, 229–30
hundred-year, 230–31, *230–31*
rock, 21, 25
timber, 21
Water buttercup, 140
Water chestnut, 141
Water clovers, 137
Watercress, 119
Waterfalls, 22, 76, *76*, *104*, 107, 125, *126*, 128–29, *129*
Water hawthorn, 120
Water hyacinth, 120, 126, 141
Waterleaf, 78, 99
Water lettuce, 109, 120, 137, 141, *141*
Water lilies, 106, 107, 109, *109*, 117, *117*, 118, *118*, 120, 122, 137, 140
Weeding, 34, 38, 57, 58, 59, 60
Wildflowers, 24, 27, *27*, 31, 33, 34, 45, 57, 184
for meadow gardens, *63*, 63–64
for prairie gardens, 66
for shade gardens, 76
for woodland gardens, 98
Wildlife, 106
attracting, 16, 47, 58, 92, 182–207
food for, 12, 16, 45, *45*, 70, 73–74, 94, 95
habitat for, 25, *25*
in meadow gardens, 46–50
at ponds, 107–09, 117
shelter for, 12, 14, 16, 60, 73–74, 94, 95, 146, 148–49
in woodland gardens, 94–95
Wiltraut, Dot, 150, *150*, 151
Winterberry, 79, 132
Witch hazel, 79, 101
Woodbine, 84, *84*
Wood sorrel, 74
Wulfmeyer, Jim, 122–23

Y

Yarrows, 26, 27, *27*, 30, 42, 59
Yellow flag, 134, *134*, 137, 138
Youth-and-old-age, 137

Z

Zinnias, 160, 178, 184, *186*, 187

Photo Credits

Front jacket: © Adam Jones

Back jacket: © **John Glover:** bottom; **Maslowski Wildlife Productions:** middle; **Visuals Unlimited:** © Luther Goldman: top and spine

© **Philip Beaurline:** pp. 68, 70, 73, 84, 92, 93, 96 background, 97 background, 98 background, 99 background, 100 background, 101 background, 102 background and left inset, 103 background, 115

© **Harriet Hadley Clark:** p. 205 top

©**Crandall & Crandall:** pp. 126, 239

© **R. Todd Davis:** pp. 18, 32 bottom, 35, 109 top, 123 both, 152 middle, 163, 188 bottom, 192 top right, 206 left, 218–9, 249

© **Richard Day/Daybreak Imagery:** p. 166

© **Alan & Linda Detrick:** pp. 76, 97 left, 147 top, 233 bottom

© **Ken Druse:** pp. 72 right, 86, 117, 118 top, 225

Jean Emmons: Illustrations: pp. 14, 19, 57, 83, 89, 114, 127, 129, 135, 162, 163, 166, 216, 217, 223, 230–1, 244, 246

Envision: © Priscella Connell: pp. 16 top, 199 top right; © Jean Higgins: p. 44; © E. Johnson: p. 34 top; © Wanda La Rock: p. 63 middle

© **Derek Fell:** pp. 2, 10, 12, 65 both, 74–5, 88, 103 right, 110, 132–3, 141, 143 left, 161 bottom, 164–5, 178 background, 179 background and left inset, 180 background, 181 background, 206 right, 222 left, 238 both

© **John Glover:** pp. 7, 15, 17, 20 top, 21, 22, 23, 24, 77 left, 81, 85 top, 131, 139 right, 143 right, 214, 237; **Designer:** Diarmuid Gavin/Wildlife, Pond, and Garden: pp. 17, 20

Green World Pictures, Inc.: pp. 50, 54–5

© **Adam Jones:** pp. 28, 30, 32 top, 33, 42, 43, 49 right, 59, 63 background, 64 background, 65 background, 66 background, 67 background, 71 left, 85 bottom, 89, 95 left, 112, 134 bottom, 147 bottom, 149, 167, 173 bottom, 176 left, 185 left, 187, 189, 190 left, 199 bottom right, 247 bottom

© **judywhite/New Leaf Images:** p. 202 top

© **Dency Kane:** pp. 9, 58, 99 left, 103 middle, 139 left, 156, 182, 184

© **Daniel Knight:** p. 90 top

© **Mary Ann Kressing:** p. 122 top

© **Alan Mandell:** pp. 104, 106, 113 background, 128 bottom, 138 background, 139 background, 140 background, 141 background, 142 background, 143 background, 216, 220 both, 221 both, 222 right, 228, 233 top, 248; **Designer:** Creative Gardens: 128 bottom; Rick

Hansen/Pacific Garden and Waterworks: pp. 104, 106, 113 background, 138 background, 139 background, 140 background, 141 background, 142 background, 143 background; John Pruden/Portland Gardens: pp. 228 top two rows of garden

© **Charles Mann:** pp. 45 right, 56, 116 top, 121, 188 top, 195, 210, 212, 234, 236, 241, 243

© **Richard Mark:** pp. 41 right, 45 left, 52, 53 both, 77 right, 80, 82, 83, 90 bottom, 91 both, 122 bottom, 152 top and bottom, 204, 205 bottom

Jennifer S. Markson: Illustrations: pp. 25, 51, 78, 136, 160, 170, 194, 196, 200, 226

Maslowski Wildlife Productions: pp. 16 bottom, 48 top, 94, 95 right, 125, 154 right, 157 top left and bottom both, 164 left, 176 right, 177 left, 198 both, 199 top left, 202 bottom

© **Pat and Bob Momich:** pp. 203 bottom

© **Clive Nichols:** 72 left, 111, 128 top, 130, 135, 172 left, 224, 232

© **Jerry Pavia:** pp. 26, 34 bottom, 102 middle, 107, 118 bottom, 138 right, 213 both, 229

Photo Nats: © Gay Bumgarner: p. 62; © Carl Hanninen: p. 102 right; © Don Johnson: p. 63 left; © Sydney Karp: p. 190 right; © John Lynch: p. 103 left; © Jeff March: p. 191 right

© **Richard Shiell:** pp. 27, 40, 41 left, 49 left, 179 right, 185 right, 192 top left and bottom right, 207, 208 left, 247 top

© **Anthony V. Smith:** p. 46 bottom

© **Hugh P. Smith, Jr.:** pp. 13, 20 bottom, 157 top right, 161 top, 172 right, 173 top, 177 right

© **John J. Smith:** p. 99 right

Tom Stack and Associates: © Thomas Kitchin: p. 134 top

© **Connie Toops:** pp. 38–9, 201

© **Mark Trela:** pp. 36 both, 37 both

© **Robert A. Tyrell:** pp. 144, 146, 171

Visuals Unlimited: © Bill Beatty: p. 199 bottom left; © David Cavagnaro: pp. 186, 206 background, 207 background, 208 background, 209 background, © John Gerlach: pp. 31, 46 top, 48 bottom, 71 right, 138 left, 191 left; ©Luther Goldman: p. 203 top; ©Stephen J. Lang: pp. 61, 159 right; ©George Loun: p. 208 right; ©Steve Malowski: pp. 47, 153 both, 155 both; © Dick Scott: pp. 14 left, 63 right; © John Sohldem: p. 97 right; ©Ron Spomer: p. 158; © Tom J. Ulrich: pp. 109 bottom, 159 left

The Wildlife Collection: © Charles Melton: p. 14 right; © Tom Vezo: p. 154 left

© **Rick & Dorothy Wiltraut:** pp. 150 both, 151